THE SECRET TRADITION
IN ARTHURIAN LEGEND

The archetypal themes, images and characters of the Arthurian
cycle and their place in the Western magical tradition.

By the same author

A HISTORY OF WHITE MAGIC
OCCULT EXERCISES AND PRACTICES
A PRACTICAL GUIDE TO QABALISTIC SYMBOLISM
THE PRACTICE OF RITUAL MAGIC
EXPERIENCE OF THE INNER WORLDS
THE OCCULT – AN INTRODUCTION
ROSE CROSS AND THE GODDESS

THE SECRET TRADITION IN ARTHURIAN LEGEND

by

GARETH KNIGHT

THE AQUARIAN PRESS

First published 1983

© GARETH KNIGHT 1983

British Library Cataloguing in Publication Data

Knight, Gareth
The secret tradition in Arthurian legend.
1. Arthur, *King*
I. Title
398'.352   D152.5.A7

ISBN 0-85030-293-5

The Aquarian Press is part of the Thorsons Publishing Group, Wellingborough, Northamptonshire, NN8 2RQ

Printed in Great Britain by Woolnough Bookbinding Limited, Irthlingborough, Northamptonshire.

5 7 9 11 13 15 14 12 10 8 6

To the memory of Violet Mary Firth,
true flower of the Earth of Avalon,
who blazed the trail in this Quest.
And to the company of Hawkwood,
who followed it.

Author's Acknowledgments

I would like to express my gratitude to Bob Stewart for permission to quote at length from the valuable esoteric report of his visit to an ancient tomb in Jersey, Channel Islands. Also to my fellow students of many years John Hall and the late Margaret Lumley-Brown and Arthur Chichester for permission to incorporate, at my discretion, unpublished material in their charge. It is very much in the tradition of Arthurian literature to make use of manuscript 'oral' material in this way, and I am happy to join the long line of authors from as far back as Chrétien de Troies, Robert de Boron and Wolfram von Eschenbach who have similarly acknowledged such help, though somewhat to the scepticism of modern scholars. Much of this material relates to the 'Atlantean' tradition and takes its validity for granted. Those sufficiently interested may glean more information of this tradition from works such as Rudolf Steiner's *Universe, Earth and Man* or W. Scott-Elliot's *The Story of Atlantis* to name but two. Those who choose not to believe it may find much of this book of questionable validity but I fear I have come far enough along the road of occult research to realize that there comes a time when it is too limiting to try to write within the framework of assumptions imposed by the current intellectual establishment. However, with recent discoveries and realizations in modern physics and other disciplines, the gap may not remain unbridgeable for too long.

This book is, in any case, intended for serious students of the esoteric tradition with the ability and discernment to reconstruct a living Mystery system based on the native legendary material of Britain.

Quotations from Malory are, for the most part, from Eugène

Vinaver's magnificent *The Works of Sir Thomas Malory* (Oxford University Press) though I have taken the liberty of modernizing the spelling. Biblical quotations are from the New English Bible; otherwise any other quotations are acknowledged in the text.

Gareth Knight
August 1982
    Feast of the Decollation of St John the Baptist

Contents

PART THREE: THE GRADE OF GUENEVERE AND THE FORCES OF LOVE

PART FOUR: THE GREATER MYSTERIES AND THE HOLY GRAIL

INTRODUCTION

1.
Grades of the Arthurian Mysteries and the Importance of Myth and Legend

Students of literature have often remarked upon the hold that the legends of Arthur and his Knights of the Round Table, their Ladies, and the Quest of the Holy Grail have exercised on the imagination of Western man.

Few suspect the real reason. This is that they enshrine a secret Mystery Tradition that stems from beyond the Western Ocean, and which was also the guiding force behind the old stone circles and ancient trackways of Western Europe.

This ancient tradition, preserved in Celtic myth and legend was recast by initiated Troubadours and Trouvères of the twelfth century, and spread all over the Christian world. It continues to speak to the hearts of men even to this day, because it stirs the creative imagination.

Arthurian legend is also unique in that it provides a complete run through from the depths of our primeval spiritual yearnings to the heights of mystical experience. It runs from the ancient tradition of the cauldron of inspiration and rebirth won from the King of the Underworld, to Galahad, the perfect medieval Christian knight, returning his soul to God after achieving the Grail Quest.

These visions complement each other and give a complete picture of the way of achievement in the evolution of human consciousness. The lower is not left behind as man advances but is maintained as the foundation for his future growth.

Thus the Arthurian Mysteries are no ascetic way. They show forth the destiny of Western man, to seek to control the planes of matter, not to shun them. They seek to use and elevate desire, not to snuff it out.

The Arthurian Mysteries divide, as do most other Mysteries, into three primary grades: the Grade of the Powers of Arthur, the Grade of the Powers of Merlin and the Grade of the Powers of Guenevere. Beyond these Lesser Mysteries are the Greater Mysteries of the Quest and Achievement of the Holy Grail.

The Grade of the Powers of Arthur is the first, through which all must pass, and indeed remain in as they pass through the higher degrees. It is the grade of loyalty, of dedication, of service. Its code is enshrined in the concept of chivalry, in the duty to serve loyally, uphold the law and right all wrongs, particularly in protection of the weak and innocent.

Following from this is the Grade of the Powers of Merlin. Those who are tested and found worthy attain to the wisdom behind the code of chivalry and service. With this comes knowledge in the use of the invisible forces, and by these means the group soul of the race may be stimulated into channels of correct and health giving activity. These initiates bring inspiration to the nations of men, that the higher destiny of mankind may be worked out.

The Grade of the Powers of Guenevere is for those who work with power, who can form and dispel the magnetic links between individuals and groups. This knowledge and power springs from a deep understanding of polarity and of that key to all practical occult work, the forces of the aura. This entails not only the human aura but that of all created beings, including the earth and land itself, and the solar and other celestial powers.

Thus the Arthurian tales may be interpreted at many levels. The Round Table itself can be anything from a model of charitable action to a great stellar pattern of psychic and spiritual forces.

The grades described are major differentiations of levels of esoteric function. The Grade of Arthur is that of most esoteric students and men and women of good will.

The Grade of Merlin corresponds to the higher initiates and here magical or psychic ability is a *sine qua non* of the Grade, although there are some who work at this level under the guise of psychology or the creative arts. The manipulation of opinion for commercial or political purposes also falls technically into this area, through the media.

The Grade of Guenevere is behind the higher initiates, and its members may be called adepts or masters. They give a particular vocational service to the evolution of human and other forms of consciousness.

These three Grades, great as they are, comprise only the Lesser Mysteries, in that they are concerned with the manipulation and control of Elemental forces; that is, the forces of the 'inner' Earth, the forces of consciousness in various units that help to form the world as it is presented by our senses.

Beyond these forces of the universe is the knowledge and experience of the 'uncreate' realities, which forms the corpus of the Greater Mysteries.

As a general rule, stories of the Knights and Ladies refer to Elemental forces and the Grades of the Lesser Mysteries. The stories of the Holy Grail and its Quest describe the transcendent forces behind the Elemental creation.

Three symbols might be held to represent the various grades:
    the Grade of Arthur by a sword;
    the Grade of Merlin by a sceptre, wand or rod of power;
    the Grade of Guenevere by a cup.

The Lesser Mysteries as a whole may be resumed under the symbol of the Round Table.

The Greater Mysteries are represented by the mysterious shape shifting symbol of the Holy Grail, veiled yet radiant, sometimes cup, sometimes dish, sometimes precious stone; in a sense all three.

The Grade of Guenevere is also, to some extent, a linking degree, partaking something of both Greater and Lesser Mysteries. It should not be thought that the grades are completely and utterly separate; they co-inhere one within the other in a peculiarly intimate way.

The Grail in an especial sense represents the powers and perceptions of the individual; how best to develop to be worthy of the right to a place in the ultimate grand spiritual pattern of the cosmic Round Table.

As human beings we are all free spirits, sparks from the Divine Fire, and we have the Grail within us. It was with us from the first, will be with us at the end, and is even with us through the long series of Elemental quests that form our lives in psycho-physical incarnation. Thus the Quest of the Holy Grail is, in a sense, a voyage or journey of self re-discovery. Ultimately to take one's seat at the spiritual Round Table is a very high calling and achievement. When all are Grail Winners, seated about a perfected Table Round, it will be the equivalent of the ultimate beatific scenes of the *Paradiso* of the initiate poet Dante. It will be as the great white *rosa mystica*, floating in the empyrean, beyond the created worlds, every petal a human spirit, with the fragrant essence of the God-head at the midst.

In the study of myth and legend history is not important. Its bearing is only indirect. We are concerned with the high imagination rather than prosaic fact, though high imagination is by no means the same as personal fancy. There is an important difference. It is the high imagination that produces the myths that speak to the souls of men in many different conditions and times. Personal or literary fancy merely interprets or embroiders these emanations of the group or racial consciousness, often distorting them in the process, but stepping them down to the needs and modes of expression of a particular place and time.

We know little of the history of King Arthur. Much progress has been made by modern scholars because to our generation, in answer to our own current inner needs, history seems important. Yet if King Arthur were indeed no more than a Romano-British war leader of the fifth century, who for a generation stemmed the tide of Anglo-Saxon advance, how much of this vision that has come down to us in Arthurian legend would he have been able to express in his times? Cadbury Castle, the iron age fort that is thought likely to have been the site of his headquarters, impressive as it is, could certainly have been no Camelot, with fairytale towers and helmed knights and fair ladies. The closest approach to a Round Table would have been the warriors seated around a central fire.

Yet myth and legend builds up around the nucleus of some great man who serves his race and times, and who has the power of vision to dream and even re-enact the archetypal dreams that are stored in the mind of the race; the dreams that hold the secret of its destiny and even, on a wider scale, the evolutionary potential of the whole human race.

The principle is exemplified also in King Richard I, of whom we have both the legend and the history. As a king he was hardly of the best. In his ten-year reign he barely set foot in his realm and his crusading adventures were largely diverted to family and personal gain. Yet, in spite of this, he had a vision that fired the imaginations of other men. Thus, as the Lion-heart he has come down to us as all that a crusader knight should be, with his red cross shield, almost the pattern indeed of a knight of King Arthur. Furthermore, in his role in the green-wood legends of Robin Hood and his Merry Men he figures as the king who will return to set all things right. In this respect he takes on another feature that is common to Arthur who, the British long believed, would return again from Avalon to restore his realm. It is a lesser form of the Messiah legend.

Later heroes of vision may also renew this myth. Sir Francis Drake for instance, although in some respects a mercenary adventurer and pirate, as intrepid world voyager and admiral against the Armada stirred the national soul so much that he also is looked upon as a sleeping hero who will return. Drake's drum is still preserved and the legend that he will return in time of national danger if it is struck has been celebrated in poem and song.

More prosaic servers of their country, even kings of the magnitude of Alfred the Great or Henry VII, have not had the charisma to be the subject of myth and legend.

The mechanism we have is of very important, powerful archetypes of racial consciousness making their presence apparent by crystallizing about the deeds of men or women of vision. The vision, however inadequately it might have been expressed in the historical event, is then celebrated by the poets, bards, balladiers or story tellers, who have the antennae of inspiration and, at a lower level, know the kind of imagery and story that will interest and inspire their contemporaries.

History has a bearing in a secondary sense in that scholars can investigate how the great tales came down to us through the generations, forming about certain heroes or archetypal figures, being swamped for a time by a new culture, then reasserting themselves through the consciousness of the conquerors, in a rich, confused tapestry of cultural streams.

Thus in the British Isles we have a pattern of race after race sweeping across from the continent, each laying down a stratum of consciousness, so that research into myth and legend becomes like an archaeological dig. Just as an archaeological site has definite layers laid down by different generations and cultures, so does the body of myth and legend build up in similar strata.

We might visualize the strata of group consciousness in tabular form, although there will be variations according to different locations. The South-east of England, for instance, saw more changes than, say, the far West, and in Scotland and Ireland different tribal and racial patterns occurred. However, the principle remains the same:

AD1485   –   from the Tudors, unity of
                    national consciousness
AD1066   –   AD1485 Norman
AD800   –   AD1066 Dane
AD500   –   AD800 Anglo-Saxon
AD400   –   AD500 Celtic or Romano-British
                    resurgence
AD50   –   AD400 Roman
500BC   –   AD50 Celtic
1500BC   –   500BC Bronze Age 'Wessex' culture
3500BC   –   1500BC Neolithic-megalith builders
8000BC   –   3500BC Mesolithic

In our considerations of Arthurian legend, because of the different patterns of culture, and the spread of the material, it seems best to refer, strange as it may seem, to a *territorial* consciousness rather than a racial or national consciousness.

From the way the Arthurian material breaks down and develops one becomes aware of the British Isles having a definite territorial unity, in spite of the major differences between the races and nations inhabiting them. In a sense, all these races, tribes and nations, and indeed inspired individuals, form the expression of the consciousness of the land, of the teritorial entity.

One might indeed envisage the whole Earth having a consciousness expressed by all the life that inhabits it, human, animal and vegetable and even the geological composition of the land mass. Thus, according to terrain and climate, various parts of the Earth develop various facets of consciousness, expressed in different flora and fauna and differing national characteristics.

Focusing upon our own sector of that consciousness we seem to have a distinct unity comprised of all the British islands, (and there are many hundreds of them), and with links that extend particularly to Scandinavia, Spain and France.

Many of the small islands have a particular importance, being a focus for a particular kind of force. Thus there are the various 'holy' islands such as Iona; those with ancient Druidic associations such as Anglesey; those with the Northern contacts such as the Orkneys and Shetlands; those of the Western Ocean contact, with legends of sunken lands, such as the Isles of Scilly; those preserving ancient ways and traditions such as the Isle of Man; those with the contacts of Norman France such as the Channel Islands, that formed part of the original Duchy of Normandy, and so on.

There is a dual polarity of man and land, interacting each upon the other. In certain locations certain types of inner experience are more likely to occur because of topographical features of sea or hill or plain or past event, so that a tradition builds around that spot and it becomes an ever powerful focus of a particular type of force. This pertains especially to ancient religious shrines or sites of tribal or national meeting.

Glastonbury, for instance, has developed as a particular focus for Arthurian legend and is regarded by some as the epitome of Camelot or the Isle of Avalon. Yet the locations of Arthurian legend are not of this world; they are places of the imagination.

As places of the imagination they can be built anew by each generation, by each individual who aspires to their contact. The great traditional Arthurian sites, the beautiful palace of Camelot, the castles of Tintagel, of Caerleon, of Carlisle (the fortress of 'the isle'), the Grail castle of Corbenic, Sir Lancelot's Joyous Garde, the Forest of Broceliande, the Lake from whence Arthur's sword Excalibur came and to which it was returned, are force centres in the imagination. This is not to psychologize them or to consider them 'merely' subjective. Those with experience of occult practice will realize the objective reality of certain 'subjective' places that have a very positive reality on the astral plane.

By building these centres in the imagination we make contact with these great inner forces. In some instances they have become associated with a physical location, and if this place then becomes a centre of pilgrimage, visited by people whose aspirations and interest accord with the place, and who are prepared to make some sacrifice in time and energy to go there, then something of the inner condition may build up around the physical centre and it may then become an outer aid to an inner contact for those who make a special effort and intention to go there.

In these days of easy transport some value has been taken from pilgrimage—which in its true form is a kind of ritual, an outer expression of an inner spiritual intention. The use of national shrines and ancient monuments as focuses for tourist interest has made sideshows out of major sites such as Tintagel or Stonehenge, but the old power lingers on and those prepared to go at other times, outside the holiday season, may experience something of the old magic, the inner contact. For those trained and sensitive to it, it is discernable even in the midst of the most rabidly commercialized centres of tourist traffic. On the other hand, to the discerning, there are many other lesser known points of contact with these inner Arthurian worlds. Any wood can become a Broceliande, any lake a gate to faeryland, for the key lies in the imagination.

It was through the powers of the imagination that the legends were first built. A bard seated by the fire with the tribe around him, or even the family elder within the immediate family circle, in the flickering half-light so conducive to imaginative reverie, spun the old tales that tell of the dreams of the race, of the consciousness of the land, of the whisper of the blood within the veins, of the destiny of humankind.

Thus the old tales are not the invention of one individual, or even the synthesis of the invention of many individuals; they are group imaginings, the imagery being evoked from very deep levels of consciousness by the bard who is sensitive to the images rising. There follows almost a weaving pattern in the evolution of these racial dreamings over the generations, for they become a tapestry of myth and legend.

First there are the story tellers, quarrying the old myths from out of the virgin group consciousness by the techniques of free fantasy combined with intention—the intention being not merely to entertain but to sustain the family or tribe by giving it a sense of identity, of belonging to a corpus of ancestral and inner powers.

In due course these inspirational tales are worked over by a body of more priestly-minded caste, who seek to codify the bardic material into a system of ritual practice, moral codes, totemic representation, observance of rites of specific heroes and gods. Thus is built a formal religious structure over the aspirations and day-dreams of the group.

In the course of time there may come, however, invasion or infiltration by another race or culture. This usually means the suppression, or at least the ignoring, of the altars and the religious beliefs of the conquered, who then tend to revert to the dreams and folktales of the unprivileged and thus re-stimulate the bardic tradition.

The new culture may, in time, lose its dynamism and then will come a movement within it to try to regenerate its power, to re-illumine its inspiration by recourse to forgotten traditional sources, which by now have been redeveloped and kept alive by the unprivileged of society.

From this comes the further cycle of working this material up into a new religious system, unless of course a new invasion or infiltration should intervene in the meantime, which however will make no change to the actual process, it will simply add a new stratum of religious consciousness on top of the existing strata.

This process has occurred over the centuries in the British Isles more or less according to the table we have already listed. As race has succeeded race from prehistoric times through to the historically recorded period we reach, in these Islands, a point of comparative physical stability in 1066, after the Norman conquest. Cultural changes then take place more in the realm of ideas.

The Norman influence might be said to be paramount during the first two dynasties, until the end of the Plantaganet line in 1485. Then at the coming of the Tudors, with their Welsh ancestry, there is the gradual forming of a unified nation of the Welsh and English. The Scottish and Irish elements follow a different time scale in accordance with their own past and ancestry but evolving toward a united kingdom in 1702.

There are, of course, many complex cross currents of internal and external origin in the long panorama of the history of the Isles of Albion. The question of Ireland is one of them.

Ireland is important to any study of the Arthurian legends because they stem, to a great degree, from Celtic mythology, even if they do not necessarily originate there, and it is the Irish mythology that has come down to us as the most intact. Ireland is, in many ways, the great 'teacher' of the West. She has suffered grievously from Norman and English greed and ambition, and the spirited independence of her people, that goes back beyond the beginnings of recorded history, manifests often as a glory in revolt and disputation which has made a united stand against the external forces difficult to sustain. It is no small wonder that troubles beset her relationship to the rest of the British Isles to this very day.

Thus, much of the modern political problems have their origin far back in time and deep within racial and territorial consciousness. Without a knowledge of such origins, any solutions based on modern political values are unlikely for they are no more than a surface skin of contemporary opinions riding over deep waters they do not begin to understand.

The racial soul of Hibernia has very ancient roots that include a slumbering magical knowledge and contacts with primeval forces beyond those that affect the mainland of Britain and the continent of Europe. Indeed the ancient Irish contacts of pre-Celtic times, and those of the incoming tribes, from the Continent, of immediate Germanic or Baltic origin, had strains that were completely antipathetic one to another.

The original population of these islands, and indeed of continental Gaul before the Celts, was what we call Iberian. These early peoples, neolithic in culture, had inherited the knowledge and power of incoming colonizers from the West, the remnants of the great antedeluvian 'Atlantean' civilization. It was these colonizers who brought, in the beginning, the great technological and astronomical knowledge that enabled a simple neolithic people to erect great stone monuments such as Stonehenge, Carnac and Avebury.

The pre-Celtic civilization was, in any case, not so primitive as is sometimes assumed, and radio-carbon dating methods have revealed that what had previously been assumed to be iron age structures, on the lines of a type of 'baronial' wooden hall, in fact date from c.4000 BC. Also, ancient trackways existed in those times which, by their structure of wooden rail ways over marshy land, indicate a far from brutish and ignorant culture.

In short, the corpus of myth that crystallized around the fifth century Romano-British hero antedates him by a considerable amount. The 'historical' Arthur is but a convenient peg upon whom to hang very ancient folk memories and ritual symbol patterns, much as the Druids were once, and indeed popularly still are, credited with the building of Stonehenge, which in fact pre-dates them by as much as they pre-date us.

Anachronisms abound in the study of myth and legend, for even the fifth-century historical Arthur is generally imagined, after Malory, in a twelfth-century context, or even later, for plate armour was not common until the fifteenth century.

However, in historical terms, our traceable contacts go back to the movements of Celtic tribes, who overran and amalgamated with the indigenous Iberians. Certain pockets of this indigenous stock still remain identifiable in the dark, stocky, round-headed type found in Wales or the Forest of Dean. The Celts were a taller, long-headed, fairer race.

The Celts who overran Ireland were of a different type again from those who infiltrated Southern Scotland, England and Wales. Nor were they the same as those erroneously supposed to have emigrated from Ireland to cover the Hebrides and mainland highland Scotland in later days. They were, however, of similar stock to those of the far North of Scotland and the northern isles.

The Hibernian Celts absorbed a stream of teaching and culture from Asia Minor and the trade routes running to Africa and Asia, and particularly from contacts filtering into northern Greece and the islands of ancient Greece. There is thus a similarity between the gods of Greece and of Ireland, together with a common feeling for beauty and war-like heroes. This is distinct from other Celtic affinities with Scandinavian gods.

Furthermore, the Celts who entered Hibernia found a more advanced civilization than pertained elsewhere in the British Isles. As is known to archaeology, the earliest megalithic works are to be found in the valley of the Boyne, of which Newgrange is an outstanding example. The indigenous population was so comparatively advanced because it had amalgamated with an ancient Atlantean colony which, in extreme antiquity, had been established there. According to this tradition the Iberians of Ireland also had a different culture from those of the mainland of Britain in that they held within their folk memory contacts with an even remoter sunken civilization, usually referred to in occult exegesis as Lemurian.

This unique blend of cultural currents from immense antiquity, allied to the Graeco-Celtic stream, is what produced the great power of the Druids in Ireland. And the effect upon the group mind of those who inherit the Irish tradition will obviously be considerable, and responsible for much of the later difficulties of Irish history.

The contribution of the earlier Atlantean cultures was of an extremely well focused power of the imagination (we are prior to the development of the concrete mind of the historical epoch), which, in short, amounted to a magical power. This magical use of the power of the imagination could mould profoundly the comparatively undeveloped early races, who, like children, were so much closer to involvement with nature, with the unconscious, with the Great Mother, than our own highly individualized souls of today.

This immensely strong, deliberately magically built, group soul of the remote past, mingled with the concrete mind contacts of ancient Greece, and the allied aesthetic ability, has produced an Irish group soul that is stronger than most others in the world apart perhaps from the Jewish—which also derives from immense antiquity in another way.

The Celtic druidism of Ireland reached its peak long before that of the rest of Britain and Gaul, and it was originally from

Ireland that the British and Gallic druids drew their teaching and wisdom.

The great problems which later beset Ireland over the centuries derive from a combination of these early great strengths. Because of the diversity of the contending currents within a group soul, there has ever been a tendency to internal dissension, exacerbated by the other races and religious authorities that have tried to interfere.

This flared to a crisis at the time of the restimulation of the group soul of the British Isles that brought about the reformulation of the Arthurian legends in the twelfth century. Henry II commenced a military involvement, licensed by the Pope who, in the politics of those times, found it expedient to try to exact unpaid tithes by the use of Plantagenet force. This has festered on in oppression, aggression, counter-aggression and mutual atrocities over the centuries.

The conflict of contending forces has also operated, and still operates, upon the religious level. Through the missionary genius of St Patrick, the Irish Christian church formed a nucleus of Celtic Christianity that inspired and informed the West independently of Rome through the Dark Ages, just as in former times the Irish Druids had been a centre of religious and cultural influence.

Although a Christianized form of Druidism lingered on, and indeed, like the Hermetic tradition, formed a link between pagan and Christian spirituality, this role of leadership was not without its cost. Had the new wine been introduced more slowly, as occurred in the rest of Europe, much conflict and suffering might have been avoided. Many of the highly magically trained Irish druids migrated to Wales, France and Brittany whence we have a rich vein of ancient tradition, much of it manifesting as the Arthurian legends.

The time may not be long before the racial soul of Ireland enters a new phase, manages to synthesize its deep conflicting roots and to work more freely with other nations of the west. The whole trend of Ireland in the past has been to esoteric teaching and knowledge, and a renewal of this, as pioneered by Yeats and Lady Gregory, may have more importance than political and commercial initiatives. It is a little premature to summarily dismiss this resurgence as a literary fad of 'the Celtic twilight'.

The Arthurian tradition therefore contains material of relevance to the evolution of nations, indeed to mankind at large, as well as to individuals. In its essence the pattern of the story comes down to us from a previous epoch, as the legacy of a civilization that flourished long before us in evolutionary time.

There is some realization of this in the ancient Greek myths of the Titans, the gods before the Olympian pantheon of Zeus and the classical gods and goddesses. Before the reign of Zeus the world was ruled by Ouranos and his fellow Titans. One of these was Albion, who was associated with the Atlas mountains of the western end of the Mediterranean. He was thought to hold the world upon his shoulders and thus to maintain it in its proper place in the heavenly scheme of things.

From the Titan Albion the ancient title of the British Isles is derived, and all who are born within their bounds are sons and daughters of Albion, no matter what their colour, race or creed.

The powers and knowledge represented by the Titans are those of a previous epoch, and it is this which in occult tradition is often called Atlantean. The Arthurian tradition embodies an Atlantean formula of initiatory experiences, the Round Table and the Holy Grail in their essence being symbols for them.

The Round Table signifies the universe and all the inner powers within it. To the outer eye it is the sphere of the stars and of interstellar space. To the inner eye it is this and very much more. In the words of William Blake, 'When the Sun rises . . . I see an Innumerable Company of the Heavenly host crying "Holy, Holy, Holy is the Lord God Almighty"', and 'The dead Sun is only a phantasy of evil Man'.

The Grail, which is intimately allied to the Round Table, is the heart of man as the alchemical crucible of evolutionary experience, insofar as its great mystery pertains to human dimensions.

The names of many of the knights and ladies and of geographical locations derive from very ancient symbols, and even embody certain power sounds of ancient magic. Although speech was not evolved beyond a very simple arrangement of sounds in Atlantean times, nonetheless these had a very great power because dedicated to special magical purposes rather than to the small change of social intercourse. One sees a similar kind of structural significance in the ancient Hebrew language, wherein each word consists of three letters only, and those letters and sounds are loaded with symbolic significance. A symbol, we might emphasize, following Coleridge's definition, is an object that expresses not only itself but a range of other inner meanings beyond itself.

The name of Arthur's royal line, Pendragon, for instance,

derives from remote antiquity. Its powerful symbolism caused it later to be carried by Celtic princes as the red dragon and by early Saxon kings as the white dragon. It still remains the emblem of the principality of Wales.

The dragon has come down in folktale as a fearsome monster, rather as the old horned gods of primitive man were transformed by medieval imagination into the devil and his minions. The dragon is a being of many parts, associated with fire and with flight, and its prototype is in the night sky as the constellation Draco. The pole star of a former age was in the constellation Draco before the Earth's axis tilted so that its projection currently points to Polaris, the pole star of our own epoch.

Arthur himself is connected to the constellation associated with the new pole star, the Great Bear, also known as Arthur's Wain. In the guise of what may seem facile and arbitrary patterns in the sky are indicated facts of very deep cosmic importance, for the constellations represent great extra-terrestrial influences that, modified by the ruling influence of the Solar gravitational field, pour forces of one kind and another into the evolving Earth and the other planets of the Solar System. The constellation of Arthur's Wain acts as a symbolic focus for a major source of evolutionary stimulation known in the East as the Seven Rishis (i.e., great seers) of the Great Bear.

A knowledge of the implications of the Table Round therefore implies an understanding of cosmic centres of influence working in conjunction with the great spiritual being behind the Sun, and in particular of the type of force focused through contemplation of the stars of Ursa Major.

These stars might be said to express themselves in human terms as the symbolism of the Table Round and the ideals of the Fellowship of Knights dedicated to a code of conduct. In its broadest sense the Round Table Fellowship is a formula that applies to each human being who has reached a particular level of evolutionary development.

The Grail implies the various powers which come to the human soul as it develops as an individual and as an integral part of the great Divine Pattern.

The Knights and their Ladies, who form the Fellowship, are archetypes of different sorts of force as expressed through human experience, and at the same time each one of them, as a particular type of force, is present within us all.

An important point to bear in mind in studying Arthurian

Legend is that each force, or human character, is presented in the round, not as an ideal archetype of perfection but as a pattern that demonstrates what may happen if the force is mis-applied.

We may draw a parallel with study of the Qabalah. The ancient rabbis drew the Tree of Life as an image of perfection, a representation of the attributes of God. Any unbalanced expression of pure forces was then accounted for by an inverted Tree of Life, reflected in the lower Waters of Chaos. This inverted Tree was regarded as that of the Shells, cosmic illusions, that which will in the course of evolutionary time, either be reformed or reduced to basic elements.

The Tree of Life and its Averse Reflection

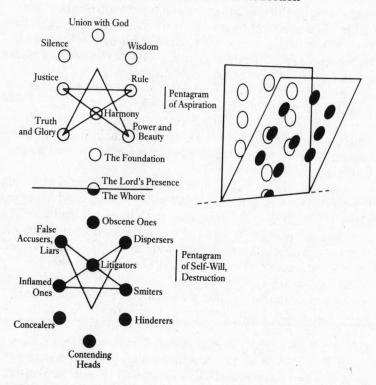

Figure 1:

In the Arthurian system it is as if a representation of this dual Tree were folded at the bottom so that the good and evil aspects of each sphere are adjacent.

This should not be misinterpreted as a philosophical justification of dualism—of evil and good as equal contending forces. Evil is fundamentally an illusion that will, in the end, be destroyed.

The effect of this portrayal of the ideal and the falling away from it in Arthurian Legend is the development of very human characters and a dramatic and complex story. It is the factor that accounts for the final break-up of the Round Table Fellowship and the disappearance of the Holy Grail. However, the Grail can be caused to reappear on Earth, and Arthur and his knights to re-awaken, but these are archetypal patterns of achieved humanity that remain the task and guide and inspiration for us.

The dual aspected treatment of the characters is largely the work of the twelfth century Trouvères who were influenced by teachings coming from the East in the wake of returning Crusaders and from Moorish Spain.

We can thus begin to draw a kind of genealogical picture of the genesis and growth of Arthurian Legend.

It begins with esoteric star lore of extreme antiquity. These traditions are inherited by the Celts in their invasion from continental Europe and become enshrined in Druidical lore and Celtic mythology.

There is a mixing of streams of influence with Roman invasion, bringing in a cosmopolitan contact with Hermetic and Mithraic ideas. There is also the founding of Celtic Christianity which develops, for several hundred years, apart from Rome. Various elements in this cultural mix, as with the ancient Irish/Greek connection, receive a new stimulus as like cleaves to like.

In the twelfth century, initiate bards of the Trouvère and Troubadour tradition deliberately search through the old material which has been suppressed under Anglo-Saxon, Scandinavian and Norman/Norse invasions. It had been preserved by Celtic and particularly Breton story tellers, many of whose forebears had fled from Wales and Ireland. They recast it into contemporary imagery and it spreads rapidly all over the Western world, including the Norman kingdoms of the South and Outremer (Palestine).

After 250 years of popular growth as long medieval prose and poem cycles it is collated by Sir Thomas Malory in the mid-fifteenth century and crystallized into permanent form by the printing press of William Caxton in 1485. The stories portrayed incorporate a certain amount of tinkering by monastic scribes but are close enough to traditional sources for this to be detected. Professor Vinaver's editing of the Winchester manuscript, discovered in 1934, also amends some of Caxton's somewhat arbitrary editing, when he set the work into type.

The story has, during the last millenium, tended to be invoked as a source of national inspiration at time of need. This includes Geoffrey of Monmouth's *History of the Kings of Britain* which sought to weld a tradition of British national history for the Plantagenet kings; and which later inspired national pride and confidence under the Black Prince in the Hundred Years War. It was also invoked by the Tudors in their coming to power.

This kind of usage, if not perhaps the highest possible spiritual use to which the material can be put, indicates its vitality over centuries and its power to touch the minds and hearts of men. That is why the study of Arthurian Legend is so important. It is a power house of evocative symbolism, embracing material that has descended through diverse cultural streams from immense antiquity.

PART ONE: THE GRADE OF ARTHUR AND THE ROUND TABLE FELLOWSHIP

2. The Titans and the Star Lore

It is to very ancient tradition that we must turn for the origin of the forces that went into the setting up of the Round Table, for it has its prototype in the night skies. It is literally well described as the 'starry' wisdom. The tilt of the Earth and the plane of its orbit round the Sun, and the position of the Sun itself in galactic space give certain images which go very deep within the soul of man.

In appearance we have a broad belt of constellations that circle the Earth, the signs of the zodiac. These are like the equator of a celestial sphere that encompasses the Earth. Between this rim of the zodiac and the central polar point, the Pole Star, about which they appear to spin, are various other constellations. These do not usually receive quite the same degree of attention as those of the zodiac. We may ignore, for our purposes, those constellations that have been named within the past few hundred years and concentrate upon those constellations listed by the ancients.

There are a number of constellations that appear below the rim of the Zodiac. These are stars of the Southern Hemisphere. Most of them are, however, visible at certain times of the year at least, to observers in the Northern Hemisphere. In fact an observer in Cairo, which is approximately 30° above the Equator, can see constellations up to 60° in the Southern Hemisphere. No constellation below this line of vision has an ancient name, so in our researches we are plainly dealing with a Northern culture, comparatively speaking. Cairo is on the same degree of latitude as the great ancient Babylonian star gazers and the traditional site of Atlantis, to the West.

In classical Greek mythology we need to go back beyond the familiar pantheon of Zeus and his fellow Olympians, to the gods whom they overthrew, who were their parents, and who are known as the Titans.

The origins of the Titans—or giant gods—is so far back in time as to have as a scenic background only the earth and sky. They were born of the primeval Earth Mother, Gaea, and fathered by Ouranos, the heavenly deep, the primeval Sky Father.

There were twelve Titans, six brothers and six sisters, and we have the strange story of how originally Ouranos kept procreating with Gaea and imprisoning all their children within her. In other words, all the archetypal forces which form subsequent life on Earth come from the starry heavens, and their evolution is held within the confines of the Earth sphere, a great cosmic crucible.

Sooner or later this primal seeding of cosmic influences into the Earth sphere had to stop and this is depicted in Titanic mythology as Gaea fashioning a flint sickle and giving it to the youngest of the Titans so that he could castrate Ouranos. The sickle is an instrument of harvesting and the keeping down of too lush a growth; its cresent lunar shape makes it particularly a weapon of the female, receptive powers. The fact that it is of flint, the stone used for man's earliest tools and also the source of sparks of fire, is also of significance. It holds within it all subsequent human civilization and technology.

A number of other important events occurred with this cessation of entry of cosmic creative influences into the Earth sphere. These were to lead to the establishment of sexual means of generation (symbolized by the birth of Aphrodite), and the establishment of the means of balance, or cosmic justice, (the Furies, or Erinyes). Other non-human generations were originated, such as a race of giants who are also mentioned in the Book of Genesis. Also the ash tree nymphs, which may signify a type of mediating angelic/elemental order; the ash tree is to this day a particularly 'magical' tree, apart from its importance in Scandinavian mythology as Yggdrasil, a Northern Tree of Life.

There were other primeval forces besides the twelve Titans. These include Gyes, Kottos and Briareos, the hundred-armed giants from the depths of the sea. Gaea produced these to assist in the changes and they thus represent very deep forces of the Earth. They are now said to guard the Titans in Tartary, a mythical world far beyond the antipodes. They are thus like Freudian censors, or guardians of the planetary consciousness from primeval upwellings.

Another offspring of Gaea was Kuklopes, who embodied

thunder and lightning—later appropriated by Zeus. Gaea later gave birth to Typhoes after the overthrow of the Titans by Zeus. Typhoes is important to Arthurian studies by virtue of his dragon form.

The dragon in subsequent myth and legend is invested with a monstrous and menacing shape. This tends to occur to all old gods when a new religious culture takes over and banishes the previous one to a repressed shadow world in its own subconscious. In fact the dragon represents a form of earth energy now lost to human knowledge.

Folk memories remain of this hidden knowledge, which accounts for the interest in ley lines and power centres associated with megalithic sites. Some of these are natural earth forces, comprising a whole range of gravitational, magnetic and more subtle force-fields. Others are man-made channels for these forces, in much the same way that physical water resources may be utilized not only as natural rivers and lakes but by dams, reservoirs and canals.

Typhoes, by his very power, has tended to be regarded as an evil figure, just as nuclear energy is adjudged by many to be an evil force today. Dangerous it might be if ill-controlled, evil perhaps in the hands of those who would mis-use it, but like all natural forces, whether physical, spiritual or psychic, intrinsically neither good nor evil.

Another side to this great Earth force is depicted in the female counterpart of Typhoes, the dragoness Delphine, who actuated the prophetic oracle of the ancient world at Delphi. It is from her that the prophetic priestesses derived their name of 'pythoness'. Her name stems from a word signifying 'womb', and the Delphic oracular priestesses sat upon a tripod over a fissure in the ground that led to the bowels of the Earth and to the creative, prophetic forces therein.

These strange creatures, and others like them, represent, not evil, but primeval forces. They were known to the ancient Atlantean prediluvian civilizations, and dim memories of them have come down to us as persistent beliefs that may seem no more than superstitions. However, their vitality expresses a deeply hidden core of truth.

Our principal concern, however, is with Arthurian developments from Titanic myth. Their common primal origins are shown in similarities borne out by the night sky. Thus the Round Table is a form of the celestial zodiac. The crest of the Pendragon dynasty stems from one of the Titanic gods. Ancient forces are also shown in similar sound patterns in names. For instance, King Uriens of Gore, the husband of Arthur's half-sister, the enchantress Morgan le Fay, is akin to the great hunter of the sky, Orion. The pattern of the Round Table knight as solar hero is depicted in the skies as Hercules. An ancient order of knighthood is to be found in the Centaurs.

The tradition of knights rescuing fair damsels—with all that this implies in deeper symbolism beyond social chivalry—is to be found in the circumpolar constellations related to the myth of Perseus and Andromeda. The strange ships of the Holy Grail are in the great, ancient constellation of Argo Navis (in modern times split into a number of smaller constellational groupings) and the spiritual forces of swans (Cygnus), eagles (Auriga), and winged horses (Pegasus) are also there. Likewise are the primeval Earth forces with the monstrous forms, Hydra, Serpens, Lupus, Eridanus, and even the Cup of the Grail itself—Crater.

By these symbols we seek to reach the same imaginative depths as were plumbed by William Blake when he wrote: 'The giant Albion, was Patriarch of the Atlantic; he is the Atlas of the Greeks, one of those the Greeks called Titans. The stories of Arthur are the acts of Albion, applied to a Prince of the fifth century.'

It is the same ancient sources, in their Greek-Irish recension, that give the stories of the ancient Tuatha de Danaan—the children of the goddess Dana—who had four treasures that have come down in Arthurian and Grail myth and legend, and later in the suits of the Tarot, and the four traditional magical instruments related to the Elemental Quarters—the Lance, the Sword, the Cup and the Stone (or Shield).

The Tuatha de Danaan, on a May Day, or Beltaine, in a mist, came 'through the air and the high air' to Ireland, from a place with four cities, each with four wise men to teach the young men 'skill and knowledge and perfect wisdom'. In the words of Lady Gregory:

> And they brought from these four cities their four treasures: a Stone of Virtue from Falies, that was called the Lia Fail, the Stone of Destiny; and from Gorias they brought a Sword; and from Finias a Spear of Victory; and from Murias the fourth treasure, the Cauldron that no company ever went away from unsatisfied.

In Arthurian legend we have these same treasures appearing. Arthur's sword Excalibur, that came from the faery workshops of the Lady of the Lake and which was returned to her at the end of Arthur's mission. The Lance that gave the Dolorous Stroke that brought the evil enchantment upon the Land of Logres in the Grail Legend. The Cup that is representative of the Holy Grail itself, although the actual form of the Grail is never seen by mortal eyes. The stone which appeared floating in the river, with a king's sword in it, to be drawn only by he who had the destiny of terrestrial kingship in the case of Arthur, or of spiritual kingship in the case of Galahad.

The Cup and Lance have even more ancient and primitive roots in the club and the cauldron. Both these were attributes of the Dagda, the ancient father of the gods. The Dagda is a Titanic figure in Irish mythology, whose functions were later taken over by Lugh Lavadha, the sun god and master of all skills. Then the club became refined into the technologically more efficient spear and, in later times still, Lugh Lavadha became humanized as the best knight in the world, Lancelot of the Lake.

The Dagda and his cauldron appears also in the equivalent Welsh branch of Celtic mythology as Bran the Blessed. Bran had a cauldron that restored slain warriors to life and which gave unlimited food—two important requisites indeed to primitive tribal man. In the Bran legends a beheading element is a major feature. This appears later in a parallel to the Grail legends as the head of John the Baptist upon a platter.

In the original Bran legends the head of Bran continued to entertain his companions for seven years in the islands of the far West before being brought to London to be buried at the White Mount, upon which the Tower of London now stands, as an unfailing guard against foreign invasion. There is a later tradition that Arthur dug it up on the grounds that he needed no such primitive aids to his defence of the realm, an act of hubris which led to downfall and the success of subsequent invasions. This is a later gloss upon the fact that the Arthurian tradition took over from the earlier Bran tradition. The cauldron is a primitive form of Grail and Bran's name appears, little changed, as Bron, one of the guardian kings of the Grail, and, as Hebron, of the kin of Joseph of Arimathea!

In one of the Welsh versions of Arthurian legend found in the *Mabinogion* (a late manuscript but containing very early oral material) we receive some idea of the dynamic of Arthurian pre-Christian Grail legend in the story of Peredur, the Son of Evrawc, a forerunner of Percivale or Parzifal.

This is a localized version of the ancient Greek hero Hercules, who is represented in the constellations as the archetypal human confronted with twelve labours, which are represented by the signs of the zodiac. The number and the nature of these labours may vary from culture to culture but they all signify the hero, forging his individuality from out of the embrace of the group soul, in the evolution of human individualized consciousness. This is recapitulated in the process of childhood and adolescence but it is also a macrocosmic task of the whole human race, in an evolution of consciousness from animal-man to angelic-man, from instinctual to intuitional modes of perception and behaviour.

In the more primitive versions of this pattern of human development, in a form that speaks to the understanding of the more group-conscious tribal man, this is best given and understood as a hunt, even a sort of treasure hunt, the reward for which is a betrothal and a raising in status to becoming the kindred of royalty. The pattern is preserved in many folk stories and fairy tales.

The *Mabinogion*, translated by Lady Charlotte Guest in 1849, has been likened to a peasant's hut built of ancient stones from a great monument of antiquity. It probably came into being from medieval storytellers putting together fragments of oral tradition, deriving from sources both ancient and contemporary that they did not fully understand.

Five of the stories relate specifically to Arthur and, in spite of the shapeless and scrappy form of the narrative, which places their literary merit below most of the old epics and sagas, they show a point of transition where myth is becoming folk tale and romance.

Of these five tales, three, *The Lady of the Fountain*, *Geraint* and *Peredur*, bear a close resemblance to the courtly works of Chrétien de Troies, though containing barbaric traits unknown to Chrétien. They may therefore derive from a common unknown French or Anglo-Norman source, of the mid twelfth century.

The others, *Kylhwych and Olwyn* and *The Dream of Rhonabwy* have no known prototype, yet some of the characters close to Arthur in later romance already appear—Kei (Kay); Bedwir (Bedivere); Gwalchmai (Gawain).

In the later recension of the legend all three are particularly close to Arthur; Kay is his foster-brother and seneschal of his castles; Bedivere as his body companion who, at the last, takes him to the Lake to return Excalibur and to await the strange barque with the three mourning queens; and Gawain as his nephew and closest in kin at the court, surpassed in prowess only by Lancelot and possibly the Cornish/Hibernian Tristram.

Kay and Bedivere also appear in a fragmentary Welsh poem wherein, in a scene similar to that of Cuchulain in Irish mythology, Arthur takes part in a ritualized dialogue seeking entry from a gate warden. This seems an early form of initiation cycle. In the dialogue Arthur names his companions and cites their exploits. Kay is credited with being a destroyer of lions and witches, and of the demon cat Cath Palac.

Three Celtic gods also appear in Arthur's retinue. Mabon is a thinly disguised Romano-British Apollo, Maponos. Manawiden son of Llyr is the Welsh counterpart of Manannan the Irish sea god after whom the Isle of Man is named, and whose father Ler or Llyr is the prototype for Shakespeare's King Lear. Lluch Llany-nnauc derives from Llugh Lamhfada, the Irish god of sun and storm and all the arts of man, who later becomes the courtly French knight Lancelot du Lac.

In another Welsh poem *The Spoils of Annwn* Arthur and his men raid the dwelling place of the pagan gods which is variously called a Fairy Fortress or a Fortress of Glass. In some lines it is regarded as an island and in other lines as a subterranean region. The various names, which include the Fortress of Riches and the Isle of the Active Door, all point to the inner planes, the astral world, and the faery and elemental forces therein.

They raid Annwn to carry off the cauldron of its lord, which is tended by nine maidens who are met with in various forms in early myth. The cauldron might be identified with that of the Dagda or with the cauldron of inspiration of the goddess Keridwen. In this version it is also a vessel for testing the courage of warriors, for it will not boil the meat of a coward. Indeed only seven return safely from this particular raid, which mystic number emphasizes that we are dealing with the fragments of an initiation ritual.

An initiation ritual is the concentration into a small compass, in symbolic form, of the tasks that are to be performed by the soul in its evolutionary journey. It is thus a device for orienting the direction of endeavour in pictorial language that speaks to the soul.

The lord of Annwn, or the Underworld, whose name is Pwyll,

is later met in more refined form as Pellas or Pellam, the keeper of the Castle of the Holy Grail, Carbonek. So although the later Quest of the Holy Grail may have been Christianized and tempered with oriental influences, at its root it stems largely from the ancient Mystery tradition of Britain.

However, it is not the primitive Arthur that has held the imaginations of men over the centuries. Certainly this level of proto-Arthurian legend provides much of the power behind the late medieval flowering of the legend into an image of an ideal society of knights and ladies in a fairy-tale land of fair palaces, stern castles, green laundes, enchanted forests, with glades and fountains and mysterious adventures. This idealized picture of twelfth-century life is the pattern that holds in the latter day imagination.

Let us therefore examine the Fellowship of the Round Table in this twelfth-century guise, but remain aware of the deep and ancient stellar lore that is embodied by it. Lore that goes back into the mists beyond recorded time to when the human race was in its childhood.

In a sense the idealizations of Arthurian legend are like the dreams of adolescence, the earlier material like the fantasies of childhood—more vivid and more threatening and immediate. We seek to explore the power behind these images of racial childhood and adolescence to find our way in the modern world, where we teeter uncertainly toward the handling of the responsibilities of cosmic adulthood, with the godlike powers over life and death that the development of the concrete mind has brought us in our technology, powers that impose either rapid growth in moral stature or self-destruction.

3. Arthur and his Kin

We will look first at the immediate kin of King Arthur. Arthurian legend in its fullness is a mass of inconsistencies, for it is the work of many hands, mouths and minds. It expands like a great embroidered tapestry over the thirteenth century in long prose romances stemming from the courtly French poems. These in turn are based on the tales of Breton storytellers at Norman courts, with their oral traditions of Celtic myth and legend containing elements of extreme Atlantean antiquity.

Because of its mode of development medieval prose romance tends not to have a beginning, a middle and an end, but a perpetual on-going. Unresolved aspects of story that are thrown up in each episode are taken up by another story teller, on another occasion, so that the whole matter grows by natural accretion.

Malory's service, in the mid-fifteenth century, with the newly invented printing press of Caxton, was to crystallize this growth at a critical point. With more or less organic consistency he gives a framework upon which the modern imagination can work. We shall therefore follow Malory's general structure, which is based on an amalgamation of the major prose romances current in his time. We will reserve, however, the licence to deviate where we choose in the case of material not well known to Malory. This includes some of the more primitive material before it was edited by later scribes who, whilst they did great service in recording the oral tradition, could sometimes not resist tampering with it, to make it accord the better with current Christian monastic belief. With a practical knowledge of occult dynamics and a longer historical perspective it is possible to detect and set to rights much of the alterations.

Arthur's Family Tree

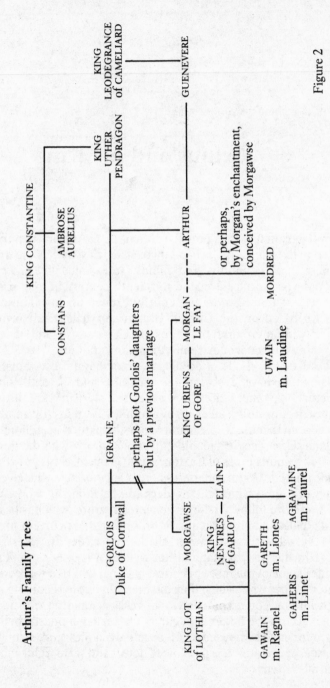

Figure 2

In the Malory story, Arthur is the son of a true king of England, Uther Pendragon. His mother is Igraine, or Igerne, wife of the Duke of Cornwall. Of this mating, which was arranged by Merlin, we shall have much to say. For the moment we may confine ourselves to the fact that Igraine had three daughters by a previous marriage; Morgawse, Elaine and Morgan. These three sisters, in their inner aspect, exemplify three grades in the Womens' Mysteries. In their outer aspect they represent three femine types:

Elaine—   the virginal type of woman dedicated to service; as nun, or nurse, or eternal 'elder sister' or 'devoted daughter'.

Morgawse—the earthly oriented mother, and woman of the world. A perfect mate; magnetic centre of attraction in or out of the family circle.

Morgan—   the withdrawn wise woman, either as crone or 'femme fatale', with knowledge of the inner powers and how to operate them. A healer and counsellor or a worker of enchantments and manipulator of glamour.

In their more esoteric development they become the Three Mourning Queens of the barge that came for the mortally wounded King after the last battle. In one sense they are the three-aspected feminine divinity, and also initiators in their own right of the mysteries of birth and death on the various planes of existence. In this respect they embody the traditional three Fates.

In Arthurian legend the three-aspected principle appears in manifold ways; not only with the three sisters, but in important relationships such as Guenevere with Arthur and Lancelot. These are expressions of principles of polarity.

At root it is a spiritual principle which manifests right through-out the psychic realms and is common in fairy tales and mnemonic devices such as the Druidic Triads. It has particular regard to principles of form and the feminine mysteries.

Traditionally Arthur's mother Igraine is an Atlantean princess, brought over from the old civilization to mate with one of the ruling line of the new civilization. Arthur therefore has within him the blood of the ancient British kings and also the sacred blood of the Atlantean priest-kings. There, according to tradition, the blood line was kept pure as it brought about a particular type of clairvoyance. In prehistoric times, when man was less individualized, the leaders of civilization were those who could communicate with teachers or leaders or racial oversouls on the inner planes. This clairvoyant faculty was implicit in the foundation of a theocracy and it was facilitated by early genetic engineering.

It makes Arthur one who is capable of action and response to inner and outer stimuli. He is no mere lusty warrior. His is the prototype of the initiate in the world; one who is conscious of the inner as well as outer aspects of life forms and forces.

Arthur received an esoteric training from an early age in order to bring out the gifts inherent in the Atlantean royal blood (*sang real*) of his mother's side. This is evident in Merlin's bargain with Uthur Pendragon to take custody of the young Arthur at birth. He is brought up, like Lancelot, under a lake. Traditionally this has been located as Lake Bala in mid-Wales. We are, however, dealing with a country of the soul, and in this imaginative geography a lake invariably signifies the astral plane.

It is this early training in seership that is in a sense his downfall. It need not, of course, have been so but, as we have said, the Arthurian cycle demonstrates both sides of any human principle —the advantages of its good use and the perils of misuse.

All gifts involve a temptation and the temptation is provided here by his half-sister Morgan le Fay. As her name implies, she is highly trained in esoteric matters. However, she is also exceedingly ambitious and so uses the powers for her own ends, rather than in dedicated service to the race, which is the proper concern of white magic.

In Malory this esoteric dedication is disarmingly quoted as her entry into a nunnery where she became greatly skilled at 'nigromancy'! There are some strange anachronisms and misunderstandings in this statement, but behind it is the fact that Morgan is of the old line of Atlantean initiates and is indeed potentially a female counterpart of Merlin.

However, whereas Merlin works on group and racial dynamics, Morgan concentrates on personal aggrandizement. One of her methods is the seduction of her young half-brother Arthur. The result of this incestuous union is the evil Mordred who, in the end, is the principal instrument in the destruction of the Round Table Fellowship.

That there was more than simply a physical liaison involved in the mating of Morgan and Arthur is to be seen in the stories of Excalibur and its scabbard. Morgan goes to great lengths to obtain these from Arthur, for Excalibur is more than a magic sword for use in battle. It is the secret and power of polarity working on the inner and outer planes. This is the significance of its provenance from, and return to, the Lady of the Lake. It is also why Merlin particularly charges Arthur to guard and cherish the scabbard, for it is as important, if not more so, than the sword itself.

In other words, if Excalibur is the power of the use of polarities according to inner principles; the scabbard is the proper containment and skilled knowledge of how and when to use these forces.

The perils of losing control of the forces of the sword and scabbard are indicated in the story wherein Morgan steals them, puts counterfeits in their place, and then arranges for her creature Accalon of Gaul, a knight whom she has glamourised with her beauty and visions of power, to fight Arthur using Arthur's true weapons. Arthur would have come to an early and inglorious end but for the specific intervention of the Lady of the Lake.

The ancient magic involved is also indicated in Mordred's birth at Beltain, May Day, and the strangely uncharacteristic tale of the slaughter of the innocents. To prevent the evil destiny from occurring, all the babies born in May are cast adrift on a boat. All perish save, of course, Mordred. This is a tale coming almost direct from ancient Greek tragedy, with Mordred as a kind of anti-hero, for it is usually the hero who is condemned and saved in this fashion according to the laws of destiny. It is also an inversion of the tale of Herod's slaughter of the innocents in the New Testament. Mordred therefore has much about him pertaining to the anti-Christ.

If placed upon the traditional Tree of Life, Mordred would hold the Gate of the dark quarter of Malkuth that abuts the evil and unbalanced forces of the Qliphoth in the waters under the Earth. In this sense, therefore, Mordred is less a human archetype, as are the other knights, than a principle of cosmic evil—an artificial creature brought to birth by the sorcery of Morgan.

In Malory, and some other sources, Mordred is said to be the son of Morgawse, but this, esoterically, does not ring quite true. Morgawse is a great, powerful and dynamic elemental figure, wife of the titanic menacing figure of one of the old kings, King Lot of Lothian, and mother of four important Round Table knights, Gawain, Gaheris, Gareth and Agravaine. She is capable of mighty lusts, as in her relationship with Lamorak, another mighty champion of the old school, but she is not one dedicated to positive evil.

If Morgawse were held to be the mother of Mordred, then it

would follow that the liaison was arranged by Morgan, manipulator of glamour, behind the scenes, entwining the great elemental passions of Morgawse with the budding adolescent emotional vulnerability of the young Arthur. Morgawse is some twenty years senior to Arthur as she, and her sister Elaine, were married at Uther's nuptials to Igraine, which followed closely upon Arthur's conception. Morgan was more nearly his contemporary, being too young to marry at this time.

Morgan herself later married Uriens of Gore, a very ancient figure, as elemental as he is human, and in a sense a King of the Gnomes. Thus does Morgan continue her involvement with magical forms of mating, although in this instance the son she bears to Uriens is a good knight, Sir Uwain le Blanchemains, who in fact turns against his mother at a later point and prevents her from murdering his half-human father.

This then is the background to Arthur's upbringing. He has a physical destiny to perform as future king of Britain, and is equipped with a knowledge and experience of the inner forces involved. These, however, are intercepted and perverted by his half-sister Morgan.

It is this which sows the seed of his later estrangement from Guenevere. In his early youth Arthur is an attractive figure as exemplified in his relationship to his foster brother Kay in the famous episode of the sword in the stone. Here, despite the attempted duplicity of Kay, who attempts to claim the feat for himself, Arthur accepts his destiny with modesty. His dismay when his foster-father Sir Ector kneels at his feet as his subject shows a disarmingly human touch and he honours throughout the rest of his life Sir Ector's request that he make Kay his seneschal.

Arthur, whose previous education has been at the hands of his foster-father Sir Ector, with the esoteric contacts of the Lady of the Lake, is now openly taken under the tutelage of Merlin during the difficult period when the lords of the country contest his right to the throne.

Arthur bears all the delays with patience, and greets with courage and fortitude the eventual outbreak of hostilities with those who will not accept him. It is in these early episodes that he wins his spurs, so to speak, as a true and worthy knight, tried in the test of prolonged combat, and also as one fit to be a king. Later the archetype of kingship which descends upon him tends to obscure the character of Arthur, but it is revealed here in his boyish optimism, skill and love of adventure.

Indeed, he has to be carefully guarded by Merlin against his own impetuosity. He could easily have been killed in a rash challenge of his youthful skills against the mighty power and experience of the great King Pellinore, but Merlin causes a sleep to fall upon his adversary, and so saves Arthur in order to fulfil his higher destiny. Thus do the inner plane powers, on occasion, protect their initiates from their own folly.

Also characteristic of ardent, knightly youth is Arthur's initial preference of the sword to the scabbard. Merlin cautions him strongly about this. In another sense this is later exemplified after a massive battle when Arthur, having won the field, seeks to continue the slaughter, until Merlin chides him 'Will you never have done?'

The story of Arthur's victory over the twelve kings who challenge his right to kingship is the remains of an ancient initiation cycle akin to the twelve labours of Hercules. This is shown in the zodiac and the constellation named after Hercules, who is the prototype of individualized man.

Having unified the realm Arthur goes to the Continental mainland. In the first instance this is to return the favours given him by his allies Kings Ban and Bors in the fight to establish his crown. Subsequently it is to quell the insolent might of the Emperor Lucius of Rome.

This is the nationalist vein in the legend, the instinct of national identity and the preservation of territorial rights and integrity. It carries within it race memories of various events, such as the formation of a separate Britain from the centralized empire of Rome under Carausius in the late third century, and, in the fourth and early fifth centuries, the attempts by Roman governors to claim the imperial throne in the days of decline of the Roman empire.

This tradition of Britain taking on the rest of Europe's organized might is rather more than jingoism. In the later destiny of nations it has been required more than once. Part of the national heritage of myth is to feed and preserve the national identity and destiny. It is no accident that the Arthurian legend, particularly in its nationally unifying and consolidating aspect, came to popularity with the Plantagenet kings. They had inherited from the conquering dynasty of the Dukes of Normandy a divided society, composed of Celt, Saxon, Dane, with the Norman ruling society also at odds with its continental kin.

Thus Geoffrey of Monmouth's *History of the Kings of Britain* was of particular importance. It is small wonder that it leaped to instant fame and acclaim. It struck a nerve in the incipient national consciousness and was exactly what the country needed—a certificate to a national identity going back to prehistoric times.

It matters not that modern historians find the work of Geoffrey of Monmouth shot through with errors, and indeed largely an imaginative fabrication. As we have said, in these matters it is inspiration fed by imagination that is important. In the event it was Geoffrey's 'history' that launched the Arthurian legend on its long modern career. The History itself was credited with factual veracity for a very long period, certainly until the time of Malory. Indeed Geoffrey's book is still in print, and even after 850 years makes a very good read.

It tells simply of Arthur's antecedents, King Uther Pendragon and his brothers Ambrose Aurelius and Constans, and their struggle against the usurper Vortigern who had disastrously parleyed with the treacherous Saxon chieftains Hengist and Horsa. Merlin also appears as the power behind the throne, a prophetic druidical type of figure.

There is no mention of the Round Table, Holy Grail or any of the other great ancillaries at the court of Arthur. His is simply presented as part of a natural line of kings that goes back to the heroic age of ancient Greece. The founder of the kingdom is said to be one Brutus, a Trojan who, after the seige of Troy, guided by an oracle of Diana, led a group of compatriots, after many adventures, to these island shores.

Early kings such as Lear and Cymbeline appear, familiar to us from Shakespeare's use of this same material via Holinshed's Chronicles, and eventually we arrive at the plateau of triumph, the establishment of Arthur. Having established a unified kingdom, Arthur is shown defending himself and his realm against the overweaning ambition and pride of a central European authority. This he conquers, marching through France and Switzerland, and he is finally crowned Roman Emperor by the Pope himself.

The triumph is, however, short lived in that news comes of Mordred's treachery at home and Arthur and his armies return to fight a disastrous civil war. At the end Arthur is borne away to the Isle of Avalon for the healing of his wounds, in accordance with Breton legend.

Geoffrey is the great reconciler between Celt and non-Celt. He uses historical antecedents such as Julius Caesar, the Venerable Bede and Henry of Huntingdon. He also uses stories from Nennius (c.826) such as those surrounding the usurper Vortigern, and he uses these to introduce Merlin, probably gleaned from current oral material and manuscripts that have not survived. He makes much of Merlin, and later produced a separate volume of 'prophecies' of Merlin. (This was the start of centuries of thriving semi-occult political literature of which the well-known surviving example is *Old Moore's Almanac*). Arthur's possession of Excalibur (here called Caliburn) is cited, together with other named weapons; Pridwen his shield and Ron his spear.

Three important themes derive from the Breton *conteurs*. First, the begetting of Arthur by Uther on Gorlois's wife at Tintagel, which derives from Cornish legend. Secondly, his victory over the emperor called Lucius, with staunch assistance from Gawain (Walwanus), which parallels a Welsh tradition of war against a vassal called Lluch. And thirdly, the abduction of Guenevere and the final battle, which is recorded in the *Annals of Wales*.

Scholars tend to deride Geoffrey's claim to the use of the ancient Breton book and assume this to be a device to conceal that he made up much of the material from his own head. To our mind Geoffrey seems to be writing along the lines of many interpreters of occult tradition, which uses a combination of intuitive clairvoyance together with similar manuscript or oral material of others in order to express inner realities and archetypal forces. This may take the guise of pseudo-history but it is the effect upon the minds and hearts of the readers and hearers that is the criterion of its value; in other words, its 'inner' accuracy. As the success of Geoffrey's book goes to show, it struck a chord that gave it very considerable influence within the group soul of the race. This is not literary fraud or academic deception although those steeped in a post-Cartesian analytical intellectual discipline may understandably tend to see it as such.

Geoffrey later, in 1151, composed a *Life of Merlin* which drew heavily on Welsh and Breton traditions, such as Arthur's departure to Avalon, where he will be cured of his wounds by the presiding goddess of the island, who is named Morgan—the redeemed or 'brighter' side of the ambivalent character of the later romances.

There was at the time of Geoffrey's writing a thriving oral tradition, for travelling and resident storytellers were a principal source of entertainment and instruction. The Bretons were particularly active in this respect because during Saxon invasions many Celts had fled from Britain to Brittany. Some became bi-lingual and earned their living telling stories at the Norman courts, using their own folk traditions as source material, and adapting them to current fashions and manners. With the Norman conquest of England many of these Breton storytellers came back with the conquerors, and there was a certain bond of sympathy between Norman and Celt in the face of the antagonism of the now suppressed Anglo-Saxons.

Furthermore, the Breton tales had an alternative tradition of stories based upon the exploits of Charlemagne—the tales of Roland and so on—which tended to glorify a central European power base. The Arthurian tales, which were more powerful in that they were older, and came from a deep racial level, as opposed to comparatively modern soldier's tales, gave a cultural stiffening to Norman and Plantagenet visions of a kingdom of England separate from the Continent. The established continental dynasties would have preferred to see England as part and parcel of the Duchy of Normandy, owing vassalage to France.

Geoffrey wrote in Latin, the language of priests and scholars. The popularity of his work demanded, however, a translation into Norman-French which the courtly classes could more readily understand. This was provided by the poet Wace, in what is a free paraphrase rather than a translation of Geoffrey's *History*. Here the Round Table appears and is compared to the Table of the Last Supper, which in medieval times was presumed to be round. There was also the Celtic tradition of chiefs or kings seated at banquets with a circle of twelve warriors around them.

Within fifty years a significant extension took place in that the work was translated into early English, so that the Anglo-Saxons could understand it. This version, by Layamon, adds a strain of Anglo-Saxon imagination and magic. Arthur's helmet 'Goose-white' could be straight from *Beowulf*, who also had a white helmet. There is also a mail corselet, which is forged by Wayland the god-smith in *Beowulf*, and by elves in Layamon.

Layamon's other additions to Wace include Arthur's dream about Mordred's betrayal. He dreams that Mordred is cutting down pillars in the hall, and Guenevere is pulling down the roof, so that Arthur falls and breaks his right arm. With his left arm, however, he beheads Mordred and cuts Guenevere to pieces. There are other versions known of this, so Layamon is here using traditional material.

Indeed we face the frustration that both Wace and Layamon

refer to contemporary oral material only to dismiss it as too unfashionable and unreliable to quote. We would nowadays wish that they had indulged themselves more in relaying these oral traditions.

In Layamon, the infant Arthur is taken, after Igraine has delivered him, by elves who bestow upon him great gifts—of strength, dominion, long life, generosity. The long life might at first sight seem disproved by events but if he is still living on the Isle of Avalon it is wholly appropriate! In Layamon, Arthur's passing to Avalon is presided over by the loveliest of faeries, the Queen Argante. A short boat with two women in it, wondrously clad, comes from the sea to fetch him.

There is a strain of ferocity in Layamon absent from the more courtly Wace. Gawain, for instance, proposes that the Queen be torn apart by wild horses. There is also an early strain of Anglo-Saxon sportsmanship, or chivalry of the chase, in that Arthur declines to attack a ferocious giant while he is asleep.

What is important above all in Layamon however, is its evidence of a unified national consciousness being forged by the Arthurian tales. This even goes to the extent of Layamon exulting in the slaughter of the barbarian hordes by Arthur. These are in fact the ancestors of the Anglo-Saxons of whom Layamon is one and for whom he is writing. However to both Layamon and Wace, Arthur is very much a model Christian king.

Thus these pre-romance annals, which provide the basis for the exploits and example of the Round Table Fellowship have their grounding in a simple patriotism.

It is this element that later helped to weld a national consciousness in the period of the Hundred Years War, when the Black Prince was fighting to resolve the final status of England in relation to France. In the same power struggle the chivalrous king was also exemplified by Henry V.

Whatever the tragedy of the wars of this troubled period, they are the external aspect of an inner link between England and France, and also with parts of the Iberian peninsular that were once part of the heritage of Queens of England. Thus there is a greater bond between Britain and France than between Britain and Germany despite greater apparent similarities of personality with the latter.

Later, the establishment of the Tudors, after the long civil anarchy of the Wars of the Roses, was helped by looking back to ancient Welsh traditions. Great hopes were placed upon the future of Prince Arthur, the original heir of Henry VII. However, the use of the name Arthur has never proved very fortunate for the later royal families of the realm—as if there were a certain sacrilege in too blatant a political use of this ancient common heritage.

This patriotic tradition is subsumed in the character of Arthur. There are elements within him of the best that has been remembered of the deeds of historical figures such as Alfred the Great, Richard the Lionheart, Henry V, the Black Prince. The fact that some of these figures come historically after the literary formation of Arthurian legend is irrelevant. The folk memories surrounding them come from the same common store as that formulating the character of Arthur. This includes the great stability, commonsense, and the encouragement of cultural knowledge and skills by the Saxon Alfred. It includes the charisma and international vision of Richard I. It includes the patriotic fervour of Henry V, particularly as portrayed in Shakespeare. These kings and the Black Prince embody chivalry, charisma, patriotic duty and fervour.

At a less immediately obvious level, the character of the king also embodies the qualities associated with the great Celtic chieftain Cassivellaunus who, though defeated and taken in chains to Rome, won the respect of the Romans by his bearing. Yet there is also a Roman strain within Arthur, something of the charisma carried by the imperator Julius Caesar, yet generalized into the ideal soldier and leader of the legions.

In counterbalance to these great qualities of kingship there is, however, a negative side, which gives the character of Arthur its human perspective and dimension. This is, in a sense, a fate that waits to entrap all human holders of high office. It is the problem of all human authority—when the person becomes overlaid by the function.

This can happen in ordinary life at relatively humble levels in a small community with well defined social roles, and can become psychologically crippling. The vicar or the school teacher, for instance, can become so identified with their function that the human being disappears behind the mask and can be stifled by it, incapable of any real human contact.

In the Arthuriad there is a poignant example of Arthur's falling into this entrapment with function. When he is first proclaimed king in his youth, against the concerted opposition of many of the great kings, dukes and barons, it is the popular massed support of the commons that provides the impetus for his final election. In the last days however, when he is away fighting on the continent, the commons side with the usurper Mordred. The implication is that Arthur has become remote from the people. The impetuous ardent heroic youth has given place to the figurehead of an aristocratic institution, preoccupied with matters that do not engage the affections of his common subjects.

In the early days the members of the Round Table fellowship go abroad radiating the benign influence of a centre of civilization and justice in an anarchic world torn by civil strife and local tyrannies of 'evil custom'. At a latter stage, however, one has a court concerned with internal accusations and internecine rivalries erupting into violence. One knight is poisoned at the Round Table, and the Queen herself accused of the deed. This in itself shows a decay of standards and values within the court society. In the end this progresses to open conflict.

Yet there have always been these stresses and conflicts of interest and ambition in the court. It is the very stuff of human intercourse. The difference is that in the earlier days of dynamism the eager aspiration of the court and the young Arthur is such as to contain and direct these conflicts into constructive channels. In the latter days, with the loss of impetus and dynamism of the whole body politic, the destructive elements of these personal conflicts take greater force to the ultimate disintegration of the whole.

In part this is a natural course of aging in any human life or institution, although all does not have to end in degradation and disaster. The old can give place to the new with grace and dignity.

However, there is a certain coldness within Arthur's attitude, barely noticeable at first, but which stems from his early 'faery' training. This becomes evident in his later difficulties with the Queen, who finds her personal fulfilment of love with Lancelot rather than with the king.

This exemplifies particular problems of the initiate, of one who has been trained in esoteric powers to a knowledge and awareness of the astral realms. To such a one there is always a kind of division of attention, between the forces of the inner worlds, and the forms they may take upon the physical. In the case of the normal man or woman of the world the inner forces are projected onto the physical plane, and onto the persons and objects therein. With the initiate they become separated.

The danger for the initiate is that by no longer being an

unconscious participant in such impulses and emotions, there can develop an element of impersonality which, if misdirected, may appear as disinterest or lack of humanity.

This is exemplified in the tradition described by Tennyson, who researched into origins widely and deeply, that at their betrothal Arthur did not go himself to claim Guenevere from her father. He sent an emissary—Lancelot. In this small incident of impersonality there is encapsulated much that in the end destroyed the whole of Arthur's Fellowship.

4. Queen Guenevere and the Court

With the Queen, Guenevere, we also have strong forces of 'office' contending with the forces of the personality of Guenevere herself.

Not only is she first lady of the court but she is the instrument of a certain group destiny, for it is through her that the Round Table comes to the court. Merlin had presented it to her father, King Leodegrance of Cameliard, when he was a stalwart lieutenant of Uther Pendragon. It then became part of the wedding dowry of Guenevere. There are very deep esoteric implications here but for the moment our concern is principally with the characters involved, and their role as exemplars of how to handle, or not to handle, various elemental forces.

Guenevere, like Arthur, is a very engaging character, and her queenly role as figurehead for all that is civilized and graceful does not transform her into a characterless idealization. She is a great beauty, and a great lady in her own right, and the inspiration of all the knights of the court.

In this she represents an important transitional role, for she embodies three phases of the role of the feminine. The earlier role is Druidical, the middle role Trouvère, and the later that of Malory.

The Druidical Guenevere, which has origins in even earlier times, is the representative of the Earth in Spring. She is the fecundity maiden, who has to be fertilized that the earth shall bring forth joy and abundance. This is the story of the Mother Earth, first as a fair maiden, the May Queen, in white or pale green, crowned with flowers, the magical virgin with whom the god or hero mates to bring back the Earth to fertility. (The fact that the king-hero Arthur fails to fertilize her is thus crucial to the later tragedy.) Then the maiden becomes the bountiful matron of the fruits of the Earth in harvest time. It is something of the measure of Guenevere's character that, although childless, she nonetheless managed to give this beneficent motherly quality to the court—helped by the attentions of Lancelot. It is only later in the human saga that the human failure of personal jealousy (at Lancelot's association with Elaine of Astolat and Elaine of Carbonek), leads to a cracking of this image. As a result the social fabric of the court, of which she forms a feminine key-stone, also crumbles. We have her being accused of intrigue and crime, and the whole Round Table splits in physical battle over her.

There is embodied in earliest myth the concept of woman as a fecundity symbol. As such she is a kind of primitive cauldron or grail bringing warriors to birth within her womb and providing the milk of their infant sustenance. Thus we have the very early ritual representations of grotesquely carved female fertility objects. Together with this concept there also goes the primitive idea that women and children are a form of wealth, chattels of private or common ownership of the men.

The transition from this primitive conception is, we have reason to believe, one of the secrets of Druidic initiation, for a knowledge of polarity working cannot possibly work practically while woman is regarded as an inferior. Indeed, the veneration of goddesses of erotic attraction, such as Ishtar in the Near East, represents a parallel development.

The esoteric traditions of Egypt, particularly the Mysteries of Isis and Hathor, also throw light on this development. The Druids probably obtained the methodology for it from Egypt. This is not as fantastic as it may sound for the ancient Mysteries of the immediately pre-Christian era were of one brotherhood in more ways than is currently realized. Pilgrimages via the trade routes took place, and new ideas were grafted onto older traditions.

The basic idea for this role of a women's priesthood was in fact a very old one, and the methods of developing the polarity (a Western form of Tantrik yoga), originated in ancient Greece and Egypt.

The Trouvères, the bards of the Middle Ages, sought to revive this knowledge, which had all but disappeared in the Dark Ages with the advent of a new ruling class based upon feudal warrior values. Indeed, with the monastic Christian interpretation of

Biblical teaching, as well as being subjugated by a feudal warrior culture, women tended to be regarded as temptations of the devil.

In the primitive society of the Druidic era women had been segregated for safety and protection but were venerated as instruments of the gods. This idea was now reintroduced upon a higher arc, and the Trouvères developed the chivalrous, romantic concept of women—a remote gracious and divine beauty, confined in a holy of holies, who might bestow grace and favour upon a sufficiently devoted suitor.

This became a major cult in the South of France and was responsible for a radical change in social customs. Women were still regarded as chattels owned by a particular male. No divorce was possible and she had no rights of her own as a separate legal entity. This entrenched legal tradition has lasted in the West until very recent times and still pertains in many parts of the world. However, initiates of the Cult of Queen Venus were generous in the matter of their wives, although when the cult spread beyond the immediate circle of dedicated followers many a minor nobleman made political and financial capital out of his wife, if she were sufficiently attractive to an overlord. Thus are all systems of human governance open to abuses of one kind or another.

It is this dynamic that we find in the relationship between Guenevere and Lancelot. In this respect they are exemplars of a new, liberated form of relationship, and initiates of a revived form of initiatory polarity working. This we shall later examine in more detail.

However, this was lost to Malory, a non-initiate, writing some four hundred years later, and by his time the story had been given a moral twist, so that Lancelot and Guenevere are made to die repentant, confining themselves to monastery and convent respectively. We miss a great deal if we accept this later interpretation of the dynamics of the Arthurian tradition, interpolated by monkish scribes.

The Christian tradition gave a soaring, lofty new dimension to Arthurian legend, with its interpretation of the Grail, but the temptation to try to suppress earlier primitive material was of little real worth.

In Guenevere, therefore, as with Arthur, we find much that relates to office—the office of Queen as opposed to that of King—and also much that relates to a symbolic overshadowing of their office by racial needs and myths of the past. In the case of Arthur this is the role of the hero-king; in the case of Guenevere it is that of Earth maiden and bright fertile mother. In terms of classical Greek mythology she is part Persephone, part Demeter. It is her Persephone aspect that is at the back of the persistent tradition of her abduction by representatives of the Underworld. In a number of variants it is when she goes a-Maying and the villain of the piece is a lusty old rustic Pan figure, slightly disguised as a minor king of Cornwall, Meliagraunce.

One of the poems of Chrétien de Troies, at the courtly literary stage of the Arthurian tradition, uses this theme in his *Lancelot* or *Knight of the Cart*. Writing in about 1170 he is drawing on Celtic sources for his main story even though his treatment of the theme is courtly.

The story of Guenevere's abduction appears decades before in the *Life of St Gildas*. The literature of saints' lives, a very popular form in those times, also served as a vehicle for much traditional pagan and Celtic material. In this version the abductor is Melwas, who is called King of the Summer Country. Her rescue is effected by Arthur, who, as solar hero, is the most appropriate according to the dynamics of early nature myth. By the time of Chrétien de Troies, who is writing this story at the suggestion of Countess Marie of Champagne, a queen of the Troubadour minstrelsy, it is Lancelot, the lover of the Queen, who rescues her.

In the Greek mythology, as in Persephone being seized by Pluto, the maiden is taken down to the shady underworld of Hades. In the Celtic tradition the underworld is an altogether brighter place, and is called Voirre, the Isle of Glass. This is an appropriate cognomen for the inner planes in that in traditional astronomy the influences affecting the sub-lunary world of Earth proceed from the surrounding crystalline spheres, moved by heavenly powers, and each representing the 'heaven' of a different planet, until ultimately the crystalline spheres of the zodiac, and the *primum mobile* are reached, beyond which are the uncreate realities of God.

Glass islands are, therefore, another way of designating various inner plane states. They correspond to the spheres of the Tree of Life, and a systematic description of them is to be found in Dante's *Paradiso*. In Chrétien's courtly version, the place of abduction is the less Elysian island of Goirre, a corruption of Isle of Voirre (glass). However, original material does remain as in the tests, such as the perilous sword bridge, that the hero must overcome to effect his rescue. These are traditional tests of initiation before the candidate is found worthy to deal with the forces that lie behind physical life.

This tradition of abduction in the later prose romances, particularly in *Le Mort Artu*, drawn upon by Malory, is made an important vehicle for the dynastic drama. This occurs in two principal ways.

One is the treachery of Mordred. Different versions make the Queen more or less willing, though the main, and more interesting, line is that she escapes Mordred and seeks refuge in the Tower of London. However anachronistic this may appear, the Tower is on the White Mount, the burial site of the head of Bran the Blessed, the mighty protective father of Welsh Celtic gods, who has, as part of his mission, the powers of the regenerative cauldron—an early form of Grail—and also the protection of these islands from invasion. This role was later elaborated in the tradition of Merlin surrounding the British Isles with a wall of brass, so that they are sometimes called Merlin's Enclosure.

The other abduction theme is a two-edged one in that it is Lancelot who abducts, yet at the same time rescues, Guenevere when she is condemned to be burned at the stake for their treasonable and adulterous liaison. Lancelot takes her to his castle of Joyous Garde where he keeps her, besieged by Arthur's forces, until, by the Pope's intercession, Guenevere returns to Arthur's court, only to be abducted again shortly afterwards by Mordred when hostilities between Arthur and Lancelot have once again broken out.

There is obviously a great confluence of different traditions here. The liaison between Guenevere and Lancelot has been going on for a long time without any accusations of treachery or adultery. Therefore in one form of tradition it is an accepted pattern of relationships. This is preserved in the Trouvère/Troubadour line.

This is unacceptable, however, to the Christian ethic of marriage, even though in practice marriage became the vehicle of statecraft and political convenience. Marriages were arranged as means of alliance between petty states, often with the principals still in infancy. These children were thus, in a sense no more than hostages. It was this abuse of the moral code that gave a fertile ground for the elevation of the ideal of love outside marriage. This is a hallmark of the Troubadour minstrelsy. Although it often may have manifested in less than ideal form, it is perhaps seen at the height of its idealism in the love of Dante for Beatrice—which gave inspiration of the highest order.

We do best in our evaluation of the character of Guenevere to see her as the paragon of Courtly Love at its height as a civilizing influence.

The tone of Courtly Love is held more in the short Provençal lyric poetry of the twelfth century than in the great Arthurian sagas in poetry and prose. This brief flowering of literature is considered by some the absolute height of European literary expression. Ezra Pound even insists that anyone who aspires to an appreciation of literature should learn Provençal in order to savour this particular art form.

The apotheosis of the movement is seen in Dante, where lyric poetry is at its most exquisite height, and many, including William Blake, have felt that this warrants learning medieval Italian. But it flourished for some hundred years and more before him in the troubadours of Limousin, Poitu, Aquitaine, Toulouse and Provence.

The lyrics breathe a sublimated passion, exalting the beauty of the lady. There were various forms, often of extreme technical difficulty. One example was the *alba* or dawn song, celebrating the parting of the lovers after a night of joy. Another was the *pastorelle*, embodying the advances of an enamoured knight to an idealized shepherdess. However, much of it is concerned with an unrequited love.

The revolutionary aspects of this poetry were that it defied church teaching and the conventions of society. It rejected or ignored the sanctity of marriage, substituting for it a relationship based on free choice, rather than political arrangement. It also, which was even more revolutionary, gave woman a higher worth and even superior status to man.

Certain heretical religious influences were major factors in the background. One was the Cult of the Queen of Heaven, or in more terrestrial terms, Queen Venus or Ishtar. Her Biblical antecedents are to be found in the term Ashtaroth—the plural form used by the Old Testament prophets to describe shrines of the goddes Ishtar—and her influence pervades the Canticles or Song of Solomon. The strongly patriarchally-minded Jews firmly repressed the feminine, but a principle so fundamental and universal can hardly remain like this for long. Elements in the mediaeval Christian church realized this and encouraged the development within the Church of the cult of the Blessed Virgin Mary. In this, a large part was played by the great mediaeval religious monastic reformer Bernard of Clairvaux, an immediate contemporary of Chrétien de Troies. However, the primary influence on the Provençal poets came from the prosperous and refined Moorish society of Southern Spain. This is exemplified in the poetry of the Andalusian Moor Ibn Hazm whose early eleventh-century poem *The Dove's Neck Ring* spells out the later code of Provençal Courtly Love. This influence extended to all Western Christendom, including the Italian states where Petrarch and Dante were its disciples.

In Southern France, however, the influence became so strong, and mixed with other heretical elements such as Catharism, that the ecclesiastical authorities took great alarm and, although the Cult of the Blessed Virgin Mary and the Courtly Love of the Arthurian tradition are longer term effects, in the short term it resulted in the bloody and brutal Albigensian crusade which effectively wiped out not only the Cathar heresy but also its fellow travellers including the creators of the Provençal love lyric.

Guenevere then, as the beautiful queen of King Arthur, to whom she was contracted in a dynastic marriage by Merlin (but with Sir Lancelot du Lac, the best knight in the world, as her lover), exemplifies the principles of Courtly Love. She is goddess—the divine feminine shown forth in human female reflection in as pure an exemplification of the concept as is to be found in the Provençal love lyrics or the poetry of Petrarch or Dante.

Charles Williams, in his comments on Courtly Love, suggests that in falling in love we see the beloved as she, or he, really is in their divine unfallen image. In this sense the process is a religious revelation, an enobling passion—not an infatuation or degrading folly.

The essence of Guenevere therefore, is to be found in parallel with Dante's Beatrice, who is no mere image of infatuation, but a guiding light, a stern teacher when need be, and instructress of the mysteries of life, and initiatrix. In Dante's poem there is a point where Virgil's inspired but earthly wisdom fails and it is Beatrice who reveals to him the Earthly Paradise and then proceeds to guide him through the heavenly spheres, until at the very threshold of the highest heaven of the uncreate realities she passes him on to the final instruction of Bernard of Clairvaux.

In our consideration of the Fellowship of the Round Table we need therefore to be equally conscious of the feminine side of it—an aspect that is often forgotten. For every knight there is a lady. So, depending from Arthur, the king, we have the knights of the Round Table—and depending from

Guenevere, the queen, we have the ladies of the Court.

In symbolic terms these functions can be visualized in relation to particular castles or palaces, where the emphasis on one or the other predominates. Thus in Caerleon we may visualize a centre for the knightly forces of the Round Table; a castle geared for war and action. Similarly in Camelot we have the ideal image of the medieval castle and palace at peace; with the emphasis on the domestic arts and an idyllic town and rural life about it.

In Qabalistic terms these centres can be placed on the Tree of Life, with the third element provided by the spiritual emphasis of the Grail Castle of Carbonek. In triadic terms this is the central balancing higher link between the male oriented Caerleon and the female oriented Camelot. One might therefore place them upon the lower Sephiroth of the Tree of Life, with Carbonek at Tiphereth, Camelot at Netzach, Caerleon at Hod, and at Yesod the astral faery forces symbolized by the Lake. Malkuth, the world of the Elements, might similarly be regarded as the forest of Broceliande, an image also used by Dante, Charles Williams, and others, for the concourse of forces we know as the physical world.

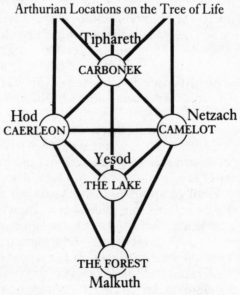

Arthurian Locations on the Tree of Life

Figure 3

We thus have a pattern of Arthurian place imagery that can be used as a basis for practical magical and meditative work. This will give an added dimension to those interested in Qabalistic 'path-workings'.

The higher levels of the Tree of Life may be conceived as principles behind these 'compositions of place'. Thus behind Caerleon is the force of endurance of the Black Pillar, and the active forces of the strength and justice of Geburah. Behind Camelot is the well ordered rule of Chesed and the Silver Pillar forces of beneficent growth, the energy of life expansive. And behind Carbonek are the spiritual transforming qualities of Daath, which bring higher forces to a lower mode of action. Beyond these again are the spiritual principles of the Supernal Sephiroth. The Paths of the Tree interjoining the Sephiroth indicate the various ways of horizontal and vertical polarity working with these forces.

There is thus a distinction between what might be called the King's Formula and the Queen's Formula, or the Caerleon Formula and the Camelot Formula, or the 'castle' formula and the 'palace' formula.

The latter embodies the art of '*court*esy', the art of the court; and this implies much more than polished manners. Rather it embraces the finer grades of feeling and a high code of honour. The expression and encouragement of these higher and finer standards are the magical function of the Court in national life.

The predominant influence in this formula is that of the Queen, who must teach and inspire the ladies and maidens of the court in the women's arts—a large part of which is the management of men, civilizing and moulding into 'gentle-men' the rough youths and uncouth squires. It achieves this by beauty, courtesy and the quality of the home environment, which applies to all levels of the realm, for every cottage in the country, however humble, is an image of the same archetype as is expressed by the court. And the woman's function is the care of that home, of the garden or home farm, of the children and of the sick.

In recent times there is a certain antagonism to what may be regarded as sex-stereotyping. However, the traditional male and female functions, which are polarised into knights and ladies in the Arthurian legends, remain valid theoretical patterns of the fabric of human civilization. A proper understanding of these archetypal patterns demands also an appreciation of their cross-polarity, and in the ideal home, be it palace or cottage, the 'male' and 'female' functions are a corporate responsibility. However, by the very facts of nature, there are some functions that are fulfilled more naturally or easily by one sex than the other.

It follows that the function of the Caerleon Formula is also an inherent part of the Camelot Formula, for the Round Table is also to be found in the Great Hall at Camelot, but there it can be regarded more as a social focus from which the knights may be called away upon their quests. Conversely, the Camelot Formula is implicit in the Caerleon Formula in that, even in the most war-like circumstances, there will be within it the women's quarters, or Bower, a miniature Camelot, or palace within the fort, a secluded haven in the alarms and excursions wherein the wounded may be succoured and the knights refreshed with the arts of peace. Thus in the midst of conflict is civilization still nurtured.

Indeed we might consider this pattern to be another specialized formula, the Tintagel Formula, which is the preservation of sacred things in evil times or within a hostile environment. An alternative title, pertaining particularly to the Queen and Lancelot, might be the Joyous Garde Formula. The Arthurian legends may thus be used to quarry various attributes of place for the conditions of human life experience.

There are two especial functions which are to be found in the Queen and the archetypes of the Ladies of the Court. In esoteric terms they might be regarded as Priestesses of the Stone or of the Cup.

The power of the Cup is the ability to inspire; the Cup of Inspiration shows the way the soul is meant to go and how to show forth its power.

The power of the Stone is a knowledge of the soul's destiny; an intuitive appreciation of character or type which gives the ability to guide and educate.

Insofar that the Ladies in the Arthurian legend derive from fundamental spiritual archetypes, it is a valuable exercise to analyse them in the way they carry out either of these dual functions of inspiration or guidance.

5. The Round Table Families

When we consider the various functions and forces of the knights and their ladies, it is helpful to group them according to their kin. In so doing we find they fall into the ambit of four principal heroes: Gawain, Lancelot, Tristram and Pellinore.

With Gawain, the nephew of the king, we may group all knights who are of the British royal house. This includes his three brothers, Gaheris, Gareth and Agravaine; also their cousin Uwain le Blanchmains, the son of Morgan le Fay. There is also the arch-traitor Mordred, and we may also include Arthur's foster-brother Kay, and the old stalwarts of the king, Lucan the Butler and Bedivere.

With Lancelot, who is a French knight, the son of King Ban of Benwick, we may associate all the French knights; his brother Ector de Maris and his cousins Lionel and Bors. Most importantly there is also his son Galahad, the Grail winner, who sits in the Siege Perilous.

With Tristram we have the Cornish connection. Tristram is the son of Melodias of Lyonesse and of the kindred of King Mark of Cornwall, who is his uncle. There are a number of other Cornish knights, such as his cousin Alexander le Orphelin, Dinadan the jesting knight, and La Cote Mal Taillé. There is also an Irish connection in that Tristram and Mark are intimately concerned with the daughter of the King of Ireland, la Belle Iseult, whose earlier Irish champion is also a knight of the Round Table, Sir Marhaus. The Saracen knight, Sir Palomides, is also closely connected with the Cornish circle.

There then remain the sons of the mighty old warrior King Pellinore. These include the first knight to be appointed to the

Round Table Fellowship by testing on a quest, Tor. There is also the mighty Lamorak, the Grail winner Percivale, and also Aglovale.

We may also consider the ladies in the same groupings. Pellinore has a daughter, Dindrane, who plays a major part in the Mysteries of the Quest of the Holy Grail.

In the Cornish circle there is the very important figure of la Belle Iseult, Queen of Cornwall and Tristram's lover. Another figure, who exemplifies true married love, is Alice la Belle Pilgrim, who marries Alexander le Orphelin.

In the French circle the most important ladies are those who form associations with Lancelot. Of principal importance (apart from the Queen) is Elaine of Carbonek, of the lineage of Kings Pellam and Pellas, the Guardians of the Grail Castle, and the mother, by Lancelot, of Galahad. There is also an important role played by Elaine of Astolat, who dies for love of Lancelot.

The ladies within the King's immediate circle include the great Queens: his mother Igraine and his half sisters Morgawse, Elaine of Garlot, and Morgan; and of course his own queen, Guenevere, whose own antecedents are from the Cornish sphere of influence, as she is the daughter of King Leodegrance of Cameliard. Indeed, bearing in mind Igraine's association with Cornwall, as Duchess of Tintagel, Cornwall plays an important role in the antecedents of the royal line.

We must also consider the ladies associated with the king's nephews. Gawain in particular is associated with many adventures involving ladies, but that involving the Lady Ragnel, who has been enchanted to look hideous, is an important one, and he is said, in one version of the stories, to have married her. Gareth is associated with the Lady Liones and the caustically tongued Linet, who is also associated with Gaheris.

Finally we must consider the faery women, the Lady of the Lake and her associates who, along with the arch-magician Merlin, play an important role behind the scenes in the dynastic role of the House of Arthur.

We will proceed to examine these various groups systematically, although in their fullness the study is a life's work and beyond the compass of a single book. The broad network of relationships is best presented in diagrammatic form as a set of family trees. (See Figures 2 and 4.)

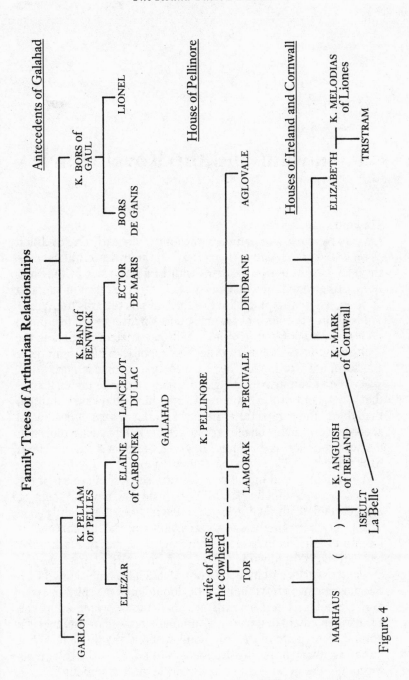

Family Trees of Arthurian Relationships

Antecedents of Galahad

House of Pellinore

Houses of Ireland and Cornwall

Figure 4

6. Gawain and the Royal House

Gawain

Gawain is a close companion of the king in the early oral tradition as recorded in the *Mabinogion*. Here he is known as Gwalchmai—the Hawk of May—and carries with him attributes of the solar hero. His strength increases as the sun rises, to reach its greatest at noon, whereafter it declines as the sun sets towards the West.

He is also the hero of an important English alliterative poem *Gawain and the Green Knight*, which has ancient origins as the 'beheading test'. Although it does not appear in Malory in quite this form it is worth while our examining it at some length.

A green giant arrives at Arthur's court to make the challenge that any knight of the court may strike him a blow on condition that the giant may return the stroke after a year. Gawain, in accordance with this challenge, strikes the knight such a blow that his head rolls across the floor. However, the giant seizes it, claps it back upon his neck, and departs in great mirth.

Towards the end of the year Gawain sets off in search of the giant's castle to fulfil his part of the bargain and, it would seem, to meet certain death. At one level this exemplifies the knightly code of honour: that a knight is as good as his word, and that this counts for more than his individual convenience or safety. At another level it is concerned with the control of the spirit of man over the elemental world, and indeed Gawain's shield is emblazoned with a pentagram, which symbolizes the dominion of the spirit over the four elements. The Elements are also aptly represented by the great green knight of the woods, although it is well to note that it is not the green giant of the 'Elements without' that he defeats but rather his own nature, the 'Elements within'. With the 'Elements without'—the green giant—he comes to an harmonious accord.

Therefore this particular story has much deep and subtle esoteric teaching.

The Anglo-Saxon author goes to some length to explain the pentagram on Gawain's shield in a way that accords with the conventional Christian piety of his times. He refers to trust in the five wounds of Christ, and the five joys of Mary. He also stresses the virtue of cleanhandedness—and it is interesting to note that the cognomen of Blanchmains is shared by two of Gawain's kin, Gareth and Uwain. The Gawain author elaborates this into an analysis of the five fingers of each hand representing the virtues of justice, prudence, temperance, fortitude—the four cardinal virtues—plus the monastic virtue of obedience; and also fraunchyse (generosity), fellowship, cleaness or purity, courtesy and mercy.

He further describes the pentagram as a sign particularly advocated by Solomon, and that if five attributes be given to each of the five points it makes a pentagram of pentagrams which, he says, is the strongest sign of protection possible.

Solomon was king of Israel, the son of David, who built the symbolic Temple later elaborated in the symbolism of Freemasonry. It was to be the permanent home for the Ark of the Covenant and the Shekinah, or Presence of God. Solomon's reputation rests on his wealth, wisdom and knowledge of magical powers.

He was plainly a student of the spiritual mysteries of other religions, and his wide ranging eclecticism extended to sending for Hiram of Tyre to help to build his Temple, and, in symbolic terms, the use of 'gold from Ophir, cedar from Lebanon.' He is also associated with the Queen of Sheba, a type of polarity priestess, the dynamics of whose working have been preserved, uncharacteristically in so patriarchal a canon, in the Old Testament as the Canticles, or Song of Solomon.

Another interesting point about Gawain's shield is that it is emblazoned on the inner side with an image of the Virgin Mary. In the context of the other material this suggests a derivation from earlier pagan forms of the Goddess. This complex of thinly disguised ancient symbolism suggests that this story may perhaps have derived from one of the warrior-priest orders such as the Knights Templar, although it has remoter origins in folk legend.

Anyway, so equipped, Gawain sets off through Arthur's kingdom of Logres and into Wales, where he passes 'Holy Head'. From thence, in the dangerous forest of the Wirral peninsula, he meets all kinds of challenge from wild animals, dragons, and evil adversaries. Added to these hazards is the hostility of the elements. He has to sleep in his armour because of the sleet and often awakes to find sharp icicles suspended over his head as a kind of 'sword of Damocles' portending his coming fate. From the Wirral he passes to a yet more strange and hostile forest full of those trees associated with the Druid religion, the hazel and hawthorn. It is thickly entangled, cold, wind-swept and dark. Eventually, however, after he prays that he may find a haven in which to hear mass at Christmas, and making the sign of the cross three times (an engaging combination of medieval piety overlaying magical tradition!) he sees a strong castle before him, on a mound behind a moat.

Gawain is given great welcome at the castle by the lord of it, a great hearty, bearded man, with a face that seems to glow like fire. His name is Bercilak, which may derive from the Gaelic *bachlach* or churl.

At Bercilak's castle Gawain spends the period between Christmas and New Year's Day, for Bercilak tells him that the Green Chapel, which he seeks in order to meet his ordeal, lies close by. Although Gawain is made royally welcome he undergoes tests of a different kind during his visit. While Bercilak goes out hunting each day Gawain is left resting at the castle. There is a custom however that at the end of each day each will exchange their winnings. Gawain presumably assumes that his own winnings refer to the minor games of chance that have already taken place. However, the gaming is rather different from what had been anticipated, for Bercilak's wife comes to Gawain's chamber each morning with the purpose of seducing him. Gawain, however, permits only the exchange of formal kisses, which he duly later exchanges with Bercilak for the spoils of the hunt.

He breaks faith, however, when she offers him a green sash that, she claims, will magically preserve him from any blow. Seeing this as a chance for him to survive his impending ordeal Gawain says nothing about receiving it, so that he does not have to surrender it to Bercilak.

On New Year's Day Gawain is taken to the Green Chapel. This, in fact, is a tumulus-like mound and here the green giant appears and prepares to cut off Gawain's head. To do this he makes three strikes.

The first time the giant stops his axe stroke in mid-air to reprove Gawain because he flinches. The second time he again stops it short of Gawain's neck, this time because he did *not* flinch.

The third time he stops short at the last hairsbreadth, having lightly nicked Gawain's neck.

Honour satisfied now that a blow has been struck, Gawain leaps to defend himself, only to find that the green giant reveals himself to be Bercilak. Bercilak commends him for his honourable conduct and says he would have gone completely unscathed but for his failing to honour his word about winning the green sash. For this he received the flesh wound but Bercilak now gives him the green sash as a token of passing the test.

Gawain regards this seal of initiation as a mark of shame, owing to his failure to win it in exemplary fashion but the court at Camelot, on hearing the tale, see things in a different light. They propose that any of the Round Table Fellowship may wear a green baldric as a mark of respect to Gawain in meeting the test of the Green Knight.

The initiatory aspect of the story is enhanced by the fact that Bercilak, the great nature figure, is accompanied at the castle by two ladies, one young and beautiful, the other old and ugly. These are aspects of the Isis of Nature, a parallel of the two consorts of Osiris, Isis and Nephthys, who stand behind the throne in the great Judgement Hall of souls in the Egyptian Mysteries of the dead. This dual female representation is also found associated with the Holy Grail.

Another great initiatory test, successfully met by Gawain, is that of the Castle of Wonders. The introduction to this test is by an extremely beautiful maiden named Orguelleuse admiring herself in a mirror. The mirror symbolizes that this is to be an initiation into the Mysteries of the Goddess of the Moon. Indeed, the Castle of Wonders is also known as the Castle of Maidens.

A ferryman takes him across to the castle—an indication of its inner plane location. The castle has an automatic aspect to it in that bow shots are fired at any knight who approaches it. It contains young girls and other women who lack husbands, together with young striplings who have not yet attained to manhood. Within the castle, which is rich and sumptuous, further magical perils await, particularly surrounding a Perilous Bed. When Gawain lies upon it he is assailed by disembodied shrieks, arrows fly at him from unseen assailants, and a mighty lion attacks him. Although grievously wounded, Gawain succeeds in killing the lion, and cuts off its claws and its head.

The Castle of Maidens is said to have been founded by a great Queen and is inhabited by herself, her daughter and her granddaughter. This is a form of describing the triple-aspected Moon goddess. One may regard the Perilous Bed, the automatic defences of the flying arrows (associated with Eros), and the feline, ravening beast in a Freudian sense. Failure of the knight to penetrate these defences and aquit himself well is, at this level, a failure in the dynamics of sexual polarity, a permanent state of immaturity; the feminine is unreleased from its egg-like shell, and the masculine is unfulfilled. At another, cosmic, level, embodying vertical rather than horizontal polarity, the earth itself remains unfructified, it stays in a state of uncultivated nature, infinite in potential, but capable of fruition only by the influx of the initiating, questing spirit, eager for self-demonstration in the waters of form.

Little is said, in Malory, of Gawain's wife, but another great aspect of initiation is held in folk lore in the story of his marriage to a fey, or faerie woman, usually called the Lady Ragnel.

In the story she is a woman of hideous aspect, whom Gawain betrothes out of loyalty to the king. However, upon his kissing her she turns into a most beautiful maiden, although with the proviso that she may be beautiful only for twelve hours out of the twenty-four—the evil enchantment must remain for the rest of the time. It is left to Gawain to choose whether he would rather have a publicly hideous and shameful wife by day who transforms into a beautiful maiden for his private pleasure by night; or a beautiful wife to be proud of during the day who at night is hideous and repulsive. Gawain however states that the choice should be the lady's, as she has to suffer the consequences of the enchantment even more than himself. This reply of Gawain's felicitously lifts the enchantment in its entirety.

Beyond the immediate lesson of personal and social relationships embodied in this story, there is behind it the deeper Mysteries of Persephone, of the Dark and Bright Isis, and also of the fair and ugly Grail bearer and messenger. It is the love and acceptance of nature, apparently red in tooth and claw, the Hideous Isis, that reveals the wondrous world of creative consciousness behind appearances, the Beautiful Isis of Nature.

All this, taken together with Gawain's early association with the king in the *Mabinogion*, makes Gawain a knight particularly associated with the native national consciousness. He is almost an equivalent of St George in a way that other great knights—Lancelot, Tristram or Pellinore, cannot quite somehow be.

Loyalty, together with the old values of tradition, is a particularly notable characteristic of Gawain, a virtue which he can, however, pursue to excess when it throws back to the old law of blood feud and vengeance. At an earlier stage of human social evolution this may be a necessary phase and virtue but when the rule of law is established it becomes a throwback, demonstrated as an unforgiving rigidity in personal vindictiveness.

Gawain does have a violent side to his nature, particularly as compared to the more courtly French knights. For instance, in the first set of Round Table quests as recorded by Malory, he kills a knight in vengeance for the death of one of his hounds. This is a somewhat severe interpretation of the old law of 'an eye for an eye, a tooth for a tooth,' even though it may have been carried out in berserk rage or the heat of combat rather than cold bloodedly. In this same incident he also hews off the head of the knight's lady when she tries to intercede.

It is to Gawain's great credit that he is genuinely capable of remorse and realization of the errors he has committed. As a result of this unfortunate episode he accepts the somewhat barbarous penance imposed upon him of riding back to court with the lady's severed head hung round his neck and thus presenting himself to the Queen. Guinevere, as mistress of the code of civilized conduct, duly admonishes him and charges that hence-forth he shall, in any circumstances, always give prior attention to the succour and assistance of ladies—and this obligation bestowed upon him places him in a particular relationship to the Queen. In fact he is sometimes hereafter referred to as the Queen's knight.

Later, however, his fealty to the Queen is put to severe test and indeed he feels impelled to abandon it when she is arraigned for treason. However, whilst at first reluctant to condemn in this most painful of dilemmas, when his younger brothers Gaheris and Gareth are killed by Lancelot, albeit inadvertently, in the rescue of the Queen, Gawain's wrath knows no bounds. It is Gawain who constantly impresses the cause of vengeance upon the king and prolongs the war with Lancelot. It is this continued skirmishing in Brittany that gives Mordred his chance to rebel in England, and Gawain later, on his death bed, bitterly repents the part which his actions have played in the break up of the Round Table Fellowship.

He dies just before the last battle, but not before writing to Lancelot to urge him to come to the king's assistance. It is from wounds inflicted by Lancelot that he dies, for outside the walls of

Joyous Garde he had constantly challenged, taunted and tempted Lancelot to come forth and fight in single combat. Lancelot, whose prowess in combat was second to none, refused for as long as he could and then, having defeated Gawain, forebore to kill him. It is a measure of Gawain's tenacity, ferocity and allegiance to old principles that, lying wounded and disabled by Lancelot, he still hurled imprecations at him and demanded a fight to the death. This happened more than once, although on the second occasion the wounds received by Gawain proved in the end to be fatal.

This was in fulfilment of an old prophecy concerning one of the great symbols associated with the Grail, the Sword that proclaimed Galahad to be the rightful claimant to the vacant Siege Perilous. Indeed Gawain's virtues are largely superceded by the advent of the Holy Grail.

Gawain's family loyalty is evident in the way that the Orkney brothers, Gawain, Gaheris, Gareth and Agravaine, are clearly discernible as a family unit in the tangled stories of all the knights. This can be expressed in the old, more bloody ways, as instinct towards family feud, and indeed they do maintain an enmity with the House of Pellinore. It is suspected that King Pellinore was responsible for killing their father King Lot; also Pellinore's son Lamorak has an illicit affair with their mother Morgawse. Vengeance to the death is therefore taken.

In the development of Arthurian romance there is a gradual change in the way different knights are described by various romancers and chroniclers. An early Celtic hero, Gawain tends to be undervalued by the courtly French writers, for whom Lancelot is the focus of interest. The Tristram stories, extolling Tristram, are a cycle in themselves which have no direct connection with Gawain. However, he comes into his own again in the superb Anglo-Saxon thirteenth century literature of *Gawain and the Green Knight*, thus getting his just dues from his own kind, now welded into one nation. It is also interesting to note how the more refined courtly writers move the antecedents of Gawain and his kin gradually further North, first to the Southern Scottish Celtic kingdom of Lothian (around present-day Edinburgh) and later to the far Orkneys, with their warlike Viking influence.

Gawain as portrayed by the French courtly writers is characterized by a certain uncouthness in love and war, and also a lack of appreciation of spiritual values. Thus in some of the stories his treatment of ladies is more inclined to physical seduction than

courtly love. He also has a fearsome reputation as a hewer of limbs
and heads in combat; whilst his experiences on the Quest of the
Holy Grail are inconsequential and negative. In short, there is a
certain philistinism about him in the eyes of the more courtly
annalists. To some extent this does reflect a trait in the British
character which puts commonsense practicalities before intellectuality, formal etiquette, or refined religious sensibilities. However, as the courtly Chrétien de Troies concedes, Gawain has an
inherent spiritual worth that shines through this lack of polish,
when he says of him, 'He who was lord of the knights, and who
was renowned above them all, ought surely to be called the sun. I
refer, of course, to my lord Gawain, for chivalry is enhanced by
him just as when the morning sun sheds its rays abroad and lights
all places where it shines.'

Gaheris and Linet

Gaheris, the second Orkney brother, who comes in order of birth
between Gawain and Gareth, combines their qualities to a certain
extent. He shares Gawain's commitment to blood feud in that it is
he and Gawain who kill King Pellinore in revenge for their father
King Lot, even though he fell in open battle.

There is a certain sense of destiny about this act. It is the
subject of prophecy that Gawain shall avenge his father's death on
Pellinore, made by Merlin on the grave of the knight slain by the
evil invisible knight Garlon. This occurs at the beginning of the
sequence of events that lead up to the striking of the Dolorous
Stroke. These matters, which form the early background to the
Holy Grail Quest have to do with the representation in Arthurian
terms of the consequences of Original Sin. Although the prophecy, the action and the motivation centre on Gawain as the bearer
of the destiny, as commonly happens, Gawain draws others into
the ambit of his involvement; in this instance his brother Gaheris.
So do the fruits of sin multiply, as apples rotting in a barrel.

Gaheris has a tendency to become involved in trans-personal
forces greater than himself. In a scene that might have come from
Greek tragedy he hews off his mother's head, having found her
with her lover Lamorak, who is of the hated House of Pellinore.

Later Lamorak is also killed by the brothers, although the
scene is never described. It is the matter of shocked rumour,
either that Gawain has done the deed, or that it was an ambush
prepared by Gawain, Gaheris, Agravaine and Mordred, with
Mordred effecting the *coup de grace*, characteristically, with a knife

in the back. Here is a clear conflict between the vows of knight-hood of the Fellowship of the Table Round and the old law of clan vengeance.

Yet Gaheris is also capable of exemplary idealism as when, with Gareth, he is ordered to guard the Queen when she is to be burned at the stake. They perform the order under protest, unarmed and without armour—an act which leads to their deaths when, in the ensuing mêlée, they are cut down by Lancelot's rescue party.

We may therefore regard Gaheris as the type of soul who is beginning to open to wider issues on the inner planes, and such a one is in a phase where it is possible to be swayed by and caught up in larger movements of group karma or destiny not of his own making. It is a time of temptation and opportunity, a critical point in the awakening of the soul, when it is becoming vaguely aware of inner plane issues but not yet sufficiently individualized, or active upon higher levels, as to be able to do much more than to drift or be swept along by the prevailing current of forces around him.

His lady, characteristically enough, is the Lady Linet, who provides unwittingly, a protracted initiatory test for Gareth with her scolding tongue. In real initiatory tests, of which formal ritual is but a reflection, the circumstances of life, laid on unwittingly by others, provide the relevant tests of soul and character. Linet constantly chides Gareth because, although she is sufficiently awakened to inner plane requirements so as to give service as a messenger between the beleagured Lady Liones and the Knights of the Round Table, she does not have the spiritual discernment to see the validity of Gareth's allocation to this quest, for to outer eyes he appears to be no more than a kitchen scullion.

This is a pattern not uncommonly seen in inexperienced occult students, who make assumptions as to how the Mysteries should be conducted and set out to try to influence, or freely criticize, those set over them. In so doing they are, however, not without useful function, in providing a testing time for their seniors whilst they learn wisdom themselves.

Gareth, the Lady Liones and Linet

This brings us naturally to Gareth, who is more of an exemplary hero. The source from which Sir Thomas Malory drew his story is unknown but it would seem to have been originally a scheme of initiation. The various tests of the hero are depicted as the conquest of knights of different colours to the eventual rescue of a fair lady and the winning of her hand in marriage.

In so far that Gareth is, to begin with, of unknown lineage, and that he later distinguishes himself in disguise, he takes on the theme of *Le Bel Inconnu*, the beautiful unknown one. This characteristic is shared by a number of other knights to a greater or lesser degree; for example Geraint and La Cote Mal Taillé. Its origin is a spiritual one and can be interpreted upon various levels. In essence it tells of the type of being who comes from another level of existence to perform certain destined tasks or to right certain wrongs. At the higher level this can be an *avatar*—and the role of Jesus the Christ demonstrates it in its highest form. At a lower level it is the role of the adept or initiate.

At the beginning Gareth comes to the Court of Arthur, half-carried by two men, no-one suspecting his close relationship to the king. He seeks a boon of the king which, to the surprise, indeed scandal, of all, is simply that he be given board and lodging for a year.

This unromantic, unambitious, almost churlish request is however granted, and implemented by Sir Kay as seneschal of the Court. Kay, however, puts his own interpretation upon this and makes of Gareth a kitchen boy so that at least he will to some extent earn his keep, and in what Kay would consider to be an appropriate, menial way. Gareth, however, accepts his role with good grace.

At the end of the year a damsel, Lady Linet, comes to the court seeking aid for her mistress, the Lady Liones, who is besieged in a tower. To the astonishment of all, Gareth claims this adventure and the right to be knighted. This is granted, much to the disgust of Lady Linet at being allocated a kitchen knave when she sought a knight of the Round Table.

Sir Kay is also put out by this turn of events and pursues Gareth and Linet to give the upstart knave a sound drubbing. To his chagrin and Linet's surprise, he is swiftly defeated by Gareth. Lancelot then arrives. A bond of friendship has been forged over the year between Lancelot and Gareth. Despite the difference in social position, Lancelot could discern the underlying realities behind the outer appearances. He duly dubs Gareth knight, and Gareth and Linet go on their way.

Linet is still not at all impressed with having Gareth as champion and taunts and scolds him continually, to the extent of even allying herself with some of his adversaries against her own best interests and of her entrusted mission.

The successive tests of Gareth indicate an initiatory system commencing with the control of the baser impulses, which are represented by six thieves. The inner plane nature of the tests is indicated in time-honoured way by the conquest of a ford, which is held by two knights. Gareth then successively conquers a black knight, a red knight, a blue knight and a green knight which may be regarded as representing the Four Elements of the created lower Nature.

There follow tests of a higher nature in that he sees the Lady Liones in the window of her tower and, as Dante with Beatrice, falls in love with the divine image, so raising the motivation of his quest from valour, and proving of the self, to love, and the abandonment or sacrifice of the self.

Just as the earlier Mystery tests of knightly valour can be failed by evil custom or by cowardice, so can the higher tests be failed by too personal an involvement, with love being grabbed at as a means of possession and the vehicle of a solely personal enjoyment.

Gareth's achievement of the earlier stages of the initiatory process is shown by his successful conquest of a knight guarding the Castle Perilous. This stands beside the sea near the Isle of Avalon, and the conquest consummates all the earlier elemental tests in one final résumé of them all, which is indicated by an ivory horn hanging from a sycamore tree. A sycamore by a well is a preliminary, since ancient Egyptian times, to the entry to the Mysteries of the Goddess. The blowing of a horn is a particularly potent means to signal entry to the inner planes, as its physical configuration implies. The rotting bodies of forty knights previously defeated enhance the mystic significance of what is to follow.

It is in the following sequence of a higher level of initiation that Gareth comes near to failing. He and the Lady Liones connive to consummate their love and arrange to meet secretly at dead of night. They are, however, interrupted by a grim-faced phantom knight with a battle axe, (in itself an ancient religious symbol of polarity), who wounds Gareth in the thigh, which is a symbolic castration. In ancient times some priests of Isis were in fact *castrati*, but in later times this barbarous element no longer applied, although celibacy was still required. As we shall discover when we discuss the Grades of Merlin and Guenevere, this early rigid code is an indication that the control and dedicated use of the sexual forces is an essential part of the Mysteries of Isis.

This is inevitably misunderstood by medieval monastic scribes and so, in Malory, Linet is described as being responsible for the production of the phantom, by enchantment, so as to preserve her lady's pre-marital chastity. The end apparently justifies the means! As an initiate of the Mysteries of Isis, Linet would certainly have been capable of enchantment, but hardly for the reasons of preserving a later social or moral code.

Gareth, at the first encounter, before fainting from loss of blood, (literally and figuratively the loss of spiritual force), manages to behead the knight. The knight, however, simply replaces it. On another occasion, or in a parallel version, he cuts the head into little pieces and throws them out of the window, but they are then reassembled by Linet.

Before the marriage may take place a further year has to elapse. During this time Gareth undertakes further quests. These are not elaborated in Malory but they culminate in a great Tournament. Here he distinguishes himself as an unknown knight, his armour constantly changing colour. Thus, having defeated the Elemental powers represented by the knights of different colours, he now demonstrates the controlled use of those forces themselves in a dedicated and impersonal fashion.

At the conclusion of the tournament Gareth marries the Lady Liones, and on the same occasion Gaheris, his brother, marries Linet. As we have said, the latter are similar initiatory types, and well suited as a pair. Tennyson, although well-versed in Arthurian origins, married Gareth to Linet, which distorts the original sense of the story with conventional Victorian sentimentality. Gareth's true mate is the Lady Liones, the idealized contra-sexual image—not the Mistress of Ceremonies, with Initiatrix of the Way.

Agravaine

Agravaine is the youngest of the Orkney brothers, and a less attractive character than his elder brothers. He is one open to being led astray by evil forces, as an accomplice of Mordred in his evil designs, and also as a willing participant in the feuding between the House of Lot and the House of Pellinore.

His type is perhaps best characterized as the spoilt, over-indulged, youngest child. Not intrinsically evil, like Mordred, but one who, through being overprotected in childhood, fails to measure up to the tests of later life. The type is well exemplified by C. S. Lewis in the character of Edwin in *The Chronicles of*

Narnia and our attitude to this type of character should be that demonstrated by Aslan and the elder children.

The condition may also apply to a nation or a generation, as well as to aspects of ourselves as individuals. Indeed all the knights and ladies may be interpreted in this triple way; as characters in their own right and how that type is expressed in a group, of whatever size, or as an element in individual psychology.

That element in the character which takes things for granted because they have been gained too easily, and which thus has egotism, conceit and resentment staining the other qualities of character, might be said to be represented by the easily tempted and corrupted Agravaine.

Mordred

Mordred is one who is intrinsically evil and he thus represents a principle rather than a person or character type. That principle moreover is demonic and represents the active evil in Arthur and in ourselves.

Mordred is engendered incestuously and adulterously against all human laws and aspirations—the product of besotted lust on one side and ambitious enchantment on the other. He is thus the Dweller on the Threshold, the karma that has been engendered, the cosmic unbalance that must be righted.

In the Arthuriad he is engendered by Arthur and has to be destroyed by Arthur, even though Arthur himself is destroyed in the process. Indeed the whole Round Table Fellowship is destroyed as a direct consequence of Mordred's plotting; for it is Mordred who is the principal agent in bringing into public light the adulterous relationship of the Queen with Lancelot.

There is indeed an averse cosmic pattern demonstrated in the scene where the Queen and Lancelot are entrapped together in her bed chamber by twelve knights led by the representative of evil, Mordred. It is also a characteristic of evil that it likes to pose as righteousness—if usually a rigid and condemning self-righteousness. This is demonstrated again and again by the evil doers in the Arthuriad such as Mordred and Morgan. Spiritual principles and rules for human conduct are used, not as personal guides or regulators, but as offensive weapons to condemn and entrap others. These are the principal methods of evil, which are demonstrated by all the atrocities that have been committed in human history under the guise of the upholding of religious or moral standards.

Yet evil only obtains its destructive power by the foibles of humans being overcome by inadequately controlled or undeveloped aspects of their own natures. Thus, although Mordred is the instigator of the final events that lead to civil war in the kingdom, the break up of the Round Table Fellowship and the destruction of the King, this mainspring of evil would not have been able to operate effectively without the lesser evils of the vacillation of Arthur, the personal indulgence of Guenevere and Lancelot, and the insatiable lust for vengeance of Gawain that fanned the embers of contention to a destructive blaze.

It is also to be noted that Mordred is a popular hero in the civil war, for the commons rise to support him. He is thus a very plausible character. As C. S. Lewis has pointed out, in *The Screwtape Letters*, the devil does not dress up in a demon-king pantomime mask to do his work. If he did, evil would be the easier to detect and avoid. It is the subtle shape-changing aspect of it, and its insidious twisting into the fibres of our being that cause it to be the great human problem. Mordred, in Qabalistic terms, holds the Gates to the Qliphoth, in the black quarter of Malkuth that abuts the Kingdom of Shells—of outworn forms, forces and desires.

The devil does not have to be conjured with fearsome and complicated rites; he is ever ready at hand—but then so is God. The choice is fundamentally our own.

In the Qabalah, aspects of evil are regarded as correspondent mis-use of divine principles. For instance the Unity of the One God in Kether becomes the Dual Contending Forces of the Qliphoth. These are, in Rabbinical terms, the distorted reflection in the 'Waters under the Earth' of the principles of divine activity and creation. They are not to be feared. The devil and evil thrive on fear. They are to be confronted in love, understanding and compassion; realizing them to be an intimate part of ourselves. This gives us a means of controlling them that is lost if we project them out and away from ourselves as fearsome external entities— or pretend that they do not exist.

In this manner should Mordred be understood by us. He is a part of ourselves, and even he can be redeemed, by understanding and love. Hate and rejection, under whatever guise, are the devil's tools and degrade the user as well as those whom they are turned against.

Uwain, (Owain or Yvain), Lunette and the Lady Laudine

This son of Morgan le Fay and King Uriens of Gore is the protagonist of one of the major poems of Chrétien de Troies, *The Lady of the Fountain*. A version also appears in the *Mabinogion*, and the story, like that of Gareth, is also an initiation cycle.

Riding into the enchanted Forest of Broceliande, which is, as Charles Williams has developed it in his poetic Arthuriad, an image of the unconscious, or of the inner planes, he comes to a massive and terrifying Elemental figure—a mis-shapen monster clad in bull's hides, surrounded by fighting bulls. This seems to be very close to the root of the powers of brute nature that give life and form in chaotic abundance—the power centre of the life force.

Properly approached this force is not to be feared, and the black mis-shapen giant hunchback leads Uwain to a magic spring by a tall pine. Upon the tree there hangs a golden bowl and by the spring there is a stone. We are still very close to the power of nature—the *kundalini* in the psychic structure of man—as is shown when Uwain uses the bowl to pour water upon the stone.

This is an instance of the most primitive form of the Holy Grail and his action is a symbolic demonstration of control of the Elements. By a spring, (which comes from the depths of the Earth), and a tree, (which is an emblem of life and stretches toward the heavens), he uses the magical golden bowl of form—which signifies also the astro/etheric aura. This is referred to in the Bible in the phrase 'if ever the silver cord be loosed or the golden bowl be broken'.

On sprinkling the water from the bowl upon the stone, a terrifying thunder storm breaks forth, with rain, gale, hail and lightning, after which in the ensuing calm the entire wood is filled with songbirds singing harmoniously. This in itself is an epitome of the dynamic forces of the psyche which, when unleashed, can be as destructive and powerful as those of the physical atom.

It is not for an individual mortal to meddle with these powers with impunity. Uwain's act is also a challenge to the Lady who owns the fountain. In the story she is called the Lady Laudine, but in esoteric fact she is the Isis of Nature. Her champion, Esclados the Red, who is swift as an eagle and fierce as a lion, immediately appears and fights a grim battle with Uwain. Thus it is one thing to become aware of, and to evoke the root powers of nature, it is another to control them; which is why there are so many warnings given about the unqualified pursuit of the powers of *kundalini* or tantric yoga. They are, however, the basis of all occult power, and indeed of life itself.

Uwain succeeds in mortally wounding Esclados, who flies to his lady's castle. He is hotly pursued by Uwain, who then finds himself entrapped with the bleeding corpse of Esclados. He is about to be attacked by the inhabitants of the castle when he is saved by a maiden, called Lunette, who gives him a magic ring which makes him invisible. Lunette acts as a kind of mistress of ceremonies in this action and so forms a similar function to the Linet of the Gareth story. Indeed the characters might be regarded as the same.

The Lady Laudine, the Isis of Nature, pitifully mourns her slain champion and lover but by the intercession of Lunette, Uwain is introduced to her. They fall in love and he becomes the new lover of the Lady Laudine and, by that fact, the new champion and defender of the magic spring. In other words he has become master of his own nature.

This concludes the first stage of the initiation cycle, the conquering of the Elements, as with the Gareth story, and there now follow the tests of putting the powers into controlled direction.

In the story the wedded pair are visited by King Arthur, accompanied by Uwain's cousin Gawain, who urges him not to neglect feats of arms too long or he will lose prowess and honour. Uwain therefore goes with them, promising to return to the Lady Laudine after a year.

However he becomes so involved in the life of a knight at Arthur's court that a more than considerable time goes by and he fails to return to Laudine. She eventually denounces him as faithless and untrue and renounces their relationship. Bearing in mind the forces that Laudine represents this not unnaturally drives Uwain mad and he runs from the court like a wild beast and lives like an animal in the forest.

In courtly French romances the losing of one's reason through love became a kind of literary romantic convention, but at root there is much more to it than that. The uncontrolled use of psychic powers can indeed lead to insanity. Similarly there is more to the story of Uwain and Laudine than a cautionary tale about a knight neglecting his ladylove for the sake of militant pursuits. There is certainly this element to it, but there are deep esoteric teachings, beyond the cautionary moral tale of social sensibility.

Uwain slowly returns to his senses through the intercession of a forest priestess but he continues to wander disconsolately in the wild woods until he finds the chance to redeem himself. He does this by joining in a terrible, if symbolic, fight between a lion and a dragon. Uwain takes the lion's side, whereupon, the dragon having been slain, the lion becomes his devoted servant.

The lion and the dragon may be held to represent the higher and lower forces of the human psyche. When the higher forces are victorious they form a vehicle of expression in the world for the spirit.

With the lion as his faithful servant Uwain undertakes more adventures, all dedicated, as is appropriate in the context, to the service of damsels in distress. Finally he fights, by chance, Gawain himself, and proves his equality with this great sun-hero, who, it will be remembered, originally started him off on this higher cycle of tests. Uwain then returns in honour to the Lady Laudine and her castle.

Geraint (or Erec) and Enide
Although he is not a direct relative of Arthur it may be appropriate to deal with Geraint here. His story is often compared with that of Uwain, which it complements to some extent. Both have parallels with the tale of Gareth and the Le Bel Inconnu formula. This is because they are all aspects of an initiation process which is concerned with the gaining of powers over the inner nature and their demonstrations. In a sense this is an Arthurian species of yoga.

Geraint, the son of the King of Estregales (Outer or Further Wales), is happily married to Enide. Such is their love that he neglects his duties as a knight. When this is brought home to him he reacts by embarking upon a perilous journey, taking Enide with him, defending her against all dangers.

The climax of this perilous journey is, once again, an inner plane test. It takes place at a castle on an island in a rapidly flowing river, within which is an enchanted garden from which no-one has ever emerged alive. As with other tests of this nature there is a warning in the gallery of severed heads of failed champions, and a challenge in the horn hanging from one of the stakes on which the heads are impaled. It is said that no-one has been able to blow this horn but that he who succeeds will be a great champion.

In the garden there is a fair lady, seated on a silver couch by a sycamore tree, (accoutrements of the Isis of Nature). She is, as in the story of Uwain, defended savagely by a red knight. By defeating this knight and blowing the horn Geraint frees him from his bondage to the garden and the beautiful lady.

The key symbol in this story is that of the horn, and indeed the apparently pointless designation of this story as *The Joy of the Court, (Cort)*, is likely to be a corruption of *The Joy of the Horn, (Cor)*. The horn is paramountly a symbol of annunciation between planes, and also has a dual sexual connotation. Viewed from one end it is thrusting and pointed, and from the other it is deep and dark—a phallus on the one hand and a yoni on the other. Its customary uses are also dual, as an instrument of the hunt it calls in the hunters for the chase, and as an instrument of the court its role is as a drinking horn. In popular religious tradition it is associated with Gabriel, the Angel of the Annunciation, and it is also the instrument in religious symbolism for announcing the end of the world, the Last Judgement and the Resurrection of the Dead.

In Geraint's story, the Lesser Mystery tests are his perilous journey with Enide, wherein he demonstrates the dual function of a knight as both lover and champion. The Test of the Horn is of the Greater Mystery that follows on from his mastery of the dual function, it raises him a plane above the polar manifestation of the sexual forces embodied by the Red Knight and the Lady of the Sycamore. The enchantment of the secret garden is no more, for it is no longer a seductive danger from which none can return. In psychological terms the return to the womb, or to the idyllic group consciousness of the animal level, is no longer an overwhelming magnetic attraction. They no longer strip the hero of his manhood, he has now won his spiritual independence and is master of the polar forces of lower nature.

Kay

The shortcomings of Arthur's foster-brother Kay are usually presented more prominently than his virtues. In the more popular stories of King Arthur, the tale of Kay trying to say that it was he rather than Arthur who drew the sword from the stone makes an early and not very engaging impression. He is, it would seem, open to the temptation to try to take the main chance.

His rough and ready tongue show his primitive origins. He is one of the earliest knights recorded in the cycle and appears as Kai in the *Mabinogion*. This aspect of him is eagerly used by courtly writers as a dramatic foil against the exemplary courtesy of the French knights. This is to some extent justified because Kay is undoubtedly rude and brash to the point of churlishness. In that he holds an official court function for life, through the intercession of his father for past favours to the young Arthur, there is in Kay an element of the officious bureaucrat and the exploiter of nepotism. However, this is redeemed in his ferocious loyalty and bravery.

The other side of the advantages gained from his office is that the privilege was well paid for in other respects. Tradition has it that Kay spoke with a stammer because as a baby he was snatched from his natural mother's breast to give way to Arthur.

His unfriendly manner is also part of his function at the court, which includes that of a gate keeper. It was his responsibility to challenge, test and reject all who were unworthy. This function in its inner plane aspect raises him to the level of the great guardian forces of the Mysteries and deities such as the dog headed Egyptian Anubis, or the three-headed dog Cerberus who guards the underworld of the Greeks. He is also an aspect of the Dweller on the Threshold—the unredeemed shadow of every soul who seeks entry to the inner worlds.

This link with higher forces shows in some of the attributes of Kay in the *Mabinogion* which include bizarre magical powers. He can go without sleep and live under water—feats which indicate an uncommon control and right of entry to the watery astral/ etheric worlds of dream. He also has a strong nature link, particularly with trees; for he can grow as tall as one if he wishes, and he is himself like a tree in that his limbs are cold but can give forth heat to warm his companions. In this respect he is a deity of the central forces of the family and tribe, the communal fire.

It is interesting to see these characteristics going through the Arthurian tradition in terms of character. This focus of warmth and jollity beneath a cold exterior is described in the prose *Merlin*: 'But of what Kay said his fellows that knew his customs ne wrought never, but he was full of mirth and japes in his speach for said it of none evil will of no man, and thereat laughed they gladly that knew his manners, and on that other side he was one of the best fellows and merriest that might be found.' (*E.E.T.S.*)

This is in contrast to another early aspect of his, which is that no doctor could heal any wound he gave, which leads Queen Guenevere to remark, in Chrétien de Trois' *Yvain*: 'Really, Kay, I think you would burst if you could not pour out the poison of which you are full.'

As with Gawain, the character of Kay is never presented in an entirely sympathetic way. These early British knights have a certain uncouth ambience that jars in the high sensibility of French courtly circles. As characters in twelfth century court poems they do however reflect original magical powers and inner plane attributes, which is a revealing demonstration of how old traditions pass from generation to generation and are capable of surviving passing fashions and being recoverable with the use of a little esoteric discernment.

The bravery of Kay is shown in an early episode in Malory where the young King and Queen are beset by five hostile kings. There are only four knights, including the King, in the Queen's party, but Kay undertakes to kill two adversaries and does so. Guenevere here accords recognition of the more positive side of his character: 'For ye spake a great word and fulfilled it worshipfully', she says.

Lucan and Bedivere

Two knights closely associated with Arthur from the earliest times are Lucan and Bedivere, and each has a close connection with the weapons of Arthur: Lucan with his spear, Bedivere with his sword. When one considers the inner plane significance of these weapons, this connection considerably expands the importance of these two otherwise minor characters.

It is with the spear, Ron, that Arthur finally slays the evil that besets himself and the Round Table, his incestuous bastard son Mordred. In this episode the spear is the ultimate righter of past wrongs, an element of cosmic justice, used once *in extremis*. This great cosmic weapon is handed to Arthur at the appropriate moment by Lucan the Butler.

Lucan is one who himself displays great faith and loyalty unto death, for before dying he loyally carries out all the last requests of the King, although greviously wounded himself. It is notable that these two knights who were with Arthur in the early stories are with him at the end.

Bedivere, (or Bedwi of the *Mabinogion*) carries the wounded Arthur on his back to the site by the shore where he will be met by the barge with the three mourning queens. He has therefore an element within him of the guide, the introductor, to the inner planes. Indeed he has something of St Christopher, whose hold on the popular imagination stems from the same archetype.

His returning of Excalibur to the Lake is a signal to the inner plane forces that the time is ripe for their intercession. The problems and temptations that beset one whose duty is to signal the end of a cycle, or to perform a deed that has high portent on the inner planes but seems inconsequential or even foolish in terms of physical plane values, are well drawn in Tennyson's poem *Le Mort d'Arthur*. The test of being able to let go of former good and glory is a formidable one that tests many human souls to the limit. At the same time it reinforces the other great test of the initiate, which is to have the faith to place his trust in spiritual rather than mundane values.

Tennyson emphasizes, in the scene of desolation after the last battle, that Bedivere, as the sole survivor of the Round Table on the battlefield, carries within himself the whole gamut of the aspirations and characters of the Fellowship. He is a great synthesizing figure and one whom it is useful to invoke as an archetypal all-embracing Round Table knight—whose destiny followed Arthur from first to last, and even beyond. In Tennyson, the King bids Bedivere to pray for his soul, and his kingship. This is an exercise that all of us today might still do, to considerable national and personal benefit.

In the Malory epilogue to the Arthuriad, Bedivere concludes his days with Lancelot and the Grail-winner Bors, and they are later joined by seven other knights. These ten spend their days in a hermitage at Glastonbury, near the Queen, who is in a nunnery at Amesbury. Beyond the superficial piety of this medieval conclusion to the tale there is a deep shadowy significance of the ten praying knights awaiting upon the death of the nearby nun-Queen. It is an aspect of the withdrawing of manifest life, of a phase of manifestation, of the ten Sephiroth of the Tree of Life pendant from the Ain Soph being taken back into the uncreate realities of God; in Eastern terms the phase of *pralaya*, between phases of manifest activity.

Bedivere continues his role as ender of phases with his attendance at the death of Guinevere, whose body is taken to Glastonbury, and then of Lancelot who is buried at his castle of Joyous Garde, his body being taken on the same bier that carried Guenevere.

In the very last days Bedivere remains alone at the Glastonbury hermitage until his own death. Another aspect of Bedivere which is easily overlooked is that, as the only witness to the passing of the King, it is he who, in his bridging function between the planes, initially tells the world of the manner of the passing of Arthur. He is thus, like Bors with the Holy Grail, a custodian, revealer and interpreter of great Mysteries.

King Lot of Lothian and Queen Morgawse

Lot, although later a knight of the Round Table, is one of the old order, who opposed Arthur's kingship. Designated as king of Lothian and of Orkney he represents the old powers of the North, stark, bleak, with berserker courage and blind loyalty to clan. The Viking marauder and Highland warrior are very much after the order of King Lot. It is appropriate that Gawain and the other Orkney brothers, with their strong allegiance to the old code, should stem from the alliance of Lot and Morgawse, although the gentler aspects of Gareth, Gawain and Gaheris show the finer sensibilities that can grow from this ancient stock.

Morgawse, Lot's queen, gives an impression of the wild north. There is, with these two, almost a harking back to vast earlier epochs of tradition—Lemurian and Hyperborean phases in the culture of consciousness on Earth. Charles Williams, in his poetic Arthurian cycle, brings out particularly well the untamed, elemental aspect of Morgawse in his poem *Lamorack and the Queen Morgause of Orkney*. As C. S. Lewis describes her in his commentary on Williams' work: 'Morgause is more like the spirit of stone itself—not, to be sure, of stone considered as a cold thing, but of stone considered as pressure, sharpness, ruthlessness: stone the record of huge passions in Earth's depth.' In Lamorack's ill-fated meeting with her, which led to both their deaths at the hands of her sons:

> The sea wind was whipping her hair about her face: yet her face outstripped her hair. One has seen faces of this quality: however they may be at rest in space, violent speed is embodied in them. As in some women things not in themselves beautiful . . . may become almost obsessively attractive, so with Morgause; the frightful energy of passion, the murderous danger, the fierce simplicities, of her face claim their slave at the first interchange of glances.

In Lamorak's own words, through Williams:

> Her hair was whirlwind about her face; her face outstripped her hair; it rose from a place where pre-Adamic sculpture on an ocean rock lay, and the sculpture torn from its rock was swept away. Her hand discharged catastrophe; I was thrown before it; I saw the source of all stone, the rigid tornado, the schism and first strife of

primeval rock with itself, Morgause Lot's wife.

There is something of the Medusa about Morgawse, and the affair with Lamorak can hardly be counted as part of the convention of Courtly Love. It is love at its most elemental—the clash of overpowering passions whose roots lie deep within past ages and ancient conflicts and desires. In another sense it is the dark side of Isis. It is small wonder that from the twin powerful ancient forces of Lot and Morgawse should spring the fourfold force in the Round Table Fellowship, the Orkney brothers, who could receive a minor Elemental allocation in their own right: Gareth—Spring, Air, East; Gawain—Summer, Fire, South; Gaheris—Autumn, Water, West; Agravaine—Winter, Earth, North.

King Nentres of Garlot and Queen Elaine
Little is recorded of Arthur's half-sister Elaine and her husband, King Nentres of Garlot. She does continue to perform a role in the Arthuriad in being one of the three Queens who conduct Arthur to the inner planes in the last days. It is not unreasonable either to associate her with the Castle of Maidens—one of the principal guardians of this focus of the feminine force. In this case her husband may be regarded as representing one of those inner plane figures, and their counterparts on the outer plane, who do not take the forefront of action but on whose presence in the background, the scene of action depends. They are the great *nirmakayas*—the mystic contemplators who keep the structure of the phenomenal world in being. In outer life the upholders of the fabric of society, calling little attention to themselves in their static, preserving roles, yet being by no means mere stage properties, for they may act as catalysts in a way that is very seldom suspected. In that they hold within their consciousness the norm of the ideal of the current phases of civilization their inner plane correspondence is with that of Christian Rosencreutz. In cosmic terms this relates to the two aspects of God—the part that remains withdrawn as observer, the All-Seeing Eye. This has also its parallels in individual esoteric psychology.

We may therefore usefully regard Elaine of Garlot, and her husband Nentres, as representative of initiates of the secret wisdom—she bringing with her the heritage of the Atlantean wisdom. Her husband's kingdom, Garlot, is held by some to be associated with the faery stronghold of the peninsular of Gower, of which the Gore of the Elemental King Uriens is a form. Thus the pair represent withdrawn initiates working in the background. Appropriately they have no children, their work being focused upon inner rather than outer affairs.

In a sense the Elaine/Nentres partnership is a halfway house, or balanced position, between the outer, fully physically committed elemental partnership of Morgawse and Lot on the one hand; and the inner, faery magical orientation of the marriage of Morgan and Uriens. The three partners thus form a dual aspected set of three Pillars—and from this basis a structure of magical work could be initiated.

King Uriens of Gore and Queen Morgan le Fay

A proper discussion of Uriens and Morgan is difficult at this stage because a full appreciation of them depends upon an understanding of the higher degrees. He is a creature at least half Elemental, and she is a priestess of the Atlantean type, skilled in magic, whose powers relate at least as much to the inner worlds as to the outer.

Uriens is a good knight of the Round Table but also what might be called a 'redeemed' Elemental being; that is, one who has been enabled to take on human characteristics. The strange old book *Le Comte de Gabalis*, under the guise of a novel, has something to say of this aspect of Elemental life, whereby an Elemental becomes attached to a human adept. In Uriens' case the adept is Arthur's half-sister Morgan le Fay, who, in the story, behaves reprehensibly towards him. In fact their son, Uwain, intervenes to prevent her destroying him.

There is in Uriens an aspect of Oberon, the fairy king in *A Midsummer Night's Dream* and imaginative re-creation of Shakespeare's portrayal can be helpful in coming to an understanding of him. Some of the old word magic is in his name, to be found also in Orion, the familiar hunter of the night skies, and in the Aur, (from which derives the archangelic Auriel) in Hebrew, meaning light. Uriens of Gore is, in fact, an 'enlightened' Elemental, or one seeking enlightenment. This Elementals can do in relation to humans able to be aware of them, much as domestic animals can be enlightened by ordinary humanity.

In another respect, Uriens is close to being what is called in magic an Elemental King—similar to the traditional Ghob, King of the Gnomes.

There is a little known tradition that besides genetically engineering the birth of Arthur, Merlin also utilized different forms of Atlantean magical mating for the births of Morgawse and Morgan. In the former case her stark Elemental qualities would suggest some kind of half-Elemental parentage. With Morgan, her formidable magical abilities would be partly due to the over-shadowing of her mother Igraine by non-human adepti on the inner planes. This particular and varied use of Igraine by Merlin throws considerable speculative light upon her unique role as a kind of human brood mare in ancient primitive magical fertility rites, of which the Arthurian story is a half-recalled part-bowdlerized memory.

The 'nunnery' to which Morgan went as a young girl, where she became 'a great clerk of nigromancy' would have been, traditionally, a colonial off-shoot of an Atlantean college run by priestesses for the education of girls of the blood line of the Sacred Clan. The memories of this kind of institution are merged with the traditions surrounding the Celtic Christian St Bride, who derives from a high priestess of the goddess Brigantia of the Hibernian Mysteries. It was she who first made Beckary a 'little Ireland' long before the institution of the Christian nunnery of St Bridget.

Morgan was Merlin's pupil in magic but also studied under another, non-human, Master who had helped to father her by overshadowing her birth. He also overshadowed her withdrawal to the 'inner Avalon' where, in the Celtic equivalent of the Qabalistic 'Water Temple of Hod', or the Eastern *devachanic plane*, she is the psychopomp of a state of being to which King Arthur, Ogier the Dane, Thomas the Rhymer and others were withdrawn when summoned by the 'Faery Queen'. This withdrawal is particularly well described in the Barge of Avalon, which, as the scholar Jessie Weston rightly says, is linked through its mourning queens with the wailing women of the Mysteries of Tammuz; and there is also a parallel in the Ancient Egyptian Boat of a Million Years in which the goddesses Isis and Nephthys stood guard.

This is the redeemed aspect of the less exemplary Morgan whose Atlantean powers, and their mis-use, are demonstrated in her powers as a shape shifter with knowledge of magical mating, as when she changed herself and her retinue into the appearance of standing stones to avoid detection after stealing the scabbard of Excalibur.

Ector

Arthur's foster-father, Ector, represents the faithful and loyal subject of the realm. He fulfils his appointed task with honour, and is also able to cooperate with the inner plane forces represented by Merlin and the Lady of the Lake. Although it is little stressed and described, and easily taken for granted, the actuality of his task demanded rare qualities of faith and dedication. In this he has close parallel with Joseph, the surrogate father of Jesus, who had to take much on trust and faith and live his life thereby. Meditation upon this parallel may bring much realization about the significance of the character of Ector. Although he is generally regarded as a minor figure in the legends it was of no small importance to be the father of the brave and mighty Kay, and guardian of the infant and youthful Arthur.

At another level his willingness to sacrifice his own firstborn son Kay at the behest of Merlin shows a parallel with the test of Abraham and his son Isaac. Ector is therefore a seed and patriarchal figure. Without him, little of the later action could have occurred.

7. Lancelot and the French Knights

Sir Lancelot, his kindred and his colleagues, are of French origin. In part this relates to Brittany—a traditional site for the Forest of Broceliande and Lancelot's castle of Joyous Garde. It also relates to Benwick which, if we take account of traditional physical equivalents to inner plane conditions, is sited in present day Belgium—the site also of Wastelands, as indeed in recent history they were to become in the 1914–18 war, when outer and inner conditions coalesced in a rare and frightening manner.

Lancelot

Lancelot was the son of King Ban of Benwick, who lost his kingdom, and died, when Lancelot was still a baby. Lancelot therefore has a symbolic initiatory attribute in being 'the son of a widow'; an attribute seen in its fulness in the story of Sir Percivale. It is not stressed in the Lancelot *enfances*, the emphasis being place on the dramatic seizing of the baby by a water faery—hence his cognomen Lancelot du Lac.

As is apparent in other parts of the Arthuriad, the Lake signifies the astral other-world and so, like Arthur, Lancelot is the subject of a special kind of initiatory up-bringing, although in his case it does not result in the aloofness or impersonality that characterize Arthur. Lancelot manages to integrate fully with the physical plane perhaps because, to provide him with company in this unusual upbringing, his cousins Bors and Lionel are also taken.

This initial training of Lancelot indicates a destiny marked out for him that is as important as Arthur's, and indeed, Lancelot does become the greatest of all knights, and a model of courtesy and knighthood. His story is also intimately connected with

Arthur and Guenevere, and also with the Grail. He not only performs commendably on the Grail Quest but he is also the father of the Grail winner Galahad. Besides his exemplary knighthood and chivalry to all ladies, his relationship with Galahault the Haut Prince exemplifies the comradeship in arms that can exist between men, and he remains an important figure even after the fall of the Round Table Fellowship as one of the ten knights who attend upon the Queen.

We shall therefore have much more to say about him and his role in our consideration of the higher grades of the Arthurian Mystery schema. For our immediate purposes he gives more than enough to consider in his function as a principal Knight of the Round Table.

At the age of eighteen he is taken by the Lady of the Lake and presented at court, and his arms are provided by her. One of his important adventures is recounted by Chrétien de Troies in *The Knight of the Cart*. Despite its over-refined courtly sentiment, even to the point of burlesque, it contains an ancient pattern of Mystery secrets in which Guenevere plays the part of the Spring Maiden and Lancelot that of the Sun Hero.

She is abducted by Meleagant, prince of Gorre. Gorre as a place name often signifies the faery other-world. It is also part of the title of Morgan's half-elemental husband Uriens. To reach her, Lancelot has to cross a river by a bridge as narrow as the edge of a sword, which is a typical description of the conscious link between inner and outer planes. He effects the rescue of Guenevere and the other prisoners and later slays Meleagant.

He is also a rescuer of prisoners of enchantment when he wins his great castle which, until his coming, was known as Dolorous Garde. On his fighting his way into it the spell is lifted, it becomes his own, and is renamed Joyous Garde. This castle is closely tied to his destiny in that it contains a mysterious tomb which only the winner of the castle can open. When he opens it, he finds that it contains the prophetic inscription that he himself will lie in it. It is from this inscription that he, for the first time, learns his true name and lineage.

The enchanted castle is a symbolic representation of the goal of every initiate, and indeed of every human soul. The self that we are born with is a mysterious castle. It holds prisoners which are aspects of our talents and gifts under enchantment before their unfolding in true maturity. When we succeed in conquering ourselves, facing reality, looking clearly at the true reflection of ourselves as we really are, without the enchanted glamours of self-deception, we then discover who we really are. This is another way of illustrating the force and relevance of the old Mystery adage 'Know Thyself'.

In some physical allocations Lancelot's Joyous Garde is located in Brittany; in others at Bamburgh Castle in Northumberland. It is, however, the citadel of every man's soul.

The rescue of Guenevere and the conquest of Joyous Garde are the principal factors in Lancelot's role as a knight and initiatory archetype of the Round Table. He appears constantly throughout the stories of the other knights and their quests because he is 'the best knight in the world' and the champion and ideal for all other knights.

Two events from the many might be chosen to exemplify two cardinal traits of Lancelot—his loyalty and love of the King, and also of his adopted country, England.

When Arthur has been unhorsed in a skirmish and his adversaries have him at their mercy, Lancelot intervenes and puts the king onto his own horse, saying: 'I will never see that most noble king that has made me knight neither slain nor shamed', whereupon the king, reseated on Lancelot's horse, looks down and 'the tears brast out of his eyen, thinking of the great courtesy that was in Sir Lancelot more than any other man.'

His love of England is expressed in the prayer and blessing he makes as the ship bears him away to exile:

> 'Sweet land, delightful, debonair, joyous and abounding in all ease and wealth, wherein my soul and life remain, blessed be thou by the mouth of Jesus Christ, and blessed be they who stay here after me, whether they be my friends or foes. Peace may they have and rest, and may God give them joy, . . . for they who live in so sweet a land are more fortunate than any others: thus say I who have known.'

His character is noble and gentle, he is a protector and rescuer of the weak, and an inspiration and patron of the younger knights of the court. This is exemplified in his special relationship with Gareth, on whom he personally confers the accolade of knighthood. Throughout all the bitterness of the break-up of the Table Round, he maintains a quiet, calm dignity far beyond the call of duty, especially in the face of Gawain's consuming rage and lust for vengeance. It is part of Lancelot's tragedy that he himself plays a part in the situation that leads to the break-up of the Fellowship by his love of the Queen—although, as we shall go on to discuss, this has been much misunderstood by later recounters of the tale. In a decaying situation it is difficult for any man to do right, the most innocently intentioned deeds go awry in their effect. Thus his rescue of Guenevere results in the killing of the unarmed Gareth and Gaheris—who were close in affection to him—and whose death fans Gawain to embittered all-destructive vengeance.

Of his encounters with the enchantress Morgan le Fay, and on the Quest of the Holy Grail, and the begetting of Galahad, we shall deal later, for they fit into a wider scene than his personal feats as a Knight of the Round Table.

Ector de Maris

The main characteristic of Ector de Maris is his brotherly devotion to Lancelot. He is by no means so accomplished a knight and he has few of the spiritual qualities that impel his brother Lancelot to the Quest of the Holy Grail. He accompanies Gawain for much of the time on the Quest of the Grail and neither of them come upon any significant adventure to speak of, so they decide to abandon what seems to be a fruitless and pointless quest. This is much the situation of the average man of the world in relation to mystical realities.

In an indirect way, however, Ector does get quite close to the Holy Grail when he is seeking his brother. When Lancelot has finally achieved so far as to be seated within the Grail Castle at a table filled with food by the Holy Vessel, there comes a loud knocking at the closed and fastened door. It is Sir Ector, who, when he learns that Lancelot is there, and of the circumstances, goes abashed away. This incident indicates the place of brotherly love in the higher Mysteries. It can reach the door of the sanctuary but cannot enter. This is also expressed in one of the 'hard' sayings of Jesus when he asks who are his mother and brothers when they come seeking for him when he is preaching. The love of God, the 'vertical' polarity as opposed to the 'horizontal' polarity of human life, is of a different order, and may appear as impersonality or even inhuman coldness to those whose dynamic is wholly 'horizontal' in outer worldly relationships.

Ector again appears at the very end of the Arthuriad, when the body of Lancelot is returned to Joyous Garde. Ector had been seeking his brother for seven years past, for he was not one of those ten who took to the encloistered life about the Queen. He does not even recognize his old comrades in their monastic guise until Bors makes himself known, whereupon in Malory, he speaks a fine elegy about the greatness of his brother Lancelot.

Bors

Lancelot's cousin Bors is an important figure not only at the Round Table but in the Quest of the Grail, for he is one of the Grail winners. His principal characteristic is that he is a family man rather than a spiritual ascetic and is the only one amongst the Grail winners to return to the land of the living. He represents the plain, loyal, faithful man, one who is not greatly gifted in feats of arms as are the great figures of Gawain, Lancelot or Tristram, but whose humanity shines through as one of the pure in heart. He shows greatly loyalty to his kinsman Lancelot, and also to the Queen, whom he champions in Lancelot's absence in the latter days of the declining Fellowship. Again, although he does not have the burning spiritual one-pointedness of Galahad his human kindness is of a quality that enables him not only to achieve the Grail but to return to bear witness of it to his fellow men.

The tests that such a character has to face are those of divided loyalties, and in the stories he is confronted with cruel decisions of conduct between conflicting calls of duty. One instance is his having King Arthur himself at his mercy in the siege of Joyous Garde, although here Lancelot intercedes to resolve the conflict. Perhaps even more of a testing dilemma is his having to choose between saving the life of his brother Lionel or going to the rescue of a damsel in distress. He chooses the latter course and is later confronted by the uncontrollable rage and resentment of his brother who has in fact survived.

Lionel

The previous incident shows the fierce, resentful character of Lionel which was apparent in the early days in his temper as a child under the Lake. He is the equivalent of Gawain amongst the French knights. In his dilemma Bors had prayed that Christ save his brother while he himself went off to rescue the maiden from dishonour. It would seem that the prayer was answered but Lionel does not see it this way, having little perception of or credence in spiritual realities. Neither does he concede that saving a maid from rape is a more pressing call than rescuing a kinsman. His code of honour and practice is plainly of the old school.

So great is his resentment that he attacks Bors savagely even though Bors refuses at first to defend himself. He kills a hermit who tries to intercede, and then kills Sir Colgrevance who also tries to avert the battle between the brothers. Having committed this dual killing Lionel advances on his brother yet again, who only at this point raises arms in defence. However, a shaft of lightning separates them, physical evidence of the spiritual power that had saved Lionel before, and Bors is led off to take up the Grail Quest.

Lionel is, however, a good knight withal, a companion of Lancelot in some of his adventures, and he is finally killed in the last days by the forces of Mordred.

Galahad

Galahad, Lancelot's son by Elaine of Carbonek, is the supreme spiritual champion—the bearer of a high destiny in exemplary fashion. As such he tends to be portrayed in a bloodless, two-dimensional way, rather as in popular pious imagination Jesus of Nazareth is imagined, watered down from the most powerful of men to a 'gentle Jesus meek and mild'. Galahad has within him all the human qualities that endear us to the best that is in Gareth, Geraint, Uwain, Lancelot and the other initiatory hero figures. His prowess at arms exceeds even his father Lancelot's, and is used directly and specifically in his one-pointed pursuit of his destiny. This destiny embraces that of the nation and of the Round Table Fellowship. It has been pre-ordained by Merlin in the inception of the Siege Perilous—the seat at the Round Table where none may sit but the rare soul who has the strength to bear tests and responsibilities of a very high order. It is the destiny of a 'Christed' one, that leads directly to the laying down of life and all external interests for the one destined objective. Such a mission is likely to be short but of unparalleled effects upon the plane upon which it is carried out. It is the supreme magical/spiritual act. Those who aspire to such a role through a false spiritual presumption risk a dire reward—that of being a false messiah. This brings either apostasy and shame, (the humiliation of failure rather than the triumph of humility), or pointless and profitless persecution, (being the victim without the transcending victory). These are the awesome lessons of the Siege Perilous.

Galahault

An important figure in Lancelot's circle appears only sketchily in

Malory. This is Galahault the Haut Prince of Sorlois—or alternatively the Faraway Isles. Originally a rival of King Arthur's he is won over by the friendship of Lancelot, which in its enduring strength exemplifies the band of comradeship between brothers in arms.

Galahault is a giant of a man, brave, kindly, honourable and impulsive. Galahault is Lancelot's confidant in his liaison with the Queen, and Lancelot his, in his love of the Lady Malehault, who at first had been enamoured of Lancelot. A vignette of Galahault's character is given in the episode where, having been troubled by portentous dreams, he seeks advice from the divination of a wizard. There he learns that he is to die within four years, and that his death will be caused by Lancelot and Guenevere. He tells nothing of this, however, to his friend Lancelot, who is waiting outside. The prophecy is fulfilled when, after Lancelot has abandoned his friend for a long period because of his involvement with Guinevere, a false report comes to Galahault of Lancelot's death, which causes Galahault to die of grief.

At the behest of the Lady of the Lake, Lancelot buries his friend at his castle of Joyous Garde, in the same tomb where he too is later to be laid to rest, so that the two comrades are re-united in death. Lancelot's great loves, with Queen Guenevere, Elaine of Carbonek, and Elaine of Astolat, are the better known stories, but it is his bond of comradely affection with Galahault that is ever in the background and attains to the sanctity and recognition of the final memorial.

Urre and Felelolie

Sir Urre is not a French knight but belongs here because he was healed of severe wounds by Lancelot. In this he plays a passive but important role in demonstrating to Lancelot the powers of his own dedication if he can only keep it in sufficient purity.

There is a deep, self-sacrificing, spiritual teaching element in Urre therefore. His seven wounds, and the syllables of his name, which are those indicating light in ancient sonic symbolism, also indicate his far from minor role. He also comes from Hungary, a connection that has important implications in the deep esoteric learning of that area of Europe—which at its heights is shown forth in the alchemical knowledge of Bohemia, and in the depths in the dark secrets of Transylvania. It is also exemplified in the modern esoteric forces surrounding the legend of the Count Rakoczi.

Urre has a sister Felelolie who represents the feminine side of the forces he bears, and in particular a devotion to healing in that she bears her wounded brother through many countries for seven years before arriving at Arthur's court in search of help and healing.

Sir Urre's mother is not mentioned by name but it is she who has laid the enchantment whereby he can only be cured by 'the best knight in the world'. Thus there is a questing, testing, element of the Feminine Mysteries in this strange tale of Sir Urre of the Mount.

8. Tristram and the Cornish Circle

Tristram and Iseult

Tristram of Liones rivals Lancelot as great knight and lover. His antecedents are of Cornwall and his great love is for the Queen of Cornwall, La Belle Iseult, who is the daughter of King Anguish of Ireland.

To some extent, in Malory, the Court of King Mark of Cornwall is used as a foil to the Court of King Arthur. Nothing at Cornwall is quite at the same level of excellence and attainment. It is more rough and ready, more rustic.

There are indeed many rural notes of the green wild wood about the Cornish court. King Mark is even said by some to have had horses' ears—and although this is an excuse for denigration and mockery of him, its origins are noble in that in the period of racial and tribal totems, the horse, particularly as black stallion or white mare, was an object of reverence in the land.

Tristram and Iseult repair to the wild wood for much of their life together, and Tristram himself is noted as a harper and a hunter. They have all the accoutrements for a pastoral idyll rather than for the more artificial conventions of the court.

There are several versions of the Tristram and Iseult story, and we shall examine it at greater length when we consider the Mysteries of Guenevere, for it is part of the mysteries of polarity working. In short, the compulsive nature of the love draught that they take transforms a romantic honourable relationship into a consuming involvement that erodes all honour and custom; one in which 'projection' rules over reality—where the worshipper confuses the godhead with the mediator, the finger for the moon.

Brangane, the maid who is in charge of the potion which they drink, is thus a priestess/initiate of the Hibernian Mysteries. Her role is similar to that of Linet and Lunette in the Gareth and Geraint initiatory stories. The tragedy of Tristram and Iseult is that the initiatory powers prove too strong for the candidates for initiation, who are overcome by them.

There are, however, greater depths contained within their story. The hunter/musician is a cosmic figure of immense antiquity, having within its ambit the Mysteries of Diana/Artemis, of Orion, or Orpheus, and of the music of the spheres. Tristram is one of the greatest knights, second only to Lancelot, and also a great lover second only to Lancelot, and it is significant that Merlin predicts their meeting in combat at a particular spot which happens to be the grave of the ill-starred lovers Colombe and Lanceor. Colombe, significantly, is another who cannot handle the forces of polarity. When her love Lanceor is killed she commits suicide over his corpse. Their double tomb is built by King Mark of Cornwall, who at root is psychopomp of the great polar forces of the Hibernian Mysteries.

Marhaus
Sir Marhaus is an important linking figure between the Round Table and the Mysteries of Ireland. He is a knight of the Round Table, as in the tale of Marhaus, Gawain and Uwain and the maidens of sixty, thirty and fifteen winters. He shows himself as a mature and wise knight who undergoes his adventures and fulfils his obligations with honour. He appears later as the champion of the King of Ireland in demanding truage from Cornwall, and is slain by Tristram. His antecedents are to be found, however, in more primitive versions of the story where he is Morholt, a great sea creature. He thus carries within him the great sea power that is a part of the Mysteries of the Western Islands, originally of Atlantis, and inherited in part by Ireland and also by Cornwall and Brittany.

Although what we are pleased to call 'inanimate nature' is in fact very much alive, that part of it which we know as the sea is a good deal more alive than any other force of nature. The secrets of the sea power are among the traditional lost secrets of Atlantis, pertaining not so much to the well known Sun Temple priesthood of the Sacred Mountain as to an older centre based upon the Island of Ruta.

The Sea Mysteries are concerned, not so much with the expression of human spirit as are the Solar Mysteries, but with the very origins of primordial life, which are based on Space and the Sea. Even in Genesis the first beginnings are said to be from Water. Thus behind Sun worship, which is the basis for most Mystery systems known to the historical period, there is an older, fiercer, and stronger Sea cult. Its vestiges are seen in the primitive Venus figures known to archeology. It is concerned with the Mother of Birth and the Mother of Death, with the Beginning and Ending of Life, particularly as connected with the Cosmos. It has links not only, in Mystery terms, with the Solar Logos but to other great cosmic systems, to the great Cosmic Universe, the Sea of Space, the Mother and Genetrix of all Life, in Qabalistic terms the cosmic Binah.

The vestiges of the Sea cult are to be found particularly in island races, and there was a great deal of early Sea worship in the British Isles before the rise of the Druids and their Solar worship. It was not the work of the Druids to revive this earlier cultus as its phase had then passed, and what remained of it had become degenerate, as do all aspects of human culture when their cycle in time is waning. However, the time is not far distant when they may return, for a new age, in a new form of expression.

Were the actual occult symbols and powers of the Sea Mysteries rightly remembered they would render available a vast complex of forces, and few would be capable of handling such power and the self-sufficiency that it would bring. It has therefore been withheld over the centuries by inner plane guardians. However, those who can train themselves to recollect and fit together the fragments that survive, may be permitted to be pioneers for those who will come after.

Certain guide lines can be given to those who aspire in this special way to be servers of the Great Mother. King Solomon followed the great Solar monotheistic teaching but found his Temple lacked much of the ancient power that had originally been given to Israel via Chaldean sources. In this, one might include the tradition of the great fish-man Oannes. However, Solomon sought to remedy this by recourse to a great master of the hidden knowledge, who has come down to us as Hiram, King of Tyre. His people, of the same line as the later sea-questing Phoenicians, had retained much of the ancient beliefs, and that is why in the Bible Solomon is recorded as having sent for Hiram to perfect the great Temple of Jerusalem.

In the British Isles also, certain parts are especially sacred to the ancient Sea worship. Many are now almost forgotten, except in some of the strange and imaginative symbols of Irish myth—of which one example might be the tales surrounding Manannan, Lord of the Sea, beyond and under which lay the Celtic other-world, Tir nan Og, and who provided the Tuatha de Danaan with supernatural food. From him the Isle of Man is named and the main centres of the Sea cult were in islands off Wales and Cornwall, although the greatest treasure house of such lore is Brittany. Traditionally itself originally an island, it remains culturally isolated, in a curious way, from both Britain and France. Many of its strange surviving customs, little understood and mixed up with the Roman Catholic faith, are remains of the old Atlantean Sea Mysteries, the last surviving secrets of which, it is said, were kept here until the cult became too debased to survive in its current form. Tradition tells of a small party of colonists direct from the Isle of Ruta who brought the Sea Mysteries to Armorica, from which the legends of Ys and similar fables derive, although now much distorted.

Palomides

Sir Palomides, the Saracen knight, is an important figure, and his baptism into the Christian faith coincides with the arrival of Galahad and the commencement of the Grail Quest. His immediate antecedents are to be found in the adversaries of the Crusaders, and he represents also the influences of the East to the Western Mysteries, which go back in time as far as the most ancient trade routes. He is a part of Tristram's circle in that he is another initiate of the extremely powerful horizontal polarity workings that can all but swamp the personalities of those who become involved in them. His love of the fair Iseult is unrequited and is an aspect of his dedication to the Quest, which is of a more abstract type than the more earthy and pragmatic Western knights.

He is also a principal follower of that unattainable creature, the Questing Beast. This strange animal, in one aspect, represents questing for questing's sake, just as love can degenerate into love for love's sake, an introspective and obsessional emotional paralysis.

Another aspect of Palomides is his role as a stranger to these shores, a citizen by choice, who takes upon himself, not without considerable difficulty, the customs and conventions of his host nation. In this respect he is important in that he foreshadows all problems of racial integration. He is thus also a great universal civilizer. His Quest is that of other cultures, and as such he treads the middle way between an abstract universalism and a narrow nationalism.

Dinadan

Another of the Cornish knights, Sir Dinadan is remarkable for his exemplary jesting and humour, which are important elements in controlling the strong forces of horizontal polarity. Emotional intensity of an obsessive nature can be controlled by humour, which has a distancing, objectivizing effect. This applies in Dinadan's case not only to the obsessive love of a Tristram, whom he follows rather after the fashion of a Sancho Panza, but to a compulsive following of a code of honour or rule of conduct. Tristram is no Don Quixote, but a formidable knight. Yet his fierce ardour, such as when he takes on thirty knights at once, or fights his friends to maintain the custom of a particular castle, needs to be questioned and put into perspective. This is Dinadan's function. This distancing from completely committed love and honour can, however, lead to a flippancy and flexibility of will that verges on cowardice, and Dinadan is no great hero even though a loveable character.

Alisaunder (or Alexander) le Orphelin and Alice la Beale Pilgrim

Tristram's cousin Alisaunder and his love Alice, provide a beautiful vignette of the code of love and honour. Even when Alisaunder is beguiled by an enchantment of Morgan le Fay he keeps true to his word, even though it is given under deception and duress. Theirs is a young love that moves smoothly through the obstacles that beset the lovers, to a fruitful union. Their first meeting is worth quoting from Malory.

'And when La Beale Alice saw him joust so well, she thought him a passing goodly knight on horseback. And then she leapt out of her pavilion, and took Sir Alisaunder by the bridle, and thus she said: Fair knight, I require thee of thy knighthood show me thy visage. I dare well, said Alisaunder, show my visage. And then he put off his helm; and she saw his visage, she said: O sweet Jesu, thee I must love, and never other. Then show me your visage, said he. Then she unwimpled her visage. And when he saw her he said: Here have I found my true love and my lady. Truly fair lady, said he, I promise you to be your knight, and none other that beareth the life. Now, gentle knight, said she, tell me your name. My name is, said he, Alisaunder le Orphelin. Now, damosel, tell me your name, said he. My name is, said she, Alice La Beale Pilgrim. And when we be more at our heart's ease, both ye and I shall tell other of what blood we be come.'

La Cote Mal Taillé or Bruin le Noire

Bruin le Noire is nick-named La Cote Mal Taillé by Kay because he came to Arthur's court in a rich but ill-fitting and gashed coat. He is a Cornish equivalent of Gareth, and of the more universal figure of Le Bel Inconnu. In fact the coat belonged to his father, who was killed in it, and he wears it until his father's death can be avenged. Thus he represents a two-fold force, that of justice that seeks to be fulfilled through all the vicissitudes of life; and also, in a more esoteric sense, the inner reality behind appearances, which, as in the case of Gareth appearing to be a kitchen scullion, may be very different at an inner spiritual level than may seem by outer appearances. Like Gareth he is taunted by a sharp tongued initiatrix, called Maledysaunt, even after he has defeated a hundred knights. She later confesses that her scorn was expressed not out of hatred but in order to turn him from danger because of her love for him, at which Lancelot changes her name to Beau-Pensaunte, and La Cote Male Taillé marries her. He also achieves distinction by defending Queen Guenevere from a lion, and assisting Lancelot to rid Castle Pendragon of four intruding knights, both of which feats may carry esoteric interpretation. He is knighted by Arthur and becomes a Knight of the Round Table.

Lanceor and Colombe

Another link with the Hibernian Mysteries is found with Sir Lanceor of Ireland, who plays an important role in the tale of Balin (or Balyn le Sauvage) with which we shall deal more fully in our consideration of the Holy Grail. He volunteers to seek out and punish Balin for his misdeeds at the court of Arthur but in this attempt is killed by Balin. This indicates the danger of attempting to take the law, particularly the cosmic law, into one's own hands. It is a temptation that has a particularly Irish dimension to it.

Lanceor is also the knight with whom the Lady Colombe is so enamoured that she kills herself over his dead body. In this we have another aspect of the very powerful forces of the polarity working of the Hibernian Mysteries, which can overwhelm the individual personality. It is not without significance that the place of their death is marked by a tomb, erected by King Mark of Cornwall, which becomes a place destined to see the confrontation between the two great champions, Lancelot and Tristram, who have also failed, each in their own way, to control correctly the forces of horizontal polarity.

9. The House of King Pellinore

Pellinore
Pellinore is one of the great kings of the generation before Arthur, and one of the pioneers of the principle of the Quest in that, before Palomides the Saracen knight, it is Pellinore who pursues the Questing Beast. The foolhardy young Arthur takes him on in combat and has to be rescued by Merlin, who causes a sleep to fall upon the mighty old king. Pellinore is, however, a staunch ally when later troubles come, and fights to establish Arthur on the throne. He kills another of the old Kings, King Lot of Lothian, in the process. It is this act that causes the enmity towards him of Lot's sons, Gawain and the others. Merlin prophecies that the spot where Gawain exacts revenge will be where the invisible evil knight Garlon strikes down an innocent wounded knight, which starts a chain of events leading to Balin striking the Dolorous Stroke.

There is also in the enmity of Gawain a Cain-like element of jealousy, stemming from when, in the early days of the Round Table, Merlin places King Pellinore in a place of honour, beside the Siege Perilous.

It will be evident from this that, far from being a symbol of equality as is generally nowadays regarded, the Round Table did have its areas of importance and precedence. The desire to make all equal needs careful analaysis as to its true aims and origins, for all life organisms are based on some kind of hierarchical organizational pattern. However, in Gawain's case, it was not a modernist desire for an ideal of equality for all, but rather an objection to the hierarchy of bloodkinship (he was senior nephew to the king) giving place to the hierarchy of spiritual function.

Tor

Gawain's sense of injustice is increased by the fine performance of Tor, Pellinore's illegitimate son, in one of the first set of quests of the Round Table Fellowship, undertaken by Gawain, Tor and Pellinore. Gawain fares comparatively badly. His excess of zeal spills over into brutality and he is sent back to court in disgrace with a maiden's decapitated head round his neck.

His discomfiture is not relieved by the fact that Pellinore is also censured for his actions when he ignores the cries of a maiden in distress because he was too intent upon his quest. This obsession with the current Quest underlines the significance of the Questing Beast as the symbol of adventure for adventure's sake, which Pellinore for many years pursued. The penalty for Pellinore is also more extreme, as it is revealed by Merlin that the lady he left unaided, who is killed by wild beasts, is his own daughter. This is not Dindrane, the Grail maiden, and she does not appear elsewhere in the legends. The lesson imparted by her presence is, however, that all humankind are of one family and that it is only lack of perception, to the point of blindness, that causes us to fail to look upon all we meet as our immediate kin.

Tor, who comes to court apparently as a shepherd's son, has, in this respect, similarities with the coming of Gareth and La Cote Mal Taillé, and above all with Percivale, his half-brother. However, despite his humble beginnings, his later prowess shows that noble blood will out, a sentiment no doubt approved by the courtly twelfth-century hearers of his tale. There is also a spiritual side to this, as there is a nobility of the spirit, of which the now almost out-moded nobility of the blood is a terrestrial reflection. Also, the fact that his step-father is named Aries—the first sign of the zodiac—and that Tor's tale appears first in the tales of the quests of the Knights of the Round Table, emphasizes the zodiacal cosmic parallel to the Arthurian fellowship.

Percivale and Dindrane

There are two important figures in the Holy Grail story in Pellinore's progeny—Percivale and Dindrane, with whom we shall deal more fully in our consideration of the Greater Mysteries.

Percivale is very much an archetypal figure representing all humanity, and as such corresponds to the innocent Fool of the Tarot. He is brought up by his widowed mother to know nothing of knighthood but, as always, blood will out, and he sets forth on a pilgrimage to become a knight. In a sequence of adventures he develops from uncouth and untutored rustic yokel to one of the foremost Knights of the Round Table who goes on to achieve the Quest of the Holy Grail.

His sister is un-named in Malory, but called Dindrane by Charles Williams, whose lead we will follow. She is present in the strange symbolic sequences of the appearance of the Ship of Solomon in the metaphysical land and sea-scape of the spiritual stages of the Grail Quest. Dindrane willingly lays down her life during the Quest by giving her life's blood to cure a chronically sick lady. She is thus a feminine aspect of the Christed one. In the religious elements that one finds shot through the Arthurian legends, like rays of sun through rain and cloud, there is a singular spiritual equality between male and female which is not found in orthodox ecclesiastical spirituality.

Lamorak

Pellinore's eldest son Lamorak is a great, rugged, heroic figure cast in his father's mould. Of tremendous force, bravery, and animal vitality, he adds fuel to the enmity of the Orkney brothers by sleeping with Morgawse, their mother. Gaheris in the end kills his mother because of this liaison, and Lamorak is later cornered by Gawain, Gaheris, Agravaine and Mordred and done to death in unequal combat.

There is, hidden within this dynastic tragedy, an esoteric teaching concerning the abuse of the feminine Mysteries and the consequent destructive evocation of the forces of the four Elements, represented by his four assailants, sons of the elemental Morgawse.

Aglovale

The last son of Pellinore, Aglovale, accompanies Percivale in leaving their mother, and meets his end at the hands of Lancelot on the fateful day when his rescue of the Queen results also in the death of his brother Tor, Gareth, Gaheris, and many other good knights. He is not a major protagonist but insofar that Percivale represents all humanity Aglovale achieves greater proportions as a guide and protector of humankind and an introductor to its higher destiny. He has an element of the elder brother and protector of the young. He is also a champion of the less privileged in that he revenges his squire who was slain simply for being his squire. Not all knights would have felt this to be an obligatory duty.

10. Other Knights of the Round Table

There is no definitive list of the knights of the Round Table and the number of knights varies, and of those named there are various anachronisms and inconsistencies according to the differing source material. Malory does give a roll call of knights on the occasion of the healing of Sir Urre which we will now give, leaving out the knights already mentioned, and adding brief notes where applicable.

King Clarence of Northumberland
Sir Barant le Apres (the King with a Hundred Knights)
King Anguish of Ireland
King Carados of Scotland
Sir Constantine:
> son of King Carados of Cornwall. He succeeded Arthur as king.

Duke Chaleins of Clarence
The Earl Ulbause
The Earl Aristause
Sir Gingalin:
> son of Gawain.

Sir Florence, Sir Lovel:
> also sons of Gawain, begotten on Sir Brandile's sister.

Sir Blamore de Glanis and Sir Bleoberis de Ganis:
> Two brothers who are noble knights with a strong sense of the importance of kinship, without the brooding resentment of Gawain. See, for example, the grace with which they concede victory to King Anguish who has slain one of their kin when Blamore is defeated by King Anguish's champion

Tristram. In the last days they left, with Bors and Ector, to crusade in the Holy Land.

Sir Gahalantine

Sir Galihodin

Sir Galihud

Sir Menaduke

Sir Villiars the Valiant

Sir Hebes le Renoumes (or Renowné or Renommé)

Sir Sagramore le Desirous:
> stepson of King Brandegoris of Eastragoire or Stangore, i.e. of non-human lineage or patronage.

Sir Dodinas le Savage:
> a well proved knight of Arthur's court.

Sir Kay de Stranges:
> saved from enchantment once by Lancelot.

Sir Meliot de Logris:
> a cousin of the Lady of the Lake, and one who joined Agravaine's plot against Lancelot and Guinevere.

Sir Petipase of Winchelsea

Sir Galleron of Galway:
> once lent his armour to Tristram. One of those who were in Agravaine's plot—the others have been listed as Agravaine, Mordred, Colgrevance, Mador, Gingalin, Meliot, Petipase, Malyon of the Mount, Ascamore, Grommerson, Curses-alayne, Florence and Lovel.

Sir Melion of the Mountain

Sir Cardok

Sir Uwaine les Avoutres

Sir Ozanna le Cure Hardy:
> one who accompanied Guenevere on her Maying expedition, the others being Kay, Agravaine, Brandiles, Sagramour, Dodinas, Ladynas of the Forest, Persaunt, Ironside and Pelleas—'Queen's Knights' with white shields.

Sir Astamor:
> 'the good knight who never failed his lord'.

Sir Gromere and Sir Grommorson:
> Caxton makes these into one knight.

Sir Crosshelm (or Cursesalayne)

Sir Servause le Breuse:
> considered a mightier warrior than Lancelot by the Lady of the Lake, but who fought only giants, dragons and wild beasts.

Sir Durnore:
    a son of King Pellinore.
Sir Griflet le Fise Dieu:
    He was made knight when a very young squire in the early days of Arthur's reign, and so well represents the aspirations of youth, and at the same time the old initiate in a young body whose antecedents go to the beginnings of time. Sometimes takes with him Dagonet, King Arthur's fool.
Sir Brandiles
Sir Clegis:
    a commander of knights in Arthur's early battle against the Roman emperor.
Sir Sadok:
    a brother of Edward of Orkney—both cousins of Gawain, so presumably King Lot had a brother.
Sir Dinas le Seneschal (of Cornwall)
Sir Fergus:
    an Earl, and companion of Tristram.
Sir Driant:
    of Tristram's circle.
Sir Lambegus:
    of Tristram's circle.
Sir Clarrus of Cleremont
    one of Arthur's knights in the war against Rome; afterwards of Lancelot's party.
Sir Cloddrus
    a 'noble knight' of the Roman campaign.
Sir Hectimere (or Askanere)
Sir Edward of Carnarvon and Sir Dinas:
    brothers of Priamus.
Sir Priamus:
    a Roman knight by birth, whose father rebelled against Rome. Christened by Tristram.
Sir Hellaine le Blank:
    Bors' son, by the daughter of King Brandegoris.
Sir Brian le Listinoise:
    'a good knight and an adventurous'. Delivered by Lancelot from Tarquin along with Kay, Brandiles, Galihud, Alydukis, Marhaus, Ector, Lionel and others.
Sir Gautere, Sir Reynold and Sir Gillemere:
    Cornish knights won upon a bridge by Lancelot when wearing Kay's armour.

Sir Guyart le Petite:
>among those defeated by Palomides in Ireland when fighting as Knight of the Black Shield. Others were Gawain, Gaheris, Agravaine, Badgemagus, Kay, Dodinas, Sagramour and Griflet.

Sir Bellangere le Breuse:
>son of Alisaunder le Orphelin.

Sir Hebes:
>originally squire to Tristram, but of Lancelot's kin.

Sir Morganore:
>Seneschal to King with a Hundred Knights.

Sir Sentraile de Lushou:
>in the service of Tristram.

Sir Suppinabilis:
>a Breton knight.

Sir Bellyaunce (Bellangere in Caxton) le Orgulous:
>won by Sir Lamorak. Brother of Froll of the Outer Isles.

Sir Nerovens de Lyle:
>won by Sir Lancelot.

Sir Plenorius
Sir Pellogres
Sir Pellandris or Pelaundris
Sir Pillounes or Pyllownes:
>four brothers won by Lancelot.

Sir Darras:
>once imprisoned Tristram, Palomides and Dinadan. Tristram had slain three of his sons and wounded two others. But he prevented forty of his kin from killing them.

Sir Harry le Fise Lake:
>one of three who fought Breuse Sans Pité—the others being Ector and Percivale.

Sir Erminide:
>brother of King Harmaunce, for whom Palomides fought at the Red City.

Sir Selises of the Dolorous Tower:
>nephew of the King with a Hundred Knights.

Sir Ironside:
>the Knight of the Red Laundes, won by Gareth.

Sir Arrok de Grevaunt
Sir Degrane Saunce Velany:
>son of King of Alenie, fought with giant of the black tower.

Sir Pelleas:
  'wedded' to the Lady of the Lake.
Sir Lamiel of Cardiff:
  'that was a great lover'.
Sir Plaine de Fors:
  overthrown by Cote de Mal Taile—with Pleine d'Amour.
Sir Mellaeus de Lile:
  son of the King of Denmark.
Sir Bohart le Cure Hardy:
  king Arthur's son on Lady Lyonors.
Sir Mador de la Porte:
  brother of Gaheris de Karehen—champion against the
  Queen in incident of the poisoned apple.
Sir Colgrevance
Sir Hervise le Forest Savage
Sir Hervis de Revel:
  chosen by Pellinore to be a Round Table knight.
Sir Marrok:
  betrayed by his wife who made him a werewolf for seven
  years.
Sir Persaunt, the Blue Knight
Sir Pertilope, the Green Knight
Sir Perimones, the Red Knight:
  brothers, won by Gareth.
Sir Dagonet:
  the King's fool.
Sir Galagars le Roux

PART TWO: THE GRADE OF MERLIN AND THE FAERY WOMEN

11. The Atlantean Background

We proceed now to consider the Second Degree, which we shall call the Grade of Merlin. It includes the powers and functions of the 'faery women' and enchantresses, of whom the most important are Morgan le Fay and the Lady of the Lake, usually called Nineveh or Nimuë. Others are the sorceress Hellawes, Lady of the Castle Nigramous; and Annowse, a sorceress who in one of the stories seduces Arthur. Nor should we forget the shadowy figure behind Merlin, called Blaise. He appears to be Merlin's master and mentor, although he is reduced somewhat to the role of a scribe or annalist in later redactions. There are also semi-human or Elemental figures such as Morgan's husband Uriens of Gore, and various lesser 'ladies of the Lake' (such as Saraïde) of whom there are many, for the Lake is no less than the astral plane, the great treasure house of images beyond the physical plane. It is sometimes perceived by ordinary mortals by the subtle perceptors that register through the pictorial imagination. There are also various places to consider that are part of this faery world of the Lake—such as the Castle of Maidens and various forests, castles and chapels of enchantment.

Merlin, Morgan and Nimuë may be fitted into the perspective of traditional occult proto-history as early teachers of the current evolution of mankind that is sometimes called the fifth Root Race. The fourth Root Race comprised the 'Atlantean' phase of human evolution of antediluvian times.

Noah's Flood is not necessarily the actual Atlantean catastrophe, but a minor repetition of it, like that which afflicted the Celts when the Baltic overflowed through the melting of ice at the end of the last Ice Age. Events such as these would, however, restimulate racial memories.

The Atlantean tradition that comes down to us in fragmentary form is the result of efforts of seership by those particularly gifted and trained at recovery of these memories. It is sometimes called reading the *akasha* or the *akashic* records.

The importance of Merlin is his role as a way-shower to a new phase, or epoch, of conscious evolution. The antediluvian Atlantean phase had brought about, as its fruits, a species of humanity well developed in instinctual wisdom but not in the individualized intellectual capacities. The consciousness of antediluvian humanity might be considered as similar to that of the higher forms of domesticated animal of our own days, particularly the family dog, or the horse, brought to the highest peak of individuality by prolonged human contact and affection.

The seat of consciousness of Atlantean man was at a 'lower' point of the brain, more towards what we might almost call a spinal consciousness. They thus tended more to a species of group consciousness rather than individual expression. This is sometimes seen, as something of a throwback, in modern crowd behaviour. In such a context the emotions are easily aroused and actions undertaken that may be very uncharacteristic of many of the individuals that compose the crowd. In its most degenerate and dramatic form it may be a lynch mob but it also applies more commonly, and at a higher mode of expression, to any theatre, cinema or concert audience. This participation in mass emotion is, however, a form of expression and experience laid down in the Atlantean phase of evolution. It should perhaps be said that the form of expression and experience is none the worse for being an ancient mode of human behaviour, and it would be a foolishly intellectualized and egoistic individual who tried to cut himself off from the roots that link him with the rest of humankind and the fund of common human experience.

This form of mentation is more easily influenced by sound, form and colour than by intellectual reasonings. Thus, much of Atlantean magical technique was founded upon the use of sound, form and colour as a means of playing upon the instincts and emotions. The modern exploiters of these old Atlantean magical techniques are to be found, not in occult fraternities, but in the creative departments of advertising agencies. Indeed, time spent studying television commercials in an analytical fashion is perhaps one of the best introductions to the use of rhythm, vowel sounds, background music or sound effects, and associated visual images.

In matters of this kind the old Atlantean ruling priesthood was highly skilled, and in the Arthurian legends they are represented particularly by Merlin, the great magician, and by Morgan le Fay the enchantress.

These methods, amounting to strong hypnotic influence over a more easily suggestible, less individualized humanity than pertains today, would have made them adept at 'shape-shifting' and at putting people into an enchanted sleep. The latter would also give the seemingly magical ability to transport them to distant places, the subjects having been rendered unconscious while they completed the journey.

Merlin is, however, no mere illusionist. He represents a humanized Western form of the ancient gods of learning and civilization, such as the Greek Hermes or the Egyptian Thoth. He is, furthermore, one of those, akin to Melchizedek in the Old Testament, 'without father or mother, without descent'.

These are the great superhuman figures who work behind the scenes of planetary evolution, sometimes appearing physically to selected disciples at particular times of opportunity or crisis, but for the most part unseen, working through chosen human intermediaries. They are known in Eastern esoteric literature as *Manus*.

In this role Merlin brought the secret teaching of doomed Atlantis, at the end of its phase, to the new world of Europe, and founded first the Hibernian Mysteries, the vestiges of which come down to us in the mythology of Ireland. Following this, and from other Western seaboard outposts, the same teaching spread to the rest of the islands of Britain and Continental Europe.

His mandate came from a great primordial being who is traditionally called Narada. It was he who brought through to the consciousness of humanity, as a guiding light, the great solar pattern – of a central life – generating point surrounded by seven circles of force. This was the pattern of the great Sun Temple of Atlantis on the island of Ruta, and the spiritual pattern of civilization upon which the Atlantean human epoch was built. This, in the early days of Atlantis, was a secret teaching, confined to the sacred clan of aristocratic priest-initiates.

At the end of the Atlantean epoch Merlin was charged to bring to the new root race a more subtle and complex form of the plan. This new pattern was that of the Round Table. This has been preserved in human consciousness over the centuries, latterly through the vehicle of the Arthurian legends. This added the

concept of corporate responsibility through individual endeavour, in place of the emphasis on hierarchy. The legends were
rendered into written form in the twelfth century but were in oral
form before that, and in the earliest times were expressed in direct
physical form by the construction of stone, wood or earthen
circles.

A further advance on the previous solar pattern is that the new
formula takes cognisance of forces beyond our immediate solar
system. With the Round Table, stellar forces and patterns are
taken into account, for it is indeed a form of Zodiac. This teaching
emanates from a cosmic centre of force that is concerned with the
universal evolution of consciousness as opposed to comparatively
localised Solar or planetary evolution. For purposes of Earth
consciousness this source of influence may be thought of as
emanating from what appear to us to be the seven stars of the
constellation of the Great Bear.

We should also mention in passing a further pattern, also of
stellar origin, but using, as a transforming agent for reception by
human consciousness on Earth, the inner forces of the planet
Venus. This formula, mediated by Melchizedek, is the formula of
the Rose Cross. The inner significance of these teachings was
esoterically reserved until their partial public revelation in the
seventeenth century. In its fullness this is an arrangement of rays
and circles in which the central rose has three sets of petals,
(three, seven and twelve), from which rays of light emanate. This
indicates the creative spiritual mystery of the inner cosmic energies finding their true destiny through being impaled upon the
equal-armed cross of space and time in the world of matter.

It had, of course, been esoterically revealed and expressed in
the Incarnation of the Logos and the crucifixion of Jesus, the
Christed one, who was rather more than an ordinary way-shower,
avatar, or *manu*. This was a unique cosmic event, the ramifications of which are still not by any means worked out or revealed,
and they are contained in the Mysteries of the Holy Grail in their
form for the New Age.

In the higher form of initiation associated with the Holy Grail,
all three patterns, of Solar sphere, Round Table, and Rose Cross,
are assimilated fully into consciousness. They are each aspects,
and developments, of the same one eternal reality. Their simplic-
ity and familiarity in various guises, sometimes sadly vulgarized,
should not blind us to their fundamental importance as keys to
conscious evolutionary development, which is the purpose be-

hind all physical life. Initiation, let it be stressed, and the Mysteries, are not for the privileged few, but for all, even though new conceptions necessarily have small beginnings.

Merlin's purpose was, therefore, to implant a pattern of consciousness into the new civilization of humanity, commencing with the Western islands of Britain. The course of the early spread of this pattern can be traced by the chain of megalithic circles across the face of Europe. Higher centres of teaching developed in various parts of the world, notably, so far as the West is concerned, in Ancient Egypt. From thence came Moses, the prime agent of the mission of the Jews as preparers of the way for monotheism and the revelation of the Messiah.

However, in the matter of Britain, the Round Table legend is the formula for the ultimate group development of individual men, ruled not by a central despotic power but by co-operation in mutual regard and love, whilst at the same time retaining the hierarchical concept of spiritual organization and kingship.

In the days of the dawn of our epoch, when these principles were first being laid down, man was far less individualized than he is now. Therefore some of the methods instituted by Merlin would be impractical, and indeed immoral, if practised in modern times. As the general run of humankind was more animal-like in those days, so did genetics, and selective breeding, play an important part in government and the social order. This was particularly important in an epoch when man was more group-minded and open to inner plane influences. Those who could best guide the destiny of their particular group were not the most intellectually intelligent or the most physically strong but those who could be most readily receptive to teachings of a higher order of consciousness from the inner planes.

Thus certain blood lines had a natural clairvoyance which was an important corollary of power and vision. This was the foundation of the concept of aristocracy and the 'divine right of kings'—a concept so deeply ingrained in human consciousness that Charles I was proud to be a martyr in defence of it. The agonies resulting from this act, on the Puritan as well as the Royalist side, indicate the depths of motivation involved, for the most part completely unrealised by the protagonists, who as in all times tended to think in immediate and pragmatic terms limited by the intellectual presuppositions of the day.

The importance of this sacred kingship, and of inherited ease of contact with the inner planes, is clearly demonstrated in the

Arthurian legend by the stories of Arthur's conception and birth, which reveal a specific policy of genetic engineering on the part of Merlin.

It is this that is behind the somewhat bizarre events that surround this part of the Arthurian story. Arthur, according to Merlin's intention, was meant to be a priest-king in the ancient tradition of Atlantis, chosen before birth, as a result of a mating carefully planned in the light of esoteric genetic considerations.

Merlin chose the two parents with great care. Arthur's father was to be Uther Pendragon, of the ancient British royal line. This line had been established by a previous Atlantean migration and held within it Hibernian and even remote Lemurian strains. It was symbolised by the 'Pendragonship'—which signified an early brotherhood of esoteric warriors whose symbolic crest derived from the constellation Draco, the Dragon, which coils its way about the Northern Pole of the celestial sphere, and at certain epochs provides from its body the North Star.

On his mother's side Arthur had the blood of an Atlantean princess, Igraine. She was one of the Sacred Clan, who had come to Cornwall and become the wife of the local chieftain. In the surviving annals that have come down to us he is known as Gorlois, the Duke of Cornwall or Duke of Tintagel.

Cornwall had especial links with Atlantis and with Hibernia, and in its legends are woven strands from ancient Irish and Cornish Atlantean settlements. These are to be found principally in the stories surrounding Tristram and Iseult and the Court of King Mark. The ancient native Cornish stock, of whom Gorlois was an overlord, is said to be descended from a pre-human, giant-like race.

Whilst not directly descended from Gorlois, something of the influence of the line of Gorlois would also have permeated the embryo of the incipient Arthur, for the physical sexual union between man and woman has a strong auric and etheric effect. Even a childless marriage has a powerful inner effect upon the subtle bodies. Thus has it been said that true marriage is a becoming of one flesh.

Over the years of her marriage to the Duke of Cornwall, Igraine would have absorbed within her subtle bodies much of the native Cornish inheritance. Her Atlantean heritage by her own birth and lineage would also have been reinforced by the earlier conception, by previous esoteric matings in Atlantis, of her three daughters Morgawse, Elaine and Morgan.

Merlin's plans also included the wife of Arthur, who was to be Guenevere of Cameliard—a district now sunk beneath the waves off the Cornish coast, which had its own strong links as an early outpost of Atlantean colonists. This had been planned since his first revelation of the concept of the Round Table, in the time of the great days of Uther Pendragon, when he entrusted it to one of Uther's lieutenants, Leodegrance ('the great lion') of Cameliard, from whom it eventually came to Arthur as part of Guenevere's dowry.

As preparation for his destiny, Arthur was taken at birth by Merlin, and placed in the custody of foster parents and under the tutelage of the Lady of the Lake. A popular tradition places this episode at Lake Bala in Wales but specific locations are only secondary links with what is essentially an inner plane condition. His foster father is called Ector, a hero's name rendered in classical literature as Hector. Ector, as father of the mighty Kay, once identified with the trees and a paragon of brave warriorship, is thus rather more than the benign yeoman usually portrayed in the children's stories of the event.

Part of Arthur's training is in warriorship, on inner and outer levels. Arthur himself shows great prowess—as in some of the stories of the *Mabinogion* for example, which are at root initiatory tests. *The Spoils of Anwyn* is a version of the Quest of the Golden Fleece and is concerned with winning certain 'treasures of Britain'.

Malory makes little of the origins of Merlin. As one of the first of the modern novelists, that is, one with a sense of a dramatic story line, he obviously felt it necessary to omit early biographical material from the all-inclusive rambling sagas of his mediaeval sources. Thus 'enfances' are omitted or glossed over in Malory's treatment of Arthur, Lancelot, Tristram and Merlin himself.

Insofar that Merlin's childhood is full of wonders Malory may have felt particularly impelled to omit them. He was writing at a time when the mediaeval world of faith, and the superstition that went with it, was beginning to crumble. There is therefore a certain secularising tendency in Malory which is of course particularly noticeable in his treatment of Merlin and the faery women.

Geoffrey of Monmouth's *History of the Kings of Britain* is the first written version of the legend of Merlin in anything like coherent form. Indeed he made much of Merlin in separate books of 'prophecies' and a *Life of Merlin* which clearly expresses

Merlin's non-human generation. (It is interesting to note in this context that Geoffrey cites Apuleius of Madaura, whose novel *The Golden Ass*, under the guise of comic ribaldry, gives the clearest account we have of the ancient Mystery cult of Isis by one of its initiates.)

According to Geoffrey, Merlin hails from Carmarthen, and although the derivation of the name of Merlin or Merdhin from the name of the town Carmarthen, or Caer Merdhin, has been discredited by some scholars, here scholastic accuracy blinds rather then enlightens. We would come to no harm in sustaining the tradition of Merlin coming from this most significant part of the British Isles, at the far South-west of the Principality of Wales. It is close to Hibernian contacts and influence to this very day, and an obvious outpost of ancient colonists from the west. It is in this district of Dyfed, recently Pembrokeshire, that the blue stones of the earlier Stonehenge derive. There is also a stone circle associated therewith, and, hard by, one of the oldest 'green roads' or trackways of these islands. Popular imagination may indeed be a more fruitful repository of ancient wisdom than the shallow accuracy of modern academic knowledge suspects.

According to Geoffrey, Merlin's mother was daughter of the King of South Wales who lived in a nunnery as a result of a strange encounter with a non-human entity who became the father of Merlin. To quote Geoffrey, this father:

> as Apuleius in writing as touching the god of Socrates doth make report, certain spirits there be betwixt moon and earth, the which we call incubus demons. They have a nature that doth partake both of men and angels, and do hold converse with mortal women. Haply one of these hath appeared unto this lady, and is the father of the youth.

It is important to differentiate between the modern usage of the word demon which, by orthodox religious influence and loss of knowledge of inner dynamics, has rendered the meaning of the word wholly evil. It would be better to revert to the older spelling, deriving from the Greek, of daimon, which signifies simply a discarnate spirit. Indeed, in the case of Socrates it is a being entirely beneficent, and has been likened to the esoteric concept of man's own Higher Self or Holy Guardian Angel.

What we have here, in effect, is a species of parthenogenesis; and virgin birth is a corpus of legend that grows about many divine and super-human figures. Nor is it without a profound inner validity. It is a mode of establishing physical manifestation for many types of higher being and is by no means unique. It is a strange fruit of the evolution of consciousness that many Christians should disbelieve the fact of virgin birth in relation to the Saviour, whilst others in the faith hold it to be a unique event never happening before or since.

The Incarnation may indeed have been a unique event of supreme and crucial importance to the evolution of the world, but the mode of certain aspects of its operation nonetheless will have had some common factors with lesser occasions; and the incarnation of *avatars*, *manus*, or other high beings dedicated to certain tasks in the aid of terrestrial evolution, may well be initiated in similar fashion.

It is interesting to compare the explanations of Wace and Layamon in these matters, highly dangerous in their heretical implications in those days.

The Norman Wace writes that Merlin's mother is the daughter of the King of Dimetia in Wales, now a nun in Carmarthen. His father he calls

> a certain order of spirit (that) ranges between the moon and our earth ... of the nature partly man, and partly of loftier being. These demons are called incubi. Their home and region is the air, but this warm world is their resort. It is not in their power to deal man great evil, and they can do little more mischief than to trick and to annoy. However, they know well how to clothe themselves in human shape, for their nature lends itself marvellously to the deceit. Many a maid has been their sport, and in this guise has been deceived. It may well be that Merlin was begotten by such a being, and perchance is of a demon born.

And Anglo-Saxon Layamon says Merlin's mother is a hooded nun, a daughter of Conaan, the king of a third of Wales, who, at the age of fifteen, dreamed whilst asleep often of a fair full knight arrayed in gold. He goes on to say:

> 'there dwell in the sky many kind of beings, that there shall remain until domesday arrive; some they are good, and some they work evil. Therein is a race that cometh among men; they are named full truly Incubi Daemones; they do not much harm, but deceive the folk; many a man in dream oft they delude, and many a fair woman through their craft childeth anon, and many a good man's child they beguile through magic. And thus was Merlin begot.'

There was a school of thought among the medieval annalists that sought to make Merlin's origins wholly evil. They taught that his birth was planned by the devil but that the sanctity of his encloistered mother foiled the devilish plot and caused her strange off-spring to be a power for good.

This does give a certain pathos to the story. It depicts a young girl's innocence and goodness defying the powers of evil. And it paints Merlin as a strange, enigmatic figure, torn between good and evil, conceived by the devil to thwart the coming of the Round Table chivalry, but by the influence of his Christian mother and her confesser Blaise, foiling the devil and helping the Round Table Fellowship instead. However, despite its dramatic merits, this is still no more than a pious distortion that makes nonsense of the original theme.

Merlin and his kind are no bastard brood of human devils, and the doctrine of incubi is a medieval distortion that reduces a very profound and little known form of polarity working between the planes to a form of mediumistic sexual perversion or auto-eroticism.

It is, of course, possible for such techniques and powers to be so degraded if dedication and control are lacking, which is why they are part of the withheld secrets of the initiatory tradition. However, without an acknowledgement of these intimate powers—which pertain to a knowledge of the aura that is part of the Grade of Guenevere—our understanding of the dynamics behind the Arthurian legend, and indeed the Mystery Tradition in general, will be sadly lacking.

In medieval times occult secrecy was largely imposed by religious sanctions. In latter days, although these sanctions became less of a threat, Victorian prudery about sex imposed an even more encloistered secrecy about the sexual element in the teachings concerning the aura. This is the cause of much of the portentous secrecy in occult circles that abounded until very recent times.

However, one cannot forever ignore the facts of life, and the time is perhaps overdue to point out that just as esoteric studies may be called the yoga of the West so there is an element in them that corresponds to tantrik and kundalini yoga—those forms of inner union that are concerned with the sexual and polar forces of the aura. These forces may at root be considered as one, somewhat after the psycho-analytical concept of libido, and this force may be expressed in many and various creative ways—from the conception of children to the creation of works of art. We need, in short, to acknowledge that the *rosa mystica* has also stem, leaf and root.

A more comprehensive consideration of these matters pertains to the Grade of Guenevere but something of these general principles is necessary to an understanding of the coming of Merlin, and the acts and motives of himself and the faery women—in particular Morgan le Fay and Nimuë, the Lady of the Lake.

12. The Planes of Consciousness

Before we can fully understand the background to the coming of Merlin it is necessary to examine some of the dynamics of the evolution of consciousness on the various levels of its expression.

Behind the vulgarized conception of the existence of *Incubi Daemones* there is the reality of a vast concourse of spiritual hierarchies of which the physical element of the human race is but a small part.

This great concourse of spiritual beings includes those who have gone through the processes and experiences of human form, who are indeed part of the human race as we know it. It also includes those of a spiritual destiny and origin other than human whose dedicated order of service is nevertheless to help the evolution of the human race and of the other forms of sentient being who share this planet. Mankind has never been without guidance.

In the normal course of the evolution of the individual human spirit there is a gradual concretion of experience, what may be called a coming down the planes. Each of these phases of experience is traditionally given a planetary name. This can prove confusing for it is easy to mistake this nomenclature for a fanciful description of the planets of the physical solar system. However, there are good reasons for utilizing this traditional planetary nomenclature and continuing to do so. We need to keep in mind however that they refer to conditions of consciousness as experienced by a 'swarm' of spirits rather than to physical objects in space.

We may therefore conceive of human spirits coming from a spiritual sphere of pure being, whence they have been virtually newly created. In fact their prime existence stems from further back in cosmic and 'uncreate' reality but to all intents and purposes they are as if they had been newly created by the great being whom the monotheistic religions of the world refer to as God.

It would be more accurate to consider these spirits, sparks from the Divine Fire, as little brothers and sisters of God. In the superior consciousness and creative aura of the great Being they are about to develop their own experience through a whole evolution.

The course of evolution of the human spirit may be conceived as a going out and a return through seven principal conditions. These seven conditions we designate with 'planetary' names from Sun (representing the immediate sphere of God) to Earth (our current normal physical consciousness) with intermediate conditions coming between. We can tabulate these as follows. Each planetary name is the nearest equivalent between the traditional associations of that planet in popular mythology and the specific type of consciousness.

> Sun—pure spirit.
> Jupiter—spiritual types, bringing about different modes of experience.
> Mercury—intuitive mind and faith—'unmanifest knowledge'.
> Saturn—the forms of concrete images and mentation, their logic and combination and control.
> Venus—the projective and creative emotions.
> Mars—the wisdom of the instincts.
> Earth/Moon—the concrete physical and its etheric matrix.

This table, together with Figure 5, deserves careful study. Each planet is a plane of human consciousness and none is in any sense better or worse than another. It is to emphasize this that we use a term like 'the wisdom of the instincts'. There is a tendency for some aspirants to knowledge of the inner or higher worlds to look down upon the instincts. However, the instincts give us a firm and reliable basis of behaviour. Indeed, in an otherwise feckless and deluded life it may be the call of the instincts, in family relationships or the following of social values, that promotes stability and all that is worthwhile in life expression.

Each level is capable of inspired use or degraded abuse, and this, we would stress, applies equally to the higher as to the lower

The Planes of Involution and Evolution

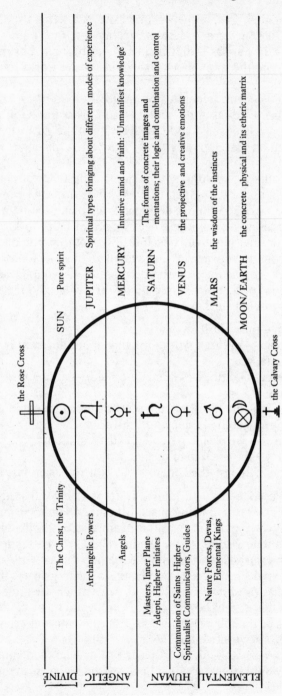

Figure 5

DIVINE	SUN	Pure spirit	The Christ, the Trinity
ANGELIC	JUPITER	Spiritual types bringing about different modes of experience	Archangelic Powers
	MERCURY	Intuitive mind and faith: 'Unmanifest knowledge'	Angels
HUMAN	SATURN	The forms of concrete images and mentations; their logic and combination and control	Masters, Inner Plane Adepti, Higher Initiates
	VENUS	the projective and creative emotions	Communion of Saints Higher Spiritualist Communicators, Guides
ELEMENTAL	MARS	the wisdom of the instincts	Nature Forces, Devas, Elemental Kings
	MOON/EARTH	the concrete physical and its etheric matrix	

the Rose Cross

the Calvary Cross

levels. In more concrete terms, a Torquemada is no less corrupt than a Bill Sykes although his motives may be 'spiritual'. Hence the reference to 'spiritual wickedness in high places' by St Paul.

Each of us has all of these levels within, although some may be more 'conscious' than others. Some may be to a greater or lesser extent repressed; others the mode of creative expression or uncontrolled abuse. This is revealed in the aura, which has its direct equivalents to these levels of consciousness in the *chakras* or psychic centres.

Referring to Figure 5, we may conceive the general course of the evolution of human consciousness to be a clockwise movement from God 'down the planes' to the nadir in earth consciousness. At each phase each spirit becomes aware of a new mode of conscious existence and interaction, and, so to speak, builds a body, or means of perception and reaction.

The sum total of bodies of expression and perception at each level constitute what we may call a 'plane' with the equivalent 'planetary' designation. There will also be different evolutionary swarms inhabiting a plane at the same time; human, elemental or angelic; and at various degrees of mastery of their evolutionary powers. These, given due training, can lead to contacts of mutual help, which is what is known as initiation.

A crucial point in this process is the passing of the lowermost point of the circle, which is the achievement of full physical/ etheric consciousness and expression. Then a direct relationship with God is possible, through the 'initiation of the nadir'. In terms of general human religious development it is here that polytheism gives place to monotheism.

In the phases prior to full physical expression there is a natural tendency to worship the higher beings who make contact with a descending 'involutionary' swarm across the diameter of the circle, so to speak. Thus does *evolving* life on any one plane help the *involving* life coming to the plane for the first time.

At the nadir, however, a direct run down the planes is possible between spirit and matter. Man is capable of realizing his own spiritual origin and destiny, and in the history of the world this fact is expressed in the great exemplary and talismanic life of the crucified and risen Christ.

We could present Figure 5 in the form of a kind of cosmic clock of the evolution of consciousness. Instead of twelve numbers around the clock, we put the planes in their planetary nomenclature in their dual aspects of involutionary and evolutionary expression.

The Paths of Involutionary and Evolutionary Consciousness

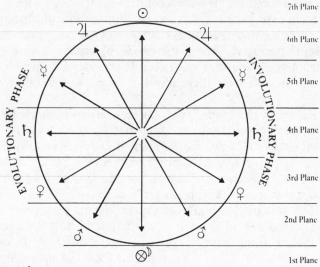

Figure 6

Referring to this diagram, inexperienced spirits are born at '12 o'clock' and proceed round on the involutionary arc of experiential consciousness, building ever more concrete 'bodies', or modes of consciousness, until at '6 o'clock' there is a swarm with a full complement of seven bodies. In other words, it is capable of conscious interaction with others on all seven levels of consciousness. There then commences, upon the evolutionary arc, the task of creatively controlling those seven modes of consciousness in a positive and integrated fashion. This means taking on individual responsibility rather than being one of a group undergoing a process.

This changeover to individual spiritual responsibility, from involution to evolution, is marked by the initiation of the nadir. Here the stamp of the Logos, as it were, is made upon the individual spirit now manifest with its full complement of seven 'bodies' and modes of action and reaction on any plane.

The initiation of the nadir accords with the general principle that major initiations function across the diameter of the circle. In general terms first and second planes are characteristically elemental forms of consciousness; the third and fourth are what we might call typically human; the fifth and sixth pertain to angelic expression, and the seventh, associated closely with God, is a paradisal form of consciousness.

A pristine swarm of spirits emerges from the paradisal state into at first, on the sixth plane, general differentiation into major spiritual types. These are drawn forth and influenced by the nature forces of a previous evolution, calling them, attracting them into matter. At a deep level the imagery of the serpent in the Garden of Eden, tempting Adam and Eve, is a pictorial representation of this.

As they proceed to the fifth plane level of involutionary consciousness, as a kind of embryonic angelic form of being, they may be influenced, across the diameter, by the saintly intercession of the human phase of a previous evolutionary swarm.

When they reach the fourth plane of consciousness the involutionary swarm can be initiated by similar 'human' beings who have experienced and conquered physical and instinctual experience. This the incoming spiritual swarm has yet to encounter. They can be prepared and instructed by the 'masters' of the fourth plane—who are achieved 'Lords of Humanity'. (It will be appreciated that we use the term humanity not confined to our own race or genus, but to denote a particular stage of consciousness).

As the new swarm of sparks descends a further stage to emotional and elemental modes of experience of the third and second planes so their guidance is taken up by angelic hierarchies. In current terms these correspond to the angelic archetypes of species, for the swarms at this stage are at what could be called animal or plant forms of existence. The development of species and the rich variety of their behaviour patterns and physical characteristics are not the fruit entirely of 'survival of the fittest', or 'natural selection'. No bird ever studied aerodynamics for example.

It follows that we should give some thought to how we treat the 'lesser' forms of life upon our planet. They are in fact forms of expression of a much higher form of life—and if we can justify extinction of species, or wholesale laboratory experimentation upon these lesser forms of life, then by the same moral categories we should be willing to submit ourselves to like exploitation and experimentation by beings 'superior' to ourselves.

An encounter with angelic or archangelic beings who thought and behaved in this fashion would be an encounter with what we would rightly call the fiendish, the devilish, the demonic—quite literally 'in-human'.

Fortunately the angels and archangels of whom we speak have passed through the equivalence of the human stage, which gives compassion and understanding. However, those humans who perform such evils, from whatever motive, have plainly much to learn as regards becoming human. They act at evolutionary peril to themselves for, in terms of consciousness, like attracts like, and cruelty inflicted by man may cause sub-human elemental or deviated angelic or discarnate human intelligences to be attracted to the suffering. These may in the end turn and devour their unsuspecting evokers.

Finally, at '6 o'clock' we come to the point where full spiritual individualization can take place—the initiation of the nadir—which is a supreme crisis point in the evolution of consciousness.

This circular pattern works in various modes, and the complete cycle can also be seen in the archetypal pattern of an individual human life on the physical plane. At physical conception the spirit awaiting incarnation is drawn into manifest existence as developing embryo. This is a response to the physical mating of two humans of a previous generation already established on the physical plane. The course of involution around the right hand downward arc of the circle represents the stages of physical birth and of dawning faculties and their control from babyhood, through pubescence and adolescence, to courtship and mating. The nadir may be represented by marriage—which is an important and significant ceremony. It celebrates the union of two separate individuals into a complementary polarity, a duality in unity. This has many symbolic echoes throughout the whole of creation, inner and outer, for all creation is effected in terms of the transmission of force from one plane to another by means of a union of opposites.

It is the mating in marriage, and in the dedication of implied parenthood, that leads to the opportunities for a subsequent generation of humankind to come forth. The growth up the evolutionary side of the circle represents the experiences of parenthood in relation to a growing family, from young infants to adolescents and their departing into the world, (the parent/child relationship reaching across the diameter of the circle). Finally there comes a period of freedom from parental ties when all the children have gone to found families themselves, and at the last a period of grandparenthood takes place and the essence of life experience is recollected in old age prior to transition to a higher mode of existence.

This is obviously a very broad and archetypal pattern and individual variations upon the theme will differ enormously. There are some who will not physically mate but will create and fulfil themselves in other ways. However, the basic pattern is worth bearing in mind when deliberating upon the consequences of issues such as promiscuity, easy divorce, sexual deviance, abortion and other moral issues. In the modern climate of opinion the main criterion tends to be that of personal convenience rather than a responsibility to other forms of life. True happiness however is to be found in service rather than in self-indulgence, for it accords with broader comsic patterns which are at the basis of our whole existence.

The sacraments of the church also take on an added significance when they are seen to mark three critical points of life. Baptism as the beginning of life, Holy Unction at the end of life, and Marriage marking the initiation of the nadir.

13. The Coming of Merlin

The medieval annals state that Merlin was not born of a human father. We may regard him as a higher being than the common run of mortal human beings of his times, incarnating into the human race by special means. That is, not by the normal means of the physical/etheric vortex set into motion by the processes of a normal physical relationship, but by a connection between a being on the inner planes and a human maiden. This is the mechanics of virgin birth and it is part of the conditions of success for such a union that utter purity of motive and dedication be the attitude of she who provides the feminine vehicle for the incarnating ego on the lower plane. The slightest deviation from this degrades the process into a subjective sexual phantasy governed by the lower vehicles and the higher contact is unable to come through. It is this aspect, unrealized in its technical function but intuitively grasped by the popular imagination that is responsible for the doctrine of the Immaculate Conception. That is, that the Virgin Mary must have been born herself without taint of original sin otherwise she would have been incapable of making herself a vehicle for the Virgin Birth of the Christ.

The birth of Merlin, and of others like him, scattered thinly through history and pre-history, was of this kind. Merlin and his like were, however, lesser teachers and guides than the unique Incarnation that occurred in the Holy Land at the dawn of our era.

In the legends, the fact that Merlin is without father attracts attention to him following certain prophecies of magicians at the court of King Vortigern. These circumstances, part history, part legend, enshrine dynamics of a deeper and earlier truth. Vor-

tigern, although a Celt, had usurped the crown from the Pendragon line and was faced with mounting dissension both from
within his kingdom and from without. He had invited the Saxon
leaders Hengist and Horsa into the land to fight the Picts but they
in turn had begun to turn on him and carve out Saxon kingdoms
for themselves. In desperate straits Vortigern had begun to build a
mighty tower and stronghold for himself on Snowdon. However,
every time they tried to build the tower the foundations crumbled.

Snowdon is a great and powerful site of the Celtic Mysteries.
Many high places have sacred connotations and Snowdon is the
highest point in Wales, and is in an area of North-west Wales that
was a focal point for the Druid priesthood. Also, because of its
location, it had strong contacts with Hibernia and the mysterious
lands and islands of the Western Ocean. It is the site of the
legendary paradisal city fortress Caer Idris. In much later years it
was the site where profound realizations of the structure and
function of the human psyche came to the poets Wordsworth and
Coleridge.

It is thus small wonder that a quisling and usurper such as
Vortigern should find that his defences could establish no foundations here. He was out of sympathy with, and outcast from, the
group soul of his race and the angelic guardians of these islands.

The wise men surrounding Vortigern decreed, however, that
the tower could be made to stand if the stones were cemented by
the blood of a child who had no human father. To the modern
mind, with its tendency to shallow intellectual assumptions, this
seems no more than a bizarre way for charlatan magicians to
preserve their interests by laying down impossible conditions.
The blood of a slaughtered virgin child of virgin birth, used for
the personal gain of a traitor and usurper has, however, a horrible
validity and reality whose dark undertones reverberate to the
depths of Hell. It would have been a deliberate attempt to thwart
the cosmic order, by perverting the means of intercession down
the planes from higher orders of creation. This is a cancer on the
body politic and on the spiritual order. It is an example of deep
knowledge and ruthless exploitation of black magic in its true
sense—seldom seen, and seldom recognized even when it is.

The emissaries of Vortigern duly find the child Merlin and take
him to be sacrificially slain at Snowdon. However, Merlin proves
more magically and prophetically powerful than the self-oriented
caucas of magical advisers to Vortigern. He reveals the true cause
of the perpetual ruin of the tower. Beneath the foundations of the

tower, he states, there is a lake; beneath the lake a stone; and beneath the stone two contending dragons.

There is, once again, more to this than a simple lesson in building technology or a crude allegory of the Saxon-Celtic struggle.

The lake, as we have already discussed, is the astral world which is at the base of physical reality. Indeed it is the foundation, in a very special manner, of a nationally magical place such as Caer Idris. Beneath the astral is a rock of spiritual reality—that same one as described by the alchemists in their mystical acrostic VITRIOL, the Universal Solvent, which is Love:

> Visita
> Interiora
> Terrae
> Rectificando
> Invenies
> Occultum
> Lapidem

And underlying this are the two polar principles, the knowledge and control of which bestows power over the whole of creation.

Thus the youthful Merlin demonstrates himself to be more familiar with the basic powers of the inner universe than even the dark knowledge of the magicians who surround Vortigern. These, despite their seeming power, can only manipulate, not create. They, like all evil, can only interfere with the cosmic order to their own temporary ends. They cannot construct and maintain such an order to the greater glory and fulfilment of all life within it.

It is at this point appropriately in Geoffrey of Monmouth's account, when the two dragons are laid bare, that Merlin launches into great prophecies—as would be expected when one, who is great enough and powerful enough, uncovers the underlying roots of appearances.

The first prophecy is of the imminent downfall of Vortigern. Accordingly, Aurelius Ambrosius and his younger brother Uther Pendragon land at Totnes the following day, from Brittany, and in a series of battles drive back the Saxons, with the sterling championship in their army of Eldol, Duke of Gloucester, and of Gorlois, Duke of Cornwall, whom we meet later in the circumstances surrounding the conception of Arthur.

In Geoffrey of Monmouth's account the Celts under Ambrosius are depicted as preserving the Christian faith against the pagan Saxons. No doubt much of the story derives from incidents of the fifth century AD, but there are, contained within the story, fragments of a much more ancient tradition in which, from the early mists of our island history, the gigantic figures of Merlin, Eldol, Gorlois, and Uther derive.

The name Aurelius Ambrosius is patently of Roman origin, along with the genealogy which credits Aurelius and Uther with being sons of King Constantine. Constantine we may confidently derive from the Roman Emperor Constantine I, who had strong connections with Britain. He was proclaimed Caesar whilst in York, where he had come with his father Constantius Chlorus. Constantine, in due time, became a very important figure in world history. Not only was he responsible for making Christianity the official religion of the Roman Empire after his conversion in AD 313, but he founded the new city of Constantinople which, after the fall of the West to barbarism, was the great centre of high civilization and the bastion of Christendom against the hordes of the East. Over the centuries it became the legendary but nonetheless real city of Byzantium, which amazed the crusaders with its splendour.

The strong British link with these origins, through Constantine, is seldom stressed but marks an important effect in the dynamics of the Mysteries of Britain, whose origins had been laid centuries, even millennia, before by Merlin and the Great Atlantean colonists.

Scholars who accuse Geoffrey of Monmouth of confusing Merlin with a Welsh bard of the Dark Ages do not realize that it is this very element which makes Geoffrey of Monmouth's history so important. Its lack of historical accuracy is made up for by its preservation of ancient oral traditions from the dawn of time. In these matters learned dissertations on historical origins of particular manuscripts are of little relevance.

The old material shines through when the victorious Aurelius is instructed by Merlin to fetch the stones to build Stonehenge. Geoffrey and other early historians may well have thought Stonehenge to have been of Druid, Roman or post-Roman origin. However, the oral tradition that Geoffrey records goes back to origins long before the Celts and the Saxons, to the time when Stonehenge was built, in the second millenium BC, and even beyond that when it was of wood and earth.

Stonehenge, according to this tradition as recorded by Geoffrey, was a monument to all who had been slain in defence of their faith and their country. In seeking a means of constructing a building 'that should stand for ever in memory of men so worthy' King Ambrose Aurelius sent, at the behest of his artisans in stone and wood, for Merlin. Merlin was obviously regarded by them as one who was custodian of superior knowledge in building great monumental structures. Merlin was eventually discovered in Gwent, at 'the fountain of Galabes that he was wont to haunt', and the significance of his being found at a fountain—a source of power and life welling up from the depths—should not be lost on us; we come upon this symbolic location again and again in the Arthuriad.

Merlin's advice was to seek Westward, and to fetch a circle of stones, already ancient and hallowed, standing on a mountain in Ireland, and called the Dance of the Giants.

Naturally the king was doubtful about their ability to move stones so large so great a distance. However, Merlin insisted on the importance of these stones, that were of great and yet more ancient Mysteries, having been carried by giants from the furthest ends of Africa to be set up in Ireland, where the giants then lived. The reason that the giants had brought them was that the stones had a healing virtue. Water poured over them and collected into baths cured the sick.

Accordingly, the king's younger brother, Uther Pendragon, was delegated, with 15,000 men, to go to fetch them.

The earliest stones of Stonehenge, the 'blue stones', were in fact transported a great distance, from the Prescelly Mountains in South-west Wales, not far from Carmarthen, Merlin's reputed birthplace. Stonehenge itself had, however, been in use long before this, with structures of wood and earth.

There is not a great deal to be gained from too close an examination of Geoffrey's geography. The esoteric truth is gleaned not so much from such detail as from the principle that the stones were of a special virtue, and had been recognized to be so from times of immense antiquity. The African giant connection suggests a line of tradition, ancient even by Atlantean standards, to memories of Lemurian life when giants walked the Earth as it then was.

This was the tradition and ancient knowledge behind the building of Stonehenge and other great megalithic monuments, besides which the actual quarrying of the stones is of comparatively recent a date. Nonetheless the site of the blue stone outcrop in the Prescelly Mountains, which overlooks on the one side a plain on which is a stone circle, river transport and one of the most ancient trackways of ancient Britain, and is within sight of the Atlantic Ocean and all its ancient Sea Mysteries on the other, is an important site of pilgrimage for the serious esoteric student.

The ancient secrets of the stones had been lost, it would seem, by those in whose kingdom they stood. Geoffrey records that the young and courageous King Gilloman of Ireland amassed an army to resist Uther Pendragon without much regard for conserving a sacred and precious heritage. Rather was it in incredulity at the seeming inconsequence of the British attack. 'No wonder the craven Saxon folk were strong enough to lay waste the island of Britain' he says, with grandiloquent anachronism, 'when the Britons themselves are such gross-witted wisacres. Who hath ever heard of such folly? Are the stones of Ireland any better than those of Britain that our kingdom should thus be challenged to fight for them?'

In Geoffrey, the location of the site is in Ireland, although the South-West corner of Wales may well have been under Irish, or other non-British settlement. The fact is that there were megalithic sites in Ireland before there were any such in England. Newgrange, and other sites in the Boyne valley, are prime examples. Their original significance would indeed probably have been forgotten in the 1500 years between their construction (c.3500 BC) and the building of the blue stone circle at Stonehenge (c.2000 BC). However, to concentrate upon any one historical period, or upon any one geographical location, constricts our view of the truth behind these matters. We are concerned with an inner wisdom, and its custodians, which makes its appearance at apparently isolated and widely different epochs and locations. To the received common knowledge of any age this ancient wisdom may seem strange and illusory; it does to many people today as it did once before to King Gilloman.

Gilloman is defeated by Uther's army and then Merlin emphasises the importance of magic by inviting the Britons to try to move the stones. In much the same way that is conjectured by archeological engineers 'Some rigged up huge hawsers, some set to with ropes, some planted scaling ladders, all eager to get done with the work, yet nathless was none of them never a whit the forwarder. And when they were all weary and spent Merlin burst out on laughing and put together his own engines.' Or, as Wace has it,

'Merlin kept silence, and entered within the carol. He walked warily around the stones. His lips moved without stay, as those of a man about his orisons, though I cannot tell whether or no he prayed. At length Merlin beckoned to the Britains. "Enter boldly", cried he; "there is nought to harm. Now you may lift these pebbles from their seat, and bear and charge them on your ships."' A similar version is given by Layamon. 'Merlin went about, and diligently gan behold; thrice he went about, within and without, and moved his tongue as if he sung his beads.'

Merlin's magical technology is traditionally held to be concerned with tapping and channelling magnetic earth currents of a subtle but powerful nature. This would be suggested by the apparent ancient obsession with being able to predict lunar eclipses, when, as with the tides of the sea, the inner geo-lunar tides would also be considerably affected. The case for ley-lines has been done no great service by over-enthusiastic advocates but those with the inner perceptions to recognize ancient power-points are well aware of the existence of an ancient system of inner power lines, now to a large extent fragmented and built over.

Anyhow, Merlin's art 'laid the stones down so lightly as none would believe' and so transported them, partly by ship, back to Salisbury plain.

Merlin continued to watch over the fortunes of the country. In course of time one of Vortigern's sons raised a rebellion, with the aid of the King of Ireland, and landed at St Davids. This is not far from the site of the outcrop of blue stones—so we may well have a telescoping of events in the fragmentary annals that have come down to us. Aurelius Ambrosius the king is sick at Winchester at the time, so the army is led by Uther, accompanied by Merlin who, as in the later Arthurian story recorded by Malory, plays, like the Druids of old, an important tactical and strategic role in times of war, advising the king or commander-in-chief how best to fight his various battles.

Whilst on the way to do battle with the invading forces, Uther and his men are amazed by a great star that appears in the sky, 'of marvellous bigness and brightness, stretching forth one ray whereon was a ball of fire spreading forth in the likeness of a dragon and from the mouth of the dragon issued forth two rays, whereof the one was of such length as that it did seem to reach beyond the regions of Gaul, and the other, verging toward the Irish sea, did end in seven lesser rays.'

Merlin, called upon to interpret this starry phenomenon,

announces the death by treachery of Aurelius. The kingship of Uther, he says, is represented by the star, and the two rays signify a son (i.e. Arthur) whose dominions shall be mighty. The seven-fold ray over Ireland signifies a dynasty through a daughter that shall rule over Britain.

The details of the prophecy we may regard as an interpolation plausible to the later annalists. The esoteric truth behind the matter is the inner 'celestial' provenance for the laying down of a dynastic line, via Uther and Arthur, through the mediation of Merlin.

Uther is made king, and Geoffrey of Monmouth states that it was because of the star that Uther was called the Pendragon—which means 'the head of a dragon'. It is in esoteric fact a profound anointing of a cosmic destiny for Uther, and originates from the deep and ancient Mysteries surrounding the ancient Pole Star and the constellation of the Dragon that encompasses the Northern celestial pole.

Something of this is realized in the annals of Geoffrey where it is recorded that Uther had two images of dragons wrought in gold: one to be kept at the most holy place in the land, (said to be the church at Winchester), and the other to be carried by him and his army. This is a talismanic act of high magic if ever there was one.

The ancient sanctity of Stonehenge is endorsed by the fact that the King Aurelius Ambrosius is said to be buried there. There is behind this fragment of legend, not so much a motivation for us to excavate the site of Stonehenge for the body of Aurelius, but rather to consider the connection between certain ancient mega-lithic works and the burial of a king. All ancient stone monuments were not built for the same purpose. Their building and the rites attached to them covered many centuries. However, in times far back the function of a divine king was to die for his people by 'entering the earth'. Something of this is preserved in the Greek legend of Oedipus, who does this very thing at Colonnus; and indeed the departure of Arthur himself to Avalon is another version of the theme. It is also an important aspect of the end of Merlin, which we shall consider shortly. We have the same principle mentioned in connection with Stonehenge by the oral tradition quoted by Geoffrey—that it is sited on a burial place commemorating the sacrifice of the leaders of the nation and continues to be used as the burial place of honour for kings.

The initial tests of Uther as king follow swiftly. In Geoffrey, this is put in the context of Saxon armies but again we have, underlying the more recent legendary history, the principles of ancient initiations of the leader and of the group of which he is the head. The starry connection with this is still preserved in Geoffrey, where Uther and his army are found in an ancient magical setting amid rocks and a hazel coppice upon a hilltop, surrounded by hostile forces.

Uther takes advice from his advisers at a particular phase of the sun and stars which, to quote Geoffrey, is 'when the Bear began to turn her chariot as it drew toward dawn'. This is not merely a fanciful way of describing the hours before dawn, it expressly mentions the great constellation behind the destiny of Merlin, Uther and Arthur. The advice on how to overcome their present perils is provided by another figure of great significance in the founding of the Arthurian epic. This is none other than Gorlois, Duke of Cornwall, whose death later seals Arthur's conception by Uther upon Igraine, almost as a sacrifice.

The traditional story of Uther falling in love with Igraine and besieging Gorlois in pursuit of his passion, aided and abetted by Merlin, is a latterday gloss upon the genetic engineering of Merlin. These are vague memories of the ways of working of the old Atlantean priesthood, which controlled the destiny of rulers and of nations. A similar system pertained in Ancient Egypt.

Merlin's aim was the selection and interbreeding of particular bloodlines that would be the basis for founding an aristocratic line of priest-kings after the old Atlantean model. The particular qualities of blood would be such as to make available a refined type of clairvoyance that would enable easier contact between the ruling family or class and the inner plane guides behind the nation. This is the basis for the conception of the *sang real*—the royal blood of the Holy Grail. At a much later date it took on a higher individualized form as the attainment of individual conscious expression of the inmost spiritual powers in the physical body.

The vestiges of this primeval practice and form of human government are to be found in the caste structures of India, the old theocracies of Ancient Egypt or, until compartively recently, in Tibet. The class system of the feudal world still retained vestiges of it, and it still lingers on strongly, particularly in Britain, where the traditions of monarchy have also been maintained. The fact is that these old value systems should be transcended rather than overthrown. There is indeed an aristocracy and royalty of the spirit that is, paradoxically, open to every human soul in a profoundly 'democratic' way.

Needless to say, the ancient methods of Merlin would hardly be appropriate nowadays. They are more apposite to the breeding of livestock or other domestic animals. However, in their epoch, they were the natural and legitimate form of human advance.

The annals also record the ancient facility for shape-shifting. This was possessed particularly by Merlin and by the enchantress Morgan le Fay. In the days of a more impressionable, less individualized, humanity, the taking on of a different appearance, by a species of hypnotic suggestion, was comparatively easy. 'I am what you think I am' is a maxim that carries considerable force, even in our own supposedly objective times. Figures in the public eye, aided and abetted by the media, carry the projected fantasies of thousands. Image building is an important factor in public relations and advertizing generally.

In the less individually evolved tribes of ancient Britain such manipulation of individual and mass psychology would have been very powerful. Thus the greater scope for the control of groups and even nations by 'magic'—which is the technique of the control of *images* in the *imag*ination, as the similarity of the words would suggest.

This technique, dimly remembered, is behind the shape-shifting legends surrounding the conception of Arthur. Uther Pendragon is aided by Merlin to take on the shape of Gorlois and spend the night with Igraine, whereby Arthur, the future king, is conceived.

In course of time Igraine gives birth and Merlin waits at a postern gate at Tintagel to take the newborn child into his custody for fosterage by Ector and the astral tutelage of the Lady of the Lake.

No more is heard of Merlin until, after the death of Uther, the young Arthur appears at court, successfully draws the sword from the stone and is acclaimed as the rightful king.

14. The Young Arthur and Excalibur

We are now well into Malory country, who chooses to commence his account, apart from a brief description of Arthur's conception, with the proclaiming of Arthur king. In spite of his antecedents and the magical backing of Merlin, Arthur has to fight for his place.

In Malory the first revelation of the unknown Arthur's kingship takes place, not inappropriately, at Christmas (also the old New Year), where, in London, at a meeting called by Merlin, the mysterious stone appears while the people are at matins and mass in the greatest church in London, which Malory speculates may be St Pauls. There is a charming quaintness in the anachronism of all this episode, wherein ancient matters of the magical and spiritual past of the realm are couched in terms of mediaeval Christianity. What is plain is that a great revelation appears at the behest of Merlin, and one that is symbolically relevant to the spirit of Christmas as we now know it. It is also important enough to be associated with the gathering of the highest in the land, at the capital city of the times, and at the most holy and dedicated place within that city.

While they are at mass, a great square stone appears in the churchyard, near the high altar, upon which is a steel anvil a foot high, wherein is stuck a naked sword by the point. Letters of gold about the sword decree that: 'Whoso pulleth out this sword of this stone and anvil is rightwise king born of all England.'

Beyond the medieval Christian trappings is the most ancient Celtic and pre-Celtic wisdom of the stone, embodied in the Lia Fail, the Stone of Destiny, which cries aloud for the rightful king. At root of all this ancient history is the bed rock of deep spiritual and psychological validity at both a personal and a group level.

After some few present have tried, and failed, to draw the sword, the Archbishop places a guard of ten knights upon it, and calls a great tourney for New Year's Day. It is on this occasion of the celebration of the New Year that the young Arthur first draws the sword that proclaims his rightful destiny.

At the beginnings of things temptations and deviations from the true and the good are always at their height and their most pernicious. This is exemplified in the Bible in the story of Adam and Eve. It is a basic principle or pattern that applies throughout all life. Even Arthur's foster-brother Kay attempts to wrest the glory from the young Arthur. It is a measure of Arthur's spiritual greatness that he forgives him this primal attempt of treachery. Like Judas, and many evil doers in times of great cosmic significance, Kay is a tool of forces greater and more malevolent than himself, and 'knows not what he does'. Much the same applies to the forces of the realm beyond Arthur's immediate family.

The great lords cannot bring themselves to accept the unknown Arthur, and acknowledgement of his kingship is postponed for a further testing on a later day. At first this is Candelmas, then Easter, and finally Pentecost. This sequence of holy days may also be looked upon as a ritual sequence, which leads up to the great spiritual outpouring of the powers of the Holy Spirit at Pentecost. Subsequently Pentecost is the time of the start of all great adventures in Arthurian legend. This is in keeping with the significance of the original Christian Pentecost that launched the apostles on their mission that heralded a new religious era.

It is at Pentecost that the spirit moves the commons to rise and cry: 'We will have Arthur as king! We will put him to no more delay, for we all see that it is God's will that he shall be our king, and who that holds against it, we will slay him.' And so it is that the true will is expressed by the lowly commons, who are not blinded by the personal and dynastic ambitions of the great lords and knights, whom ambition so easily corrupts.

There is a personal interpretation applicable here too, in that the cells of the physical/etheric body have an immediate response to the incoming spirit that may be resisted by the 'higher' faculties of entrenched ideas. Often wisdom can be 'instinctual' as well as intuitive or intellectual and there is a close inner link between the highest and lowest personal subjective levels, which is often overlooked or unrealized in western esotericism.

Arthur is soon crowned, and his principal knights established.

These are initially Sir Kay as Seneschal of England; Sir Baudwyn of Britain as Constable; Sir Ulfius as Chamberlain, and Sir Brastias as Warden of the North. Students of the fourfold magic circle will see a hint here of magical foundations. The king himself forms the central point of an elemental cross or, alternatively is the apex of a pentagram.

Things do not initially run smoothly. At the coronation, which is held at the following Pentecost at Caerleon, his brothers-in-law come. These are King Lot of Lothian and Orkney with 500 knights; King Uriens of Gore with 400 knights; and King Nentres of Garlot with 700 knights. They are accompanied by the young King of Scotland with 600 knights; the King with a Hundred Knights; and King Carados with 500 knights.

Arthur receives them with great joy and offers them gifts, only to find himself rebuffed and forced to defend himself, with 500 loyal men, in a tower.

Merlin intercedes, and lays evidence before the rebellious kings that Arthur is indeed the true son of Uther, and their rightful overlord. Some are convinced but the opposition of others crystallizes around King Lot. Even in these early days the soothsayer, whatever his reputation, does not automatically receive respectful attention to unwelcome news. Thus, although some of the kings marvelled at Merlin's words and believed what he said, some, including King Lot, laughed him to scorn and called him a witch.

Merlin counsels Arthur to confront his ill-wishers, which he does, to answer their fears and misgivings. This must always be done in the face of evil, for much of it is based, and thrives upon, misunderstanding, lack of or poor quality of communication, and a combination of fear and pride—all of which can be allayed only by fearless and frank confrontation.

However, this still fails to convince the hard core of opposition, even when Merlin solemnly advises them that their cause cannot prevail.

'Be we well advised to be afraid of a dream reader?' says King Lot, whereupon 'Merlin vanished away'. So will all spiritual or inner plane communicators in the face of disbelief. This is a law of inner nature which demonstrates the importance of faith and the self-fulfilling aridity of agnosticism or unbelief.

There follows a great battle wherein Arthur is advised by Merlin to use the sword drawn from the stone when he has greatest need of it. In the course of battle King Lot strikes Arthur down, but the young king is rescued and re-horsed by four knights. He draws his magic sword, which 'was as bright in his enemies' eyes that it gave light like thirty torches'. It is here called Excalibur, although in the subsequent story Excalibur is the name of the sword drawn from the Lake to replace the original one, which he loses fighting King Pellinore. In reality it is the same sword, for the symbolism of the sword represents his own inner spiritual dynamic—the spirit striking down through matter to express the spiritual will, in which it is similar to the Qabalistic concept of the Lightning Flash.

In Malory, battles and skirmishes continue for some time, with Merlin as strategist and tactical adviser. He is also able to command the victorious forces to withdraw, in the cause of mercy and humanity. 'With that came Merlin on a great black horse and said unto King Arthur, "Thou hast never done. Has thou not done now? Of three score thousand this day hast thou left alive but fifteen thousand! Therefore it is time to say 'Halt' for God is wrath with thee for thou will never have done."'

At length Arthur's cause prevails, aided by the fact that his opponents' lands are invaded by 'lawless people' and 'Saracens'. It is another spiritual and psychological law that those whose motives express dissension by that very fact bring dissension upon themselves as well as upon others.

There come to Arthur tests of varied character. First is the arrival of Lot's wife, Morgawse, at his court. It is as a result of an infatuation with her that the evil Mordred is conceived. (In Malory, Morgawse is the mother of Mordred; other sources prefer Morgan. The symbolic truth, and preservation of the traditional character types, would be served by regarding the infatuation as brought about by the enchantments of Morgan, but the actual fleshly deed expressed by the elemental Morgawse.)

Arthur's fall from grace in this respect is followed by an ominous dream of great portent. He dreams that monsters enter the land, burn and slay all the people and eventually defeat him. Indeed he dreams truly for it is as a result of his fall that his dynasty and the Round Table Fellowship is destroyed, by the newly conceived arch-usurper Mordred.

In order to forget the dream, but in a sequence of appropriate synchronicity, Arthur rides off into the forest where strange and significant adventures befall him. He chases a hart until, outpaced and over-exerted, his horse falls dead. (In esoteric psychological terms, this signifies the falling away of the Lower Self for truths to be revealed directly to the Higher Self.) As he sits unhorsed in the midst of the forest he sees the Questing Beast. This is the strange animal from whose insides the sounds of a pack of hounds emanates. It is followed closely by the mighty King Pellinore whose destiny at that time was always to pursue it. Later, after his death, this role fell to the Saracen knight, Palomides.

The nature of the Questing Beast has been variously interpreted. Some see it, by its juxtaposition to the conception of Mordred, as an emblem of incest. However, in a wider context it is rather more than this. It is a kind of false questing—a questing for the sake of questing. It is King Pellinore's destiny before the establishment of the Table Round, of which he later becomes a stalwart member. He represents the type of the kings of olden time, before the reign of Arthur, dimly groping towards the standards and ideals which Arthur and his destiny embodied.

This also is the significance of the Questing Beast in relation to Palomides, the Saracen knight. Palomides desperately desires to be accepted as a true knight, but cannot be so until he arrives at a true conception of reality. This is represented by his baptism into the Christian faith, after which the Quest of the Holy Grail commences. It is also his maturing realization of the spiritual reality behind knighthood, rather than a preoccupation or bedazzlement with the glamour of its outward show. Palomides is also the footloose wanderer and the new phase begins for him when he is able to commit his loyalty to a particular standard—in this case, the Round Table Fellowship of Logres. Therefore in another sense it is a growth to maturity and spiritual responsibility.

In Arthur's first encounter with Pellinore, Pellinore seizes the fresh horse that is brought for Arthur. He also refuses to give up following the Questing Beast to allow the young Arthur to pursue it. He is one of the old powers, not hostile to the young king as Lot and the others, but continuing in his own old ways, pursuing his own destiny uncognisant of the significance of the signs of change.

As with the young Arthur, portents of the future are not always as they seem. This is emphasized in a practical way by Merlin, who appears at this time and prophesies, first in the appearance of a young boy and then as an old man. Arthur tends to believe the pronouncements of the old man but to disbelieve those of the boy. The lesson that Merlin teaches is that we should not be ruled by superficial appearances but seek the truth behind the shifting pattern of the world before us.

At this point, at the beginning of Arthur's career in arms, Merlin prophesies the nature of Arthur's death, and also of his own disappearance. At the same time he reveals Arthur's true birth to him. Arthur is reunited with Igraine, his mother, and learns of his own right to kingship as son of Uther Pendragon. All this is highly unlikely as the plot for a convincing story but it is symbolically fitting. These facts had already been announced by Merlin to the lords at large, so it is hardly likely that Arthur would not know of them but, at this juncture, when he is about to take up his destiny as king, it is symbolically fitting that a reiteration of the circumstances of his birth and eventual death should be given. Although events of daily life are not predestined there is a general shape to our lives through overriding inner factors—'There is a destiny that shapes our ends, rough hew them how we will.'

There then follows a more serious encounter with Pellinore, who has set himself up at a fountain (that is, at a source of inner power) to fight all who attempt to come there. He slays a knight called Sir Miles, whose squire seeks aid at the newly-founded court of Arthur. A young squire, Griflet, who is of the same tender years as Arthur, begs to be knighted and allowed to challenge Pellinore. Against Merlin's advice Arthur allows Griflet the adventure but as Merlin has predicted he is sorely wounded by Pellinore.

At the same time as these events of confrontation with the old order in his own kingdom, twelve knights come from the established Emperor of Rome demanding tribute or Arthur's death.

The impetuous young Arthur, hearing news of Griflet's downfall, arms and horses himself secretly in the night to go himself to seek vengeance on Pellinore at break of day at the fountain. Merlin knows all his hidden intentions however and, as occult masters of his calibre often do with their charges, arranges a symbolic lesson through the circumstances of life. Arthur sees Merlin apparently being chased, in peril of his life, by three ruffians. He goes to save him, only to be dismissed by Merlin with deflating and ominous words.

'Ah Merlin', cries Arthur, very proud of himself, 'here had you been slain for all your crafts, but for me'.

'No', replies Merlin, 'not so, for I could have saved myself if I had wanted. But thou art more near thy death than I am, for thou goest towards thy death if God be not thy friend'.

However, the youthful Arthur insists on continuing with his

resolve to fight Pellinore. He aquits himself well but the strength and skill of the mighty old king are too much for him and after a lengthy pitched battle Arthur is saved only by the intervention of Merlin, who casts a deep sleep upon Pellinore.

Such has been the conflict that Arthur's mighty sword, taken from the stone, is split into two pieces. Thus is the importance of this encounter symbolically underlined. The sword represents the spiritual power of the whole being of man, and Arthur's destiny would have been rudely shattered by his foolhardly encounter with the old forces but for the intervention of the watchful Merlin, who has an overriding stewardship for the destiny of the race.

As Merlin predicts, over Pellinore's sleeping form, the old king is not an evil man, but simply the strongest currently alive. From his line will come the mighty Lamorak and also Percivale, one of the winners of the Holy Grail.

After three days in a hermitage waiting for his wounds to heal, which may also be regarded as a period of inner preparation, Arthur has his sword restored to him in greater measure when Merlin takes him to the Lake.

> So they rode till they came to a lake that was a fair water and broad. And in the middle Arthur was aware of an arm clothed in white samite, that held a fair sword in that hand.
>
> 'Lo,' said Merlin, 'yonder is the sword that I spoke of.'
>
> So with that they saw a damsel going upon the Lake.
>
> 'What damsel is that?' said Arthur.
>
> 'That is the Lady of the Lake' said Merlin. 'There is a great rock, and therein is as fair a palace as any on earth, and richly beseen. And this damsel will come to you anon, and then speak ye fair to her, that she may give you that sword.'
>
> So anon came this damsel to Arthur and saluted him, and he her again.
>
> 'Damsel,' said Arthur, 'what sword is that yonder that the arm holdeth above the water? I would it were mine, for I have no sword.'
>
> 'Sir Arthur', said the damsel, 'that sword is mine, and if ye will give me a gift when I ask it of you, ye shall have it.'
>
> 'By my faith,' said Arthur, 'I will give you what gift ye will ask'.

On the promise and its fulfilment much hangs, for it is the commencement of the events that lead up to the giving of the Dolorous Stroke and the whole Mystery of the Quest of the Holy

Grail. Of this later. We have given this passage in full for it has a verity and sense of the magic of far off days and things.

The Lake is the whole astral/etheric plane behind physical appearances and is usually only entered by ordinary man in dream or inspired imagination. Arthur has lost his own spiritual force by his feckless impetuosity in adventure and in love. The breaking of his sword in ill-advised battle with Pellinore is but another aspect of his losing his integrity by begetting Mordred upon one of his half-sisters. He can, however, being broken in this way, yet rise to greater things by the taking up of a sword not his own, in dedication to a greater ideal.

In this is the mechanism of many a religious conversion or initiation. The heart and will is broken by its own ineptitude and in that condition of humility and repentance opens itself to higher spiritual forces and aspirations. In this are encapsulated the whole deep mysteries of the Fall of Man from Paradise and the opportunities of subsequent redemption.

Before Arthur can rise to grasp and fulfil his mighty destiny he has to be humbled and come empty-handed in supplication for the means to continue. Arthur then takes the mainspring of his future destiny from the Lady of the Lake—the mistress of the inner worlds who is at the same time the Queen of Faery. She is also the goddess Isis or Queen Venus at the heart of Mystery cults throughout the ages. She has been Christianized in the cult of the Blessed Virgin Mary, and also in the traditions of certain saints, particularly Mary Magdelene and various local adaptations of old dynamics such as the Celtic St Bride or Brigit.

These are very ancient Mysteries that pre-date Christianity historically, although in their true sense all such spiritual matters are outside time. Something of their power and pattern is to be found in certain ballad lore, for instance, that of Thomas the Rhymer, the fourteenth century Scottish poet and prophet. His ballad poem records a meeting with the fairy queen and his going off to fairyland with her. This is a perilous undertaking for any mortal, for the disregard of certain rules can lead to strange consequences. Faery reality is not the same as mortal reality, thus treasures taken may readily turn to leaves or ashes when illicitly brought back to earth. Similarly, time does not exist in fairyland, or at any rate not in the same way. Thus one has the tradition of those who return after what seems to them but a night and a day to find they have been gone for seven or even a hundred years.

There is also, of course, a more common psychological truth in this, in that those who, for whatever reason, are reluctant to face reality in the physical world, may divert themselves too much to dreams of what might have been. They may then be bypassed by time and fail to mature to adult responsibility, or may delay that maturity to a greater or lesser degree.

The astral world, or world of faery, is, however, not a plane of mere subjective illusion. Whosoever's destiny leads them there can take strength from its forces and inspiration from its wisdom. On the other hand preoccupation with its glamours can prevent effective action and the full flowering of humanity. Thus its potential is double-edged.

Merlin, be it noted, also refers to the Lady of the Lake, as having her palace 'within a rock'. Here again is a memory of ancient Mysteries that go back to the origin of the stone circles and megalithic tombs of ancient kings—and which are relevant also to the end of Merlin himself.

The acquisition of this new power represented by Excalibur has to be controlled and directed with true dedication by Arthur. His first impulse on receiving it is to seek out Pellinore forthwith and be revenged on him. However, Merlin advises against this and Arthur, growing in wisdom, allows himself to be guided by him.

There is an even greater lesson that he has to learn however. In a significant passage that follows Merlin asks Arthur:

'Like ye better the sword or the scabbard?'

'I like better the sword', said Arthur.

'Ye are the more unwise, for the scabbard is worth ten of the sword; for while ye have the scabbard upon you ye shall lose no blood, be ye never so sore wounded. Therefore keep well the scabbard always with you'.

The reason for this, as we shall see later, is that the scabbard is that which contains the sword. A sword unsheathed is an awkward and dangerous object; it needs to be within its scabbard, except in the rare occasion of combat, for everything a sword touches it will cut. The virile force of the spirit is similar. It needs must be contained and the scabbard therefore signifies the power, knowledge and wisdom of its containment.

The gift which the Lady of the Lake elicits from Arthur in return for Excalibur contains a further great mystery, for she subsequently demands the head of Balin, the 'knight of two swords', the giver of the Dolorous Stroke which lays the land waste. This pertains to the beginnings of the Grail story, which we shall consider under the Greater Mysteries.

15. Merlin and Nimuë

According to popular story, Merlin becomes besotted with the Lady of the Lake or one of her damsels, called Ninyve or Nimuë. There is more to this, however, than would at first meet the eye.

To begin with, Merlin has foretold his going in this manner, which he repeats at the beginning of Caxton's fourth book: 'he told King Arthur that he should not endure long, but for all his crafts he should be put alive into the earth.'

It is, however, *because* of his subtle crafts, and not in spite of them, that he disappears into the ground. This is an ancient memory of the function of a priest king of primitive times.

As an instance, we quote from a clairvoyant reading obtained at an ancient tomb to give an idea of the ritual process involved. The seer was Bob Stewart and the contact was made at the tomb of a king at Les Monts Grantez, Jersey.

> This ancient prehistoric tomb is in an elevated and fairly isolated position, very well preserved, and only recently excavated by archeologists (1912) who found it 'comparatively undisturbed'.
>
> The King buried here had achieved his merge with the environment, and was still available as an inner entity for dialogue and interchange of communication. After an intiial contact made by tuning to the site in meditation, the King later appeared (away from the site itself, as the contact unfolded or decoded itself) as an older man, very brown, with curly hair and black beard, and spiral cheek tatoos. His eyes appeared like large black stones, due to the visual effect of tatooing or colouring around the deep eye sockets. He

wore clothing made of skins, a tight tunic and trousers tied around with sinews. In communication he may be addressed as 'Earth-man' and 'Stone-King', the nearest modern language equivalents to two magical names. The first was his identity as king before physical death, the second an after death name of transformation. He was the leader of a tribe or extended family of about fifty or sixty people at the time of his physical death, although he implied an influence over a greater number, through an obscure concept of family relationship that seemed to extend beyond the Islands to both Britain and Brittany. Some time was spent attempting to elaborate this relationship, which was apparently of great importance in his culture, but which seems obscure to the modern intellect. The basic pattern was one in which various 'kings' could rule extended tribes and families over large distances, without ever conflicting with one another. The patterns of social behaviour and warfare that resulted from this system were not similar to the modern concept of 'territory' or 'conquest' in any way, but seemed to be derived from 'loss of face' or a concept that meant 'change of roots in the family ground.'

The discarnate King was responsible for communicating 'earth-peace' to his people, this being an energy that resulted from his merging with the actual environment, and finally emerging 'on the other side' of it as an entity of wholeness or integration, that is able to link and mediate through various stages of human and non human evolution. After initial contact, the old king was (and still is) present as a father figure . . . exactly as he was to those who linked with him thousands of years ago, when this system of inner working was fully operational. There were several obscure intimations, difficult to translate into a contemporary world or universe-picture:

1.   The King is now part of the solar system (?) or Universe (?), linked through the *stones* and the special structure of the dolmen and mound, which became an earth-power gate or amplifier for his awareness . . . a focus in which his differing view-point may be translated into one which is accessible to physical humans still on the planet.

The curious and difficult point about this concept is the accompanying awareness that (to the King) the solar system is *inside the structure of the stones and in the very bones of the Earth itself* and is in no way external or removed from it. He is able to communicate this awareness very clearly indeed, and it seems to have been essential to his peoples' development. The effect of this awareness on the modern consciousness is rather disturbing . . . and is quite different from the generally accepted reality-patterns currently used by mankind trying to relate to existence.

2.   The purpose of the dolmen or passage grave is extremely precise and 'scientific'. A sealed chamber of massive stones, which have to be over a certain mass or size, is buried beneath a mound of earth. This causes certain natural processes to occur, directly due to the shapes and nature of the structure itself. This is usually aided by the knowledge and co-operation of the being or beings buried alive within it. The aim is to achieve an integration with the earth environment, moving through it to other states of awareness (which are *in the earth*, according to the King . . . or more strictly speaking . . . the Earth is *outside the stars*, and is the gateway to them.) The actual physical structure is womblike, and was identified as a returning to the Mother. There is strict time rotation involved in the process, and a guardian was placed to ensure that there was no disturbance during this period of gestation prior to inner re-birth. Other people were also interred, either at the same time, or at later stages of the development of the merge. The King suggested quite jovially that the process was voluntary, but implied a system of family obligation which could not be avoided, or rather a system which cast out those who did not merge when their time was due. This shocking occurrence was the greatest 'loss of earth root' that anyone could visualize . . . and was the equivalent of vile and obscene anti-human crime. The thought of anyone *not* wanting to merge was repulsive in the extreme, and the process was a sought after privilege that was retained through certain family ties, and could be passed on through a female line of descent.

Once the inner integration process had occurred, the chamber was then used for consultation and initiation. Entry was made through a tiny crawl passage, usually kept sealed and guarded by a restrained soul. This Guardian was a deliberately tied sacrifice, a human who was bound for a specific period to remain in an interim state close to the outer world, to defend the chamber against break in and tampering. After a certain number of years (solar cycles) the guard was free, and was replaced or rendered unnecessary by the success of the King's merging. In a 'fully achieved' chamber only the King remained, but he could link to specific ancestors in spirit ('Fathers in the deep that earth is outside'). The supplicant crawled in, and was left in the total darkness to communicate with the King.

The pattern is found clearly in modern magical practice, where the King is seated in the West and one approaches him from the East, through the Pillars. The interesting point is that this King is fully able to relate to modern magical technique, and has various things to teach or communicate.

In a simple magical operation, designed to open up his specific contact in a completely different place, far from his earth-site, the King calmly informed the operator of a mistake in the pattern of the ritual. When this error was corrected, the contact became much stronger.

The simple basis of this fraction of magical teaching was as follows. In the tomb, the King is magically 'in the West', that is, at the end of the chamber, seated, and giving out the fullness of his awareness, from his position in the depth of the womb. When an attempt was made to place him by image in the West of a modern magical Temple, he informed the operator that this was quite wrong . . . and that the operator should be in the West, visualizing the King approaching at the East. When this was done, the inner imagery reverted to the King's own Tomb . . . as if the two 'Wests' had become face to face. Prior to tuning the energies in this manner, the link had been rather difficult and sporadic, causing the operator to be kept awake at night, to be aware of the King at unrequired moments, and giving a general sense of lack of tuning, searching and semi-blindness. Once the King's operational suggestion was adopted, the contact could be turned on or off at will, and became extremely balanced and clear.

The rule or pattern of tombs of this sort was general for all the dolmens and passage graves that are found in the Western culture, which can still be seen today. Some are empty and failed, but others retain their inner contact, and can be used. One most interesting aspect of these curious 'generators' is that the flow is *two way*. The inner King, locked in the earth that is outside the stars learns about your awareness, and transmits it back to his people . . . while you learn about their awareness, and bring it forward into your own self. The King occupies a middle or mediating 'point' in this process, conveying a type of awareness that makes nonsense of the normal conception of 'time' and 'space'. To the King, 'time' is only valid as the rotational phase prior to his merging with the Earth . . . it has no meaning in his original outer life, nor any meaning in his evolved inner state.

On attempting to convey the meaning of flow of Time, the response from the King was the equivalent of 'there is no line of such a shape. There is only turning until you are inside the Earth. From the little turning to the great turning that is inside the little turning. Inside the great turning is earth-peace.'

The flow of time referred to in the last paragraph might perhaps be represented by some of the spiral and maze patterns found on megalithic sties at Newgrange and elsewhere.

There are, as the report says, many such sites, some in a more effective state of operation than others. Certainly the author is aware that two Anglican clergy with particular psychic gifts and a specialized sense of vocation have been made aware of 'guardians' bound to old sites in the West of England. They had been bound there by magical means and remained there as captive souls until released, by the appropraite sacraments, from their centuries of spiritual bondage. They were apparently not priest kings but lesser mortals, victims of human sacrifice, probably in a later, degenerate phase of the system.

On a more positive aspect, some of these ancient sites seem able to operate as 'windows in time'. At the ancient site of huge megaliths at Hagar Qim and Mnajdra, near Qrendi, in Malta, which were ancient temples, I have personally received the strongest and most friendly impressions. The sense of communication across time was particularly strong and seemed two way! One could pick up something of the attitudes of these ancient people and they too, it would seem, could gain something from the contact across time. Again, our usual conception of time as a linear phenomenon is called into question.

Personal notes of the occasion read: 'From my psychic impressions it seemed largely a cult of the Sun and the Sea and I found that maintaining a sympathetic frame of mind brought through a certain amount of teaching. A common decoration in prehistoric temples is the spiral. I was led to contemplate the shell of one of the species of snails that frequent the locality.

'Here plainly was the significance of the spiral, a revolution or unwinding, out of a central point to bring forth life. And to go back to a consciousness of origins one can follow the spiral in the reverse direction, boring a contemplative hole to the very origin and centre of things.

'This is not a lesson that lends itself easily to verbal description, but those who wish may find a surprising amount of revelation if they trouble to contemplate an actual snail's shell—studying the lessons and patterns of nature as our remote fore-runners did.'

This going back to the central starting point of the spiral also holds within it a deep truth that tends to be eschewed by many modern esoteric expositors of the west. This is that the way to the stars is, as the old king said, best commenced by going into the Earth. Christ himself descended into Hades before his resurrection and ascension, and the way he showed is repeated in the great cosmic system of Dante's *Divine Comedy*. It is also stressed in Rosicrucian alchemy (visit the interior of the Earth, in purifying you discover the hidden stone). By attempting, through a misplaced sense of 'purity', to rise upon the planes away from the Earth, if the Holy Grail is achieved it remains floating nebulously in thin air, bringing no joy, comfort or healing to the physical world and the 'spirits in prison'.

There are many ancient sites throughout Western Europe similar to those described and by no means all are exploited as popular tourist attractions whose magic is overlaid by a patina of litter and human banality.

For instance, at a site more specifically assocated with Merlin, the stone circle of Gors-Fawr beneath the Prescelly Mountains outcrop which contains the blue stones of the type found at Stonehenge, personal notes record the following: 'When one visits the area one is immediately impressed that this is an important site esoterically. In the plain before the mountains is a stone circle—said by the local guide books to be the only stone circle in Wales. This seems hard to credit, but if true suggests a particular importance is attached to the site. The stone circle is not particularly impressive or massive as stone circles go, but it has a quality of peace and ancient calm about it such as I have experienced similarly only in the rock temples of Hagar Qim and Mnajdra in Malta, buildings comtemporaneous with the circles of Stonehenge. Around about one is a great semi-circle of mountains with jagged outcrops so that one is reminded of the alternative title of Stonehenge as the Giants' Dance.'

The legend of the disappearance of Merlin is thus closely connected with the lore of the old stone circles and the various lines of psychic force that criss-cross the country, the so-called ley-lines. We should not allow ourselves, however, to be limited to intellectual structures based upon projected lines from one earth or stone work to another. The old magic works equally well in otherwise unremarkable fields, woods and hedgerows, particularly in relation to certain types of tree. The conjunction of oak, ash and thorn, old lore preserved in Kipling's children's tale *Puck of Pook's Hill*, can open the inner eye and ear to much imagery that leads to intuitional revelation.

The same applies to groves of willow or yew, or to woods of beech. Indeed many different types of contact can be made by anyone who has developed the capacity to still the mind by regular meditation and make it receptive to the myriad forces of nature. All that is required then is the faith to 'look' and 'listen' with humility and love, and the gates will open.

Any words that crystallize in the mind will be one's own but they will have been stimulated at a deep—and objective—level. Visual images will be even more valid and powerful, for this level of consciousness best works in pictures, accompanied by emotion.

Thus at a particular unfrequented spot where there are two natural pillars formed by an oak and an ash set in a thorn hedge the following words crystallized in the mind. 'When Nimuë, the earth maiden, has learned all the star lore of Merlin, and Merlin has learned the earth lore of Nimuë, then the two will go hand in hand in a cosmic marriage to the stars taking with them the children of the Earth.' Together with these words was a strong image of the dark-mantled Merlin in his traditional robe and tall hat of stars, and the young floral and earthly maiden simply clad in the natural colours of Earth.

In this respect there was an element of the inner meaning behind the fragmentary story of Blodwenn, the maiden constructed entirely from flowers. In the act of writing these words there comes a strong scent of flowers perceptible even to the physical senses; the sense of smell is indeed the most subtle of the physical perceptions. Thus the old magic is very much alive and powerful, even if it remains a closed book in the face of our modern intellectual arrogance.

There are thus deep Mysteries hidden in the story of Merlin and Nimuë that are not at all so simple as the bald narrative of Malory. Nor does Tennyson's malignant Vivien ring mythologically true.

A more complete version, which Malory chose to abbreviate considerably, although he used it as a source, is to be found in the French Merlin romances.

Here Nimuë is described as being the daughter of a vavasour named Dinas—a thinly disguised Dionysos—with whom the goddess of the woods, Diana, used to come and speak, 'for he was her god-son.'

We can do no better than to quote from the description of the scholar Vida Scudder, whose book *Le Morte d'Arthur of Sir Thomas Malory* (Dutton & Dent, 1921) has been for too long out of print. Although it may have been bypassed in some respects by more recent scholarship, the imaginative sympathy of the author for her material causes it to come alive in a very special way that is absent from most academic texts.

Merlin appears in the shape of a young squire; Nimuë in the form of a little maid 'but twelve years old'. This number is, in this context, more mystical than chronological in intent. Together they perform an enchantment that is an evocation of the ideal society of humankind and a reconstruction of the Earthly Paradise or Garden of Eden.

> For behold! Out of the forest comes a carole of ladies and knights and maidens and squires, "each holding other by the hands and dancing and singing: and made the greatest joy that ever was seen in any land" . . . And presently, in the midst of the wild wood, appears an orchard, wherein was all manner of fruit and all manner of flowers, that gave so great a sweetness of flavour that marvel it was to tell.

This is no mere infatuation of a magician for a fairy maid. It is a great and pre-ordained work of redemptive magic. Similarly Merlin's disappearance from the Earth into the world behind outer nature is no falling under a false enchantment but a deliberate sacrificial and sacramental act.

As Vida Scudder puts it, although she does not appear consciously to realize the deeper implications:

> . . . when she spoke to him of her longing to know how to create the magic tower of air, he bowed down to the earth and began to sigh. None the less he did her will, and on a fateful day they went through the forest of Broceliande hand in hand, devising and disporting; and found a bush that was fair and high and of white hawthorn full of flowers, and there they sat in the shadow. And Merlin laid his head on the damsel's lap, and she began to caress gently till he fell on sleep, and when she felt that he was in sleep she arose softly, and made a circle with her wimple all about the bush, and all about Merlin. And when he waked he looked about him, 'and him seemed he was in the fairest tower on the world and the most strong; and he said to the damsel; "Lady thou hast me deceived, but if ye will, abide with me, for none but ye may undo these enchantments" And in truth she stayed by him for the most part, "Ye be my thought and my desire", says she, "for without you have I neither joy nor wealth. In you have I set all my hope, and I abide none other joy but of you".

Her impulse is thus love and not self-will. And, whether 'deceived' or not, Merlin was well aware, before and after the fact, of the implications of this profound magical union.

Thus the mediaeval and later accounts of this liaison between Nimuë and Merlin give the bare bones of the event in terms of the symbolism of the courtship of a man and a maid. It is, however, to the symbolic overtones of this event that we must look for a deeper appreciation of the consequences of this union between cosmic magician and astral priestess of the Isis of Nature.

Something of this has been captured in the poetic cycle by Charles Williams *The Region of the Summer Stars* where, in *The Calling of Taliessin*, the protagonist Taliessin meets with Merlin and Nimuë, (although here called Brisen), on his way to Byzantium which, in Williams, is the source of the manifest God-head. The meeting is on the verges of the Forest of Broceliande which is pictured as taking up most of the western coast of Britain and extending into the sea. It is the 'middle earth' of faerie, which has been mapped somewhat glibly by the popularisers of the 'subconscious' over the past few decades, or which in esoteric textbooks is sometimes called the astral plane.

In his comments upon Williams' poetic cycle C. S. Lewis describes it well.

Broceliande is what most romantics are enamoured of; into it good and bad mystics go; it is what you find when you step out of your ordinary mode of consciousness. You find it equally in whatever direction you step out. All journeys away from the solid earth are equally, at the onset, journeys into the abyss. Saint, sorcerer, lunatic, and romantic lover all alike are drawn to Broceliande, but Carbonek (the castle of the Holy Grail) is beyond *a certain part of it only*. It is by no means the Absolute. It is rather what the Greeks called the *Apeiron*—the unlimited, the formless origin of forms. Dante and D. H. Lawrence, Boehme and Hitler, Lady Julian and the Surrealists, had all been there. It is the home of immense dangers and immense possibilities.

However, it is not with the glamorous mysteries of the astral worlds that Merlin and Nimuë/Brisen are concerned when they meet Taliessin and prophecy what is going to happen to Britain. They are intent upon bringing through high spiritual forces to the earth plane. This is a function of the archetypal white magician and of that inner body of them known in esoteric primers as the Great White Lodge.

In other words, the whole group soul of the race will be uplifted to the point where workaday Britain becomes the Land of Logres, when the Grail is nationally achieved and the enchantment falls from the face of the land—the enchantment that currently obscures the whole Earth in a mist of delusion and renders the fruitful barren and the creative earth a jungle or waste.

Talliessin, in Williams' poem, is allowed to see them enact the great enchantment which is a preliminary to this. While Merlin performs the great conjuration of contacting the inter-stellar cosmic spiritual forces, the Lady of the Lake forms the negative pole of the battery, so to speak, by growing to a huge naked figure who becomes at-oned with the whole landscape, cultural and topographical, of Europe and the Near and Middle East—the cradle of Western civlization.

The end papers of Williams' original book give this symbolism in pictorial form. The symbolic nuances are very complex and need not detain us, but in general terms, her breasts are equated with the milk of learning at the great mediaeval University of Paris; in Rome are her hands where the sacrament is constantly performed, emblematic, besides its ecclesiastical significance, of all the manual acts of man, which should be equally sacramental. Jerusalem is the creative sexual centre; Caucasus the 'rounded bottom' of creation, representing physical enjoyment of all kinds,

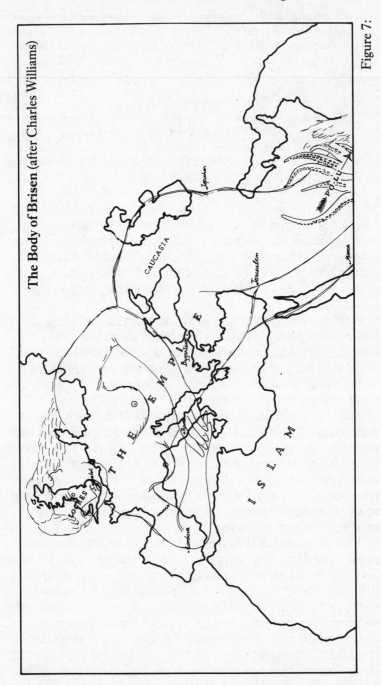

eating, drinking, the pleasures of the flesh.

In Logres lies her head, and the conception and intuition of where the human race should be going—and this concept embodies a tradition that goes back to the Isles of Britain being the Holy Islands of the continent of Europe in early historical times—and many believe to this day that these islands do have a spiritual destiny to perform in showing other nations the way.

Much of this takes us into the deeper Mysteries of the Grail, to which we shall return. However, the concept of Broceliande, and its counterpart, the Lake, and the workings of Merlin and the various Ladies of the Lake, opens the door to an intermediate reality and concourse of forces that, by its nature, tends to be glamourized by the emotions and undervalued by the intellect.

It is similar to the powers Wordsworth experienced on the top of Snowdon, described in *The Prelude*, where he and his companions emerged into clear moonlight and saw below them a sea of mist. Through gaps in the mist emerged the sound of roaring waters. To Wordsworth—and to latterday psychologists of the subconscious and superconscious—this was an excellent image of the whole human mind. To Charles Williams and to Dante and to the Renaissance magicians and Platonists it is, however, more than this; it is also an objective form of reality from whence the whole process of physical nature is brought into being.

In another way of looking at it, the Lady of the Lake is the Isis of Nature, the Goddess behind the Veil. She represents that energy which produces upon earth a pattern derived from 'the third heaven', traditionally the celestial sphere of Venus, the Higher Isis, or Divine Love.

The sword and the scabbard, the spear and the cup, stem from the energy source and comprise the power and knowledge of its directed use and containment. In their power and reality they are powerful symbolic weapons which are man's magical inheritance. They can be used powerfully both for good and for evil, like the more familiar forces of physical nature, be they drugs or explosives.

16. Morgan le Fay

The part that Morgan le Fay plays in the Arthuriad is one of the attempted usurpation and misuse to her own personal ends of the inner forces which properly belong to the kingdom and to those who rule it.

In this she is partially successful, in spite of Merlin's advice and warnings to Arthur about the importance of guarding the sword and its scabbard, which represent, *inter alia*, Arthur's spiritual integrity and mandated destiny.

The sequence where Morgan gains control and temporary possession of Excalibur and its scabbard follows the not uncommon prelude to astral adventures: Arthur is drawn far into the forest in pursuit of an animal, in this case a great hart.

He is accompanied on this occasion by Morgan's husband, Uriens of Gore and by her lover Accalon of Gaul. Eventually their horses drop from beneath them, signifying the falling away of lower physical consciousness, and the hart is brought down—though by hounds that are not Arthur's. This occurs at a water-side, and a little ship, apparelled with silk down to the water, comes to them and lands on the sands with no earthly creature therein.

When they step onto this magical ship upon these enchanted waters they are, as night falls, suddenly illuminated by a hundred torches. Twelve fair damsels appear to welcome them and lead them to a chamber where a feast is richly laid. It is all very much like a mirror image of the food-giving qualities of the Holy Grail. After the companions have supped they are each taken to a separate, beautifully bedecked bedchamber and there they fall asleep.

When they awake the enchantment is over. Uriens finds himself in his bed at home in the arms of his wife Morgan le Fay. Arthur finds himself imprisoned in the dungeon of a false knight, a traitorous usurper, the cowardly and merciless Damas. Accalon finds himself in great peril, lying within half a foot of a deep well from which issues a high-jetting silver fountain.

A hideous dwarf comes to Accalon and reveals that he is from Morgan, and that she requires him to fight a battle for her, to the death. She will however, says the dwarf, obtain for him Arthur's sword Excalibur so that he is assured of victory. To this proposal Accalon agrees. In fact the proximity of the magic fountain is a symbolic indicator that this illicit source of power, with its dangers, is already his. The kundalini power, the magic sword, and a fountain, are closely associated symbols that are virtually interchangeable.

The battle that is being set up is to settle the differences between the evil Damas and his noble brother Outelake. Damas, too cowardly to fight himself, is now able to coerce the imprisoned Arthur to fight for him as a condition for his freedom and that of other knights that Damas has imprisoned.

Outelake is however currently wounded through the thighs and cannot fight for himself. Morgan therefore arranges that Accalon shall be his champion, and at the same time sends to Arthur a sword that appears to be Excalibur and its scabbard, while Accalon is given the real ones.

Fortunately the Lady of the Lake becomes aware of what is going on and arrives at the scene of battle. Because of the switch of magical weapons, in spite of his natural skill and courage, Arthur is gradually hacked to pieces. Eventually the false sword breaks in his hand but he continues to fight weaponless, with his mailed fist and his shield.

Here the Lady of the Lake intervenes with an enchantment of her own. She causes Accalon to drop Excalibur and it is seized by Arthur. He now realizes what has occurred and also snatches the true scabbard from Accalon's side, which has so far protected him from injury.

As a result Arthur soon overcomes Accalon. They have fought in disguise and now their true identities are revealed to each other. Arthur spares Accalon on realizing that the treachery is on the part of his half-sister Morgan. She, he discovers, had been in possession of the real Excalibur and its scabbard for a twelve-month without his knowing it. Accalon dies later through loss of blood—an ebbing away of his own spiritual forces which is not unconnected with his attempted, if unwitting, usurpation of the forces of Arthur's destiny.

In the meantime, expecting Arthur dead and Accolon victorious, Morgan prepares to kill her Elemental husband Uriens with his own sword while he sleeps. The symbolic overtones of this should be evident; it is an enchantress' way of working death by turning Uriens' own vital and spiritual forces against himself.

However, their son Uwain is told of the plan by the damsel whom Morgan had sent to fetch Uriens' sword. Uwain stays Morgan's hand as she is about to strike and she pleads for mercy, saying that a fiend had tempted her. Uwain agrees to spare and forgive his mother provided that she abjures such wickedness.

At this moment there comes the news of Accolon's death. Realizing that all is about to be discovered Morgan leaves the court. She makes straight for the abbey where the wounded Arthur lies and obtains entry to his chamber while he sleeps. To her chagrin he sleeps with the drawn sword Excalibur in his hand so she cannot take it without waking him. She is, however, able to steal the scabbard.

When Arthur wakes, the treason is discovered and Sir Outelake and Arthur ride in pursuit of her. A cowherd by a cross, (who would seem to be a thinly disguised priest of Isis), tells them which way she has gone. She and her forty outriders proceed swiftly through the forest, and onto a plain where there is a lake. Here, in this obviously magical inner territory, she throws the scabbard into the deepest part so that Arthur shall never be able to regain it. Thus he loses his invincibility and the knowledge of how to control his genius and destiny; factors which inevitably result in his eventual downfall.

To avoid capture Morgan turns herself and her men into the likeness of great stones until Arthur departs. Something of her treachery, spite and twisted sense of values is revealed immediately afterwards when she comes upon a captive knight who is being taken to a fountain to be put to death by drowning, for adultery. Again it is interesting to note the symbolic connection between a fountain and the sexual forces.

She discovers that the captive is Manessen, the cousin of Accolon, and therefore releases him and allows him to kill the knight with whose wife he had lain. She then bids Manessen ride to Arthur's court with a message of her defiance and abiding spite, and returns to her own country to build her defences against any reprisal.

Morgan's further attempts at disrupting the court of Arthur fall more appropriately into the next grade of the Arthurian cycle, the Mysteries of Guenevere, which concern the secrets of polarity working. In these matters Morgan is rightly considered the epitome of the evil and selfish sorceress. However, as we have said, all the Arthurian achetypes are double-faced, showing their good and their evil potentialities, although some are portrayed facing more to one way than the other. The archetypes, like individuals, are however capable of redemption, and in the end Morgan the mischief-maker becomes Morgan the healer—which is a right and dedicated use of the powers of the scabbard. The wounded Arthur is finally borne away in the mystic barge to the Celtic Otherworld, to be tended by Morgan and her sisters under the tutelage of the Lady of the Lake.

PART THREE: THE GRADE OF GUENEVERE AND THE FORCES OF LOVE

17. Polar Forces in the Aura

The Grade of Guenevere is concerned with the knowledge and use of the forces of polarity. As polarity is the basis of all manifest existence it therefore must be regarded as a higher degree than that of Merlin or of Arthur which are concerned, respectively, with the dynamics of the group, and of the individual within the group. As in real life, however, all aspects are interdependent; one degree cannot be worked in isolation from the others. Therefore it is more a question of emphasis upon different aspects of the ideal whole human being. In this respect esoteric grades are like subject areas in the training of a doctor; pharmacy, anatomy and hygiene may be different disciplines, and perhaps studied in a particular order, yet each forms an essential part of the qualified practitioner.

The Grade of Guenevere is very much concerned with the polar forces as exemplified in the relationships between the various knights and ladies, and particularly in the relationships between herself, the King, and Lancelot, 'the best knight in the world'.

The Queen is the hub of the social life and structure of the whole court. In a wider sense she represents the courtly virtues that make up peaceful and civilized life as opposed to the military and political concerns of Arthur and Merlin. When the work of Arthur and Merlin is done, and peace and justice rule, it is the Queen who reigns over the ideal society that then develops.

In the earlier stages of creating the realm, and bringing it to peaceful order, she represents a coherent body within the court from whence the knights go out upon their adventures, and to which they return when their quests are completed. In the perfect pattern each knight has a lady and each has a place at the Table Round. In a sense Guenevere represents the Table Round and the Table Round represents Guenevere. It was no coincidence that the Table Round was part of her dowry, brought to Arthur's court by their marriage.

In another sense the Round Table, Guenevere, and the Court represent the scabbard of the sword. The sword is drawn to right wrongs in the land and then returned to its scabbard when balance has been restored. This is the group aspect of the sword, the vitality and spiritual essence of the Court.

It also has an individual aspect, in the vitality and spiritual essence of each knight and lady at the Court. They are the forces of polarity, the secrets of personal power, to be found in the dual forces of the human aura.

There is a particular glyph related to the Tree of Life which is known as the Lightning Flash. This concerns the descent of power in the creation of life and it is frequently depicted with a handle, like a sword. (Fig. 8)

The Sword of the Spirit, or Lightning Flash

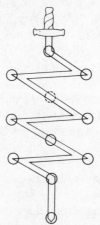

Figure 8

This can be applied to the aura of the indiviudal and gives the pattern for a 'yoga of the West'. It indicates power points and dynamics within the psychic organism. At the same time the scabbard can be visualized on a similar basis: dark, chased in silver with strange runes and cosmic symbols, winged at its top like a caduceus. (Figure 9)

The Scabbard of the Sword
of the Spirit

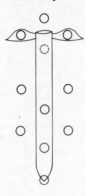

Figure 9

In the scabbard, the polarities, flashed out by the drawn sword of the spirit in action, are contained in balance within the central line of spheres of the Tree of Life. The Tree of Life is a universal figure commonly used in the Western Mystery Tradition. It corresponds to the psychic centres that align with the spinal column and which are studied in considerable depth by the various forms of yoga in the Eastern Mystery Tradition.

The various systems of yoga vary in detail and emphasize various aspects of the complex psychic anatomy of man. In general, however, they may be synthesized into a common pattern of psychic centres, (chakras, lotuses, or wheels) as shown in Figure 10. These follow the line of the spinal column from the base of the spine to a point above the crown of the head. They are power centres in a triple column of psycho-spiritual energy which gives the basic functions of life and which, when consciously aroused, (having passed the nadir of the base of the spine) gives superconsciousness and extended perceptions and powers on the inner levels. This process is known as awakening and arousing the serpent power of kundalini.

The serpent Kundalini may be symbolised in Western terms as a dragon. Indeed, as it is a dual aspected it is clearly referred to in the two dragons, one red and one white, that fight under the stone beneath the waters under Vortigern's tower. In Qabalistic terms the symbolism is most apt: the stone refers to Malkuth, the pool of water to Yesod, and the Tower not only to the psychic correspondence of the spinal column but to the Tarot Trump that is

The Psychic Centres

Symbol	Sanskrit	Location	Powers	Kabbalah
(	sahasrara	above the head	} spiritual powers	Ain Soph
·	nirvana	top of the head		Kether
◉	ajna	brow	Powers of Fire of the Wise	Binah-Chokmah
○	visuddhu	throat		Daath
✡	anahatra and hrit	heart	Powers of Air	Geburah-Chesed Tiphareth
▷	manipura	navel	Powers of Fire	Hod-Netzach
☽	svadisthana	genitals	Powers of Water	Yesod
□	muladhara	base of spine	Powers of Earth	Malkuth

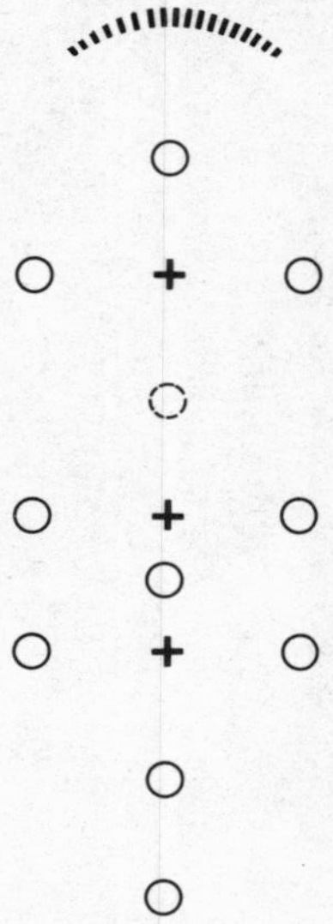

Figure 10

traditionally allocated to the 27th Path that runs between Hod
and Netzach—the Lightning-struck Tower. In other words, this
early story of the young Merlin is an account of his revealing and
raising the powers of kundalini, the 'pendragon power', in the
racial soul of the peoples who inhabit Britain.

On a more personal level the raising of the kundalini power has
its equivalent in Arthur's obtaining Excalibur, first from the
stone, and then from the Lady of the Lake. In this sense, one
might, as in Figure 11, visualize the sword rising from the depths,
with its hilt at the Muladhara chakra (or the Sephirah Malkuth) at
the base of the spine. Here it is the sword awakening control over
the Elements. It will be seen from Figure 11 that the lower
chakras are referred to the four Elements, plus the fifth Element,
the 'aether' or 'Fire of the Wise', which is their synthesis.

The Elemental Sword

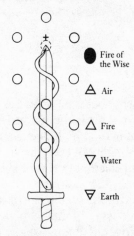

Figure 11

As this represents the rising power of the vital forces, the
serpent Kundalini, or the dragon power, we may distinguish it
from the descending sword by visualizing it with a wavy shape to
its blade. This will also be a reminder of its polar aspects—for it is
a balance of consciousness between opposite functions on the
Tree of Life. In Eastern terms it is of three-fold structure—
positive, negative and their balance (*ida, pingala,* and *shushumna*).

Also as the scabbard represents the knowledge of the appli-
cation of the powers of the sword, it may be visualized as
descending from beyond the topmost sphere of the Tree of Life,
rather like an extension of the Sahasrara chakra. (Figure 12)

The Spiritual Scabbard for
the Elemental Sword

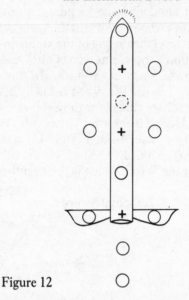

Figure 12

There is a polarity between the Elemental Sword and the Spiritual Scabbard. This is the Arthurian equivalent of the dual aspected nature of man. The Lower Self develops from physical birth into the personality of everyday life; and the Higher Self is the individuality, projector of the seed atom of the Lower Self into physical existence in the first instance. In esoteric theory this is frequently depicted in the symbolism of two triangles that unite to form the six-rayed star of the complete human being. This represents the spirit functioning wholly in earth conditions with the higher and lower aspects fully integrated. (Figure 13.)

The Union of the Higher and Lower Self

Figure 13

Although easily depicted on paper it is not so easily achieved in life but it is the concern and goal of all humanity in the long term, whether or not they consciously realize it in the current personality.

The union of the Higher and Lower Selves frequently manifests to lower consciousness in terms of a contrasexual image. Thus to a male personality it produces the concept of the 'ideal woman'. Conversely, the feminine personality will project an image of the 'ideal man'.

These are the polar points of a powerful dichotomy that exists in every human being. One may see the major difficulties that may result when the ideals of this 'vertical polarity' are expressed in terms of 'horizontal polarity' in a social and physical sexual context. The contra-sexual image is projected upon a member of the opposite sex who acts as a screen upon which this subjective image is projected and objectified. These are the mechanics of a devastating unrequited love or, if the projection is mutual, of a grand passionate love affair that takes no account of social conventions or practical realities.

With good fortune, a long standing personal relationship that develops in maturity may follow, but if the two personalities are unsuited in practical terms then disillusion and a break-up of the partnership will follow. If this is prevented by social convention or by premature pregnancy, then the domestic results can be most unhappy, even tragic.

Similar factors apply very often with the archetype of the 'ideal child' which is projected by some parents upon their offspring. Its 'vertical' basis is the desire for the birth of spiritual consciousness—the point of radiance in the centre of the interlaced triangles—the babe in the manger at Bethlehem. Needless to say, no normal child can possibly live up to it, which may result in subsequent recrimination and estrangement between the generations. This problem is also a twofold one in that the human child will have projections of the ideal father and mother against which to measure the parents. This can pass off harmlessly as an idealization of sports or entertainment stars, or even a favourite aunt or uncle, but again can cause problems before the attainment of maturity, which is not always in direct correlation with advancing physical years.

It follows that in the Arthurian legends, the relationships between knights and ladies are of importance in teaching the polarities of the human aura. This is enshrined particularly in the great panorama of the conventions of Courtly Love, which are no mere relic of the twelfth century social custom, but the symbolic wisdom of the secrets of vertical and horizontal polarity as received in the Western Mystery Tradition.

The tradition of Arthur, Lancelot and others, being brought up by the Lady of the Lake enshrines an ancient teaching of the proper direction of the virile forces in a growing youth.

The archetypal origins of the Lady of the Lake go far back into pre-history. She is the vestigial memory of a great hierarchy of matriarchal powers that were ancient even in Atlantis, and whose role in the early mists of time was to help bring through the necessary adjustments to a primordial humanity when the differentiation of the sexes was established as the means of continuous procreation of the race. A very dim memory of these antediluvian events is contained in the Bible story of the animals going into Noah's ark two by two.

When the original Merlin sought to establish the Mystery traditions of Atlantis in the Isles of Britain, the 'faery women' also were there. These were Atlantean female chiefs and high priestesses of ancient cults, of which the Lady of the Lake in her various aspects, Morgan le Fay, and Arthur's mother Igraine are memories.

Their forces and powers can be picked up even to this day and may be found in symbolism encountered and reproduced by feminist esoteric groups. As with other very ancient contacts this can cause a certain disorientation from contemporary conventions and beliefs. In some respects this can be helpful, for civilization is never static and works in a spiral process of evolution, so that modern movements have parallels in former times at the corresponding sweep of the spiral. Individuals in sympathy with currents of change may well contact these old forces. They are, however, by definition, archaic, and therefore require adaptation to the needs of the present and immediate future. This is not always successfully realized by the idealist sensitives who contact them. As a consequence one may well witness odd behaviour in individuals or groups who fail to adapt the old forces into their new form adequately. A considerable degree of discretion and discrimination is called for in this delicate process of pouring the waters of life from an old chalice to a new one. Not for nothing is the Tarot card that depicts this process known as Temperance. Many 'New Age' groups receiving age old contacts do however react in an unbalanced way. They become completely out of sympathy with the group soul of the race and are consequently unable to form and maintain the necessary fruitful polarity. That is, they are far from 'temperate'.

The old forces can be particularly disruptive and disconcerting in that they take for granted old and outworn conceptions of the role of the individual in relation to society. And indeed those who contact them may be used not at all for their own benefit, but for obscure racial and genetic purposes concerned with the preservation of certain blood-lines. Their attitude to humanity, in short, is similar to that of a live-stock breeder without the emphasis of Jesus on the role of the shepherd as concerned for the individual lost sheep, which is the contribution of the Christ to the dynamics of human evolution at a later point in time.

It is for reasons such as this that in modern esoteric circles in the Western Mystery Tradition emphasis is placed on the importance of the Initiation of the Nadir and the proper contact and realization of the Christian initiation before the depths of archaic racial Mysteries be sought. The importance of the Arthurian legends as a whole is that they do span the whole range of human evolutionary experience. They encompass the spiritual heights of the Holy Grail along with the primeval memories of ancient myth and Atlantean lore and magic. The whole range of these contacts needs to be expressible by the whole man.

In terms of the human aura, neo-paganism tends to seek the ideal man in the centres below the diaphragm, whilst the prissier type of esotericism concentrates on the centres above the torso, seeing the ideal human being as rather like one of those cherubs, all head and wings, in Victorian paintings. Whilst each view has its merits, and indeed some profound insights, they tend to lack the linking centre. They need the 'heart' that can encompass wholeness and differentiation of polarities. The image of the Sacred Heart of Jesus is, in fact, a healing, unifying symbol that enshrines an important principle of the Yoga of the West.

The function of the Lady of the Lake in relation to Arthur is the direction of the dawning virile forces of puberty into idealistic channels. Operating from the inner planes she guides the fantasies of youth into the formulation of a pure contrasexual image, based upon herself as a priestess of the feminine archetype. This should have the intended result of orientating the personality towards its own higher self, the better to enter upon its subsequent work of destiny. It should also give the personality of the young man the balanced control of inner polar forces with which to act as an initiator to the bride of his choice when he attains manhood. That is to say, having established a working cycle of inner vertical polarity, he should be able to link with a female human being to extend the cycle into a functioning horizontal polarity. This, in the case of Arthur and Guenevere, will also have wider effects and implications, for they also have a polarity to express as Heads of State that will affect the realm and people they rule. Thus much depends upon a full and satisfactory relationship between them—and the failure to achieve this to the fullest extent is a factor that aborted the full attainment of the Holy Grail and broke up the Fellowship of the Round Table.

To understand this form of education in polarity working we need to consider the difference in the auric forces of man and woman. In symbolic terms of the Tree of Life this stems from the first manifestation of force from the androgynous spirit and whether this is directed first to the male or to the female pole. In Qabalistic terms this means to either of the Supernal Sephiroth, Chokmah or Binah.

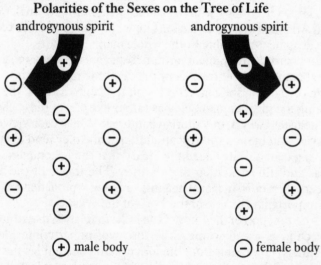

Figure 14

In Figure 14 it will be seen that although the polarities of the functional side pillars remain the same, there is an alternative polarity upon the levels of consciousness of the Middle Pillar.

This reversal of polarities as the force of the spirit comes down the planes of intuition, mentation, emotional and physical expression, ultimately determines the physical sex of the body.

This is what tends to give, in general terms, the emphasis of positive expression of the intuition and the emotions to women and intellectuality and physical force to men. The difference in the sexes is not one that is brought about simply by environmental factors and upbringing, although these will obviously have a conditioning effect. There will also, of course, be variations of sexual emphasis, for polarity can vary to some degree, particularly on the inner planes.

Much of this knowledge has not been adequately expressed in terms of the Western Mystery Tradition. In the East it has an extensive, if confused and incomplete, literature in the ancient texts of tantra and kundalini yoga.

Part of the excessive secrecy that has attended Western occult groups of the immediate past now appears to have been probably a result of repressive nineteenth century attitudes towards sex. Little on sexual magic appears in the published documents of the Hermetic Order of the Golden Dawn but that there was an inner teaching on this subject is strongly suggested in the dismay of Moina MacGregor Mathers on the publication by Dion Fortune of *The Esoteric Philosophy of Love and Marriage*. This innocent contribution to what is now a vast literature of sexual liberation was held by Mrs MacGregor Mathers to be a betrayal of the innermost secrets of the occult lodges.

Be this as it may, Dion Fortune went on to expand the teaching, in somewhat disguised form, in her novels. She states quite categorically that her *Mystical Qabalah* gives the theory but her novels give the practice. 'Those who study *The Mystical Qabalah* with the help of the novel get the keys of the Temple put into their hands. As Our Lord said: "Know ye not that your body is the temple of the Holy Ghost?"'

How successful she was in presenting the material in this form is open to debate, as she herself says. She went on, however, after the publication of the novels, which were not a commercial success, to produce papers for circulation in her group, some of which have regrettably never been published in wider form. For instance, *The Circuit of Force*, of which only a fragment appeared in a published collection of her essays, although it was published in full in *The Inner Light Magazine* during the early war years. And *The Principles of Hermetic Philosophy*, although of varied quality, from the later *Monthly Letters*, has never been given the dignity of print.

General principles are, however, available in various expositions of esoteric theory and practice. The principles of yoga enshrine the subjective use of the polarities of the vital force, generally known as Kundalini. This is the same force which is raised by spiritualists seeking phenomena by sitting in a linked circle. At another level, and in a different form, it is a group dynamic raised by Pentecostalist ceremonies in various churches—whether or not it is controlled by the Holy Spirit. Again it is brought into controlled function and structured form by exponents of ceremonial magic. It is also the 'animal magnetism' or 'vital fluid' postulated by early Mesmerists and the alchemical writers, as Mrs Attwood and her father realized, in her *Suggestive Enquiry into the Hermetic Mystery*.

Beyond the limits of its concentrated use in techniques of the expansion of consciousness, it also forms the very fabric of social relationships, between individuals and groups. This led some of the alchemists to describe this *prima materia* as being everywhere and overlooked or disregarded. In any relationship with any other being, be it physically intimate or otherwise, or with any group of which we form a part or stand in relationship to, there is an exchange of subtle force. This occurs at many levels and the mechanics of it are revealed by a study of the human aura.

The aura, in its most dense form, might be called the magnetic field of the human body. At the same time its various levels, from the centre to the periphery, from above the head to below the feet, and from front to rear, have correspondences with the complete range of experience of the human psyche extended through different levels of consciousness and physically through time and space.

Energy activates the aura from two sources: spiritual energy from above and elemental energy from below. (Figure 15)

The disciplines of yoga aim consciously to affect these energy streams. This is achieved in part by a regime of diet and posture, which tends to reverse the polarity of the physical and etheric levels. Yoga techniques also act by visualization of the etheric currents in the aura and psychic centres, and thereby manipulate the subconscious mind. By these means normally automatic functions such as the heartbeat and breathing can be consciously controlled.

There is a fundamental difference however between the

The two Energy Sources in the Aura on the Tree of Life

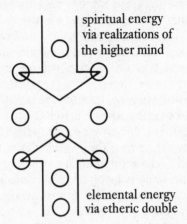

spiritual energy
via realizations of
the higher mind

Figure 15

elemental energy
via etheric double

assumptions and aims of the yogis of the East and the initiators of the West. This is exemplified particularly in the principal meditation postures and the positioning of the basal psychic centre. In the subjectively oriented Eastern systems the Muladhara chakra, the seat of kundalini power, is located at the base of the spine. In the objectively orientated Western systems it is placed beneath the feet. The Eastern yogi meditates in a squatting position with his feet tucked up so that they are either in close contact with, or physically above, the base of the spine. This effectively closes the circuit to elemental energy from the Earth. The Western postures, which are seen at their best in statues and pictures of Ancient Egyptian god-forms, consist of sitting or standing, with the lower limbs extended. Thus is formed a contact with what may be imagined as the centre of the Earth.

The Western initiate visualizes himself standing on the Sephirah Malkuth, with its quarters of citrine, olive, russet and black representing the four Elements manifesting in Earth, and he may imagine it as if it were the planet Earth surging through space. An objective magnetic flow is received by this means, a current from the Earth's aura, which rises into the personal auric system.

The Eastern system shuts off the Earth contact to make of the aura a closed circuit open only to the higher spiritual forces. This is certainly effective but demands a strict regime of seclusion that

does not generally accord with Western conditions and aspirations.

When the Western system taps the etheric currents of the
Earth through the centre beneath the feet it raises them to the
personal Moon centre, which on the Tree of Life is located at
Yesod. In the aura this is the psychic centre associated with the
sexual organs. From here the power needs to be raised yet further
to the heart centre; that is, from the personal sexual magnetism to
the mid-point whereby, through the building of images subject to
will, it can be consciously controlled and directed.

The 'magnetic' force of the aura, which is symbolically situated
at the Yesodic centre, (or Svaddisthana chakra), is a powerful
factor in all social interchange, particularly where bodily contact
or close proximity is involved. This does not necessarily imply a
sexual liaison or love affair, (although that is indeed a powerful
form of magnetic interchange), but, rather, ordinary social contacts, particularly in groups where some degree of emotion is
generated, for instance at theatre, dancehall, cinema, or sports
arena.

On the personal level the currents of this magnetic flow will
affect how well or ill people can live or work together. When aura
reacts with aura it is rather after the fashion of musical notes
played together. If the vibrations are in tune, (which could be
expressed in terms of mathematical ratios) then harmonious
relationship results; if not, then the relationship brings discord.

In addition to this there is the factor of amplitude. One aura
may be more powerful than another. A particularly powerful one
gives what is generally known as 'charisma', resulting in powers of
leadership or, at a more superficial level, the ability to be 'the life
and soul of the party'. Some auras give out a great deal of
energy—which can in certain circumstances prove overbearing.
Others may soak up energy from others, which in its extreme form
is a species of vampirism.

In general terms, however, magnetism flows from the higher
charged to the lower charged, and from 'positive pole' to 'negative
pole', and both parties benefit. A state of equilibrium is soon
reached, after which they will cease to benefit, although if they
part for a while the need will be realized again. Hence the need of
certain types of person for parties and social gatherings, and of
others for solitude, or nature contacts.

This magnetism, then, is accompanied or activated by personal
contact and the release of emotion. The art of kundalini yoga is to

release it without the stimulus of another person. In Western techniques of meditation or magic this is done by formulating clear, deeply emotive images in the imagination, which stir the soul to the point of emitting magnetism.

This is simply a matter of applied psychology, but it is the tool whereby contact may also be made with denizens of the astral light, or the other planes of existence. These beings, to those with the necessarily developed organs of perception, are as objective as contemporaries upon the physical plane.

Thus did the Lady of the Lake make contact with the young Arthur and Lancelot. And the same principles apply with regard to the sexual fantasies of the youthful male. There is, technically, no such thing as a male virgin after the age of puberty. As Jesus said, if a man lusts after a woman he is as accountable as if he had physically lain with her. Hard words, perhaps, as a goal for moral standards, but a precise statement of astral reality. The solidity and drag of the physical plane is a considerable protection, and the world would be a dangerous place if all our fantasies were immediately objectified.

In the ancient system of awakening and controlling these forces—when interchange between the planes was easier because of less developed individualization—the desires of youth would first be aroused on the inner levels by dreams of an ideal faery woman. This would then be developed by a mature older woman on the physical plane, who would instruct him in the techniques of courtship, physical and emotional, after which he would be properly equipped to woo and awaken to sexual response his future bride. Something of this pattern is still to be observed in rituals of primitive societies.

The young girl would normally remain virgin, in the astral as well as physical sense, until awakened by a male. This process is in modern times somewhat confused by the assault of the media whereby, for better or worse, innocence is soon lost.

In the Arthurian legend we see this process being perverted by the wiles of Morgan Le Fay. After the raising of Arthur's elemental forces by the Lady of the Lake they should have been consolidated and directed by Morgan so that he could then the better awaken his bride Guenevere. Morgan used him, however, for her own ends. This resulted in the birth of the evil Mordred, the loss of Arthur's own spiritual integrity, and the consequent failure to form a fruitful union with Guenevere. This had a blighting effect upon the Round Table Fellowship and the whole realm, in spite of the remedial measures set in train by Merlin.

In these matters it is important to distinguish between what is inelegantly, although accurately, called 'sex magic' and physical sexual intercourse. Sex magic is by no means the same as sexual licence—although if control is lost it could quite easily become so. On the contrary it requires considerable control to maintain and direct sexual forces at the higher levels. If the force overspills and descends the planes it may be 'earthed' by physical sexual intercourse but in this case it is generally no longer magic— except insofar that the conception of a child is the most profound magical act that can be performed, for it creates the spark of independent life upon a lower plane by the union of opposites.

However, the polarities of magical groups are not formed with the procreation of children in mind, which is rightly confined to the sacrament of marriage. It is where these principles are misunderstood however, and more force generated than the unsuspecting parties can handle, that infatuations take place, leading to liaisons, betrayals and scandals that not infrequently beset 'spiritual' leaders and groups. Much the same process can occur in the more prosaic field of psycho-analysis where this phenomenon is referred to as 'transference'. It can also occur in other situations, particularly in relation to doctors, nurses, teachers or clergy—wherever, in short, archetypal projections can take place.

Maturity and mental health in its full sense might be said to be the ability to relate to people and events without projecting one's own psychic content upon them.

The deliberate manipulation of projections, by inducing others to project them, is very much the *modus operandi* of advertising and political propaganda. To a lesser extent it is also that of magic when it is used objectively upon others. In this context however, magic is usually of dubious value and motivation, for true white magic is concerned with the evolution of consciousness towards maturity, objectivity and freedom from glamour and illusion.

Putting this into the context of the Arthuriad we find the young Arthur being induced into an early objective polarity with an inner plane being, the Lady of the Lake, thereby picking up from her the inner contacts that would enable him to polarize with the realm as a whole, and also with his queen, thereby conferring a similar regal power upon her.

Morgan le Fay, however, 'skilled in nigromancy', for reasons of personal ambition and desire to seize such powers to herself, diverts the polar flow into a projection upon herself, instead of focusing Arthur's attention, awareness and polar flow onto a maiden of his own age destined to be his queen.

As a result, whatever his positive virtues as a warrior and leader of knights, Arthur has a coldness towards women, for his polar forces are not directed towards them in the right way. Thus he cannot fully relate to Guenevere and she is left, a queen in name only, barren and unfulfilled. Consequently there is no heir to the throne and no continuation to the Pendragon line that Merlin had so meticulously engendered. The son and heir of Arthur and Guenevere would also have become the achiever of the Holy Grail, subsequently ruling a redeemed and unenchanted Logres.

We are left with a situation where Arthur, of the line of the Pendragon through Uther, and of the Atlantean priest-kings through Igraine, is wedded to Guenevere who has brought with her the dowry of the Round Table. However, the flowering of this tremendous potential plan is blighted in the bud by the interference of Morgan le Fay, who diverts Arthur's forces to her own ends. This is symbolically described in the stories of her stealing Excalibur and its scabbard.

The complications of relationship that follow are the efforts of Merlin and the powers whom he represents, to rescue and restore something of the original plan and high destiny.

Guenevere is therefore duly fructified and awakened by Lancelot, the best knight in the world, who had also been astrally initiated in youth by the Lady of the Lake. Through his help Guenevere can act as queen in the sense of leader and focus of the court and the Round Table Fellowship, although it still leaves the problem of there being no heir to the throne. Instead of Arthur being father of the Grail winner his seed has been diverted by Morgan to produce the evil Mordred who, in the end, expresses his perverted powers by usurpation of the throne, abduction of the queen, overthrow of the religious hierarchy, and revolutionary arousal of the commons.

Merlin therefore brought about a mating between Lancelot and Elaine of Carbonek, one of the maidens of the Grail Castle. By this means Galahad was brought to birth. However, there was no mate for Galahad to relate to, who would probably have been Lancelot's daughter, perhaps by Elaine of Astolat, in the original plan. Therefore the Grail, when it was won, instead of being a Cauldron of Plenty in tune with the fruits of the Earth, became a Cup of Spiritual Illumination divorced from Earth, that virtually slew those few who were able to drink from it. In this, Bors, the broadly based human family man, (although the monkish scribes tend to denigrate this), is the real achiever, for he came back as a witness of the Grail's existence. He was not able, however, to pass on the fruits of his vision to the group as a whole. Percivale and Galahad, like Enoch, 'walked with God and were not'. The great chasm between spiritual and earthly reality caused by the Fall, and the expulsion of primeval man and woman from the Earthly Paradise remained.

Later, Lancelot's liaison with the maiden who, in the normal course of events might have been his true lady, Elaine of Astolat, ended it tragedy. She dies of unrequited love, her body being floated down the river as a token of the failure in destiny of the whole court.

18. Sexuality in Magic and Psychism

There are, in the panorama of relationships in the Arthuriad, important lessons in the handling of the sexual forces, and the Arthurian legend teaches through the examples of failure as well as of success.

Magical work should only be undertaken by a person with a full range of experience of human life, particularly of human relationships maintained and fulfilled. If the life forces are deflected back up the planes before they pass the nadir of physical experience the personality may well be blighted in its self expression. This inhibition of natural expression may well help to establish inner plane contact but the price can be too high, stunting the ability for really deep and powerful work through chronic immaturity.

The factors involved differ for each of the sexes. There is a peculiar aridity that is physically noticeable about an unfulfilled woman. This is because the failure to complete the circuit of force through the aura results in magnetic starvation. This does not occur in men, (except in certain types of homosexual). In man the problem is one of congestion of force if no circuit for the flow can be found. In man the excess will be expressed through the lower centres in some form of demanding occupation. In a woman of little life experience these forces may never come down. (Figure 16.)

It follows that the virgin female should first be addressed to her spiritual nature, the suitor taking on the projection of the ideal man. Then follows the stimulation at the mental level as to how this ideal may be given expression in terms of current circumstances, from which follows emotional arousal, and finally the

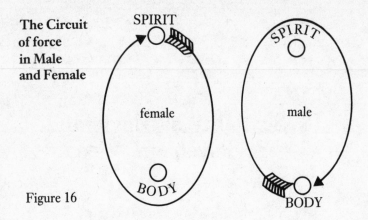

The Circuit
of force
in Male
and Female

Figure 16

awakening of her instincts and senses to all the powers of her body.

In the virgin male the senses are ready to run riot, and so need to be drawn upward and linked with the idea of beauty so that sexuality is directed above the level of brute sensual gratification. This was the function of the Lady of the Lake in relation to Arthur, Lancelot and his kin, operating through the imaginative fantasy.

These associated ideas of sexual expression and beauty then need to be objectified by polarization with a mature woman, who can lead him to an understanding of the proper expression of these creative forces within him. This is done, not by directing his sexual desires upon herself but by holding forth an ideal of courtesy and service expressed initially for her sake. Then he is fitted to approach a maid of his own generation in courtship.

This process can be conceived as operating upon three levels. (Figure 17).

In this schema it will be seen that the projection of the contra-sexual image may operate at three levels—at one pole directly upon an ideal vision, at the lowest pole directly upon a member of the opposite sex, or intermediately, (that is, magically), upon one who is aware of what he or she is doing and may divert the projection. The diversion can be upwards towards a disembodied ideal, or downwards to a member of the opposite sex, which can be either the priest (or priestess), or another third party. It is this mechanism that largely takes up the burden of Dion Fortune's magical novels.

There are of course many variations upon this basic theme, as

The Three Levels of Projection of the Contrasexual Image

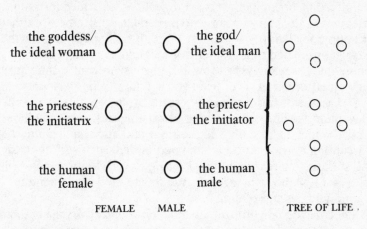

Figure 17

exemplified in the Arthurian legends. After the arousal of Arthur's powers by the Lady of the Lake, Morgan le Fay should have taken over as priestess/initiatrix of Isis, and raised them upward. Then Arthur would have had the full run of racial dynastic forces through his own blood line impressed with the forces of the faery world by the intercession of the Lady of the Lake, and these drawn into polarity with womankind as a whole by Morgan, complete with a full conscious realization of its possibilities through contact with the spiritual realms. He would then have been ideally suited to initiate the maiden Guenevere as his bride and queen of the realm.

Instead, Morgan, envious of his dynastic powers and the inner world contacts brought by the Lady of the Lake, directed his forces toward herself. Thus was the evil Mordred begotten as a result of this premature downward flow, leaving Arthur unable to relate to womenkind of his own generation. Guenevere would have remained unfulfilled but for the intervention of Lancelot.

This failure of Merlin's plan through Morgan shows the fundamental importance of dedication in higher magic. It is not generally realized by those who aspire to magical work, that the aroused psychic forces manifest as desires, images, temptations,

aspirations within the retort of the invoker's consciousness.
Consequently, failure to be able to control the direction of this
flow will result in all sorts of inappropriate projections—in terms
of affection or antipathy. It is projections of affection upon a
member of the opposite sex who is participating in the work that
accounts for liaisons seemingly quite out of character with the
ideals formulated by an esoteric or religious aspirant. These may
sometimes be justified by avowals of the discovery of karmic links
or mutual destinies, even twin souls, but even in the somewhat
rare cases where such claims are true (and in this area self-
deception is rife), the breaking of existing ties, responsibilities
and loyalties in this life, the betrayal and social and domestic
disruption of the innocent, is no part of dedicated service to the
Mysteries. Where true destiny is being served circumstances will
clear for it without the need to ride rough-shod over the rightful
claims and feelings of others.

Except in certain little understood forms of tantrik yoga or their
Western equivalent, physical sexual union is not a part of magic. It
may, however, be a means of 'earthing' high psychic voltages and
thus can act as a kind of safety valve. This presupposes that the
participants have mature sexual relationships, though not necessarily with each other. High magical potencies can not be handled
by the immature or the unfulfilled. The sense of fulfilment and of
forces in balance that comes as a result of a successful magical
working is similar to that experienced after physical coitus and
results from similar reasons—the balancing of contending or
complementary polar forces.

We speak about these matters as they relate to magic because
magic is, by definition and intention, a microcosm or focus of the
life forces generally. The same facts apply to many forms of
human activity and relationship. Polar relationships exist at all
levels of human interchange. They occur particularly in all forms
of teaching. The teacher stimulates and awakens that which is
latent in the taught—whether this be an individual or a group. In
the case of successful rapport the polarity is alternating. Having
stimulated the individual or group the teacher is stimulated in
turn, changes polarity, and brings through from his or her own
inner resources knowledge and insights suited to the situation
and immediate needs. In the case of a good polar relationship the
teacher may feel inspired, and the taught likewise, as trans-
personal dynamics are contacted by the induction of their mutual
response. This applies also to the musician, actor or dancer giving

a performance, or the extempore speaker or preacher, as well as to the magus in the occult lodge.

What can also happen is that the 'horizontal' polarity between the teacher and taught may give rise to 'vertical' polarity, at first within the participants themselves, which, in rare instances can lead to 'peak experiences', never to be forgotten moments where a horizontal polarity is evoked between the particpants at a higher level than the normal level of the conscious mind. This may be represented diagrammatically.

Possibilities of Relationship between Higher and Lower Selves

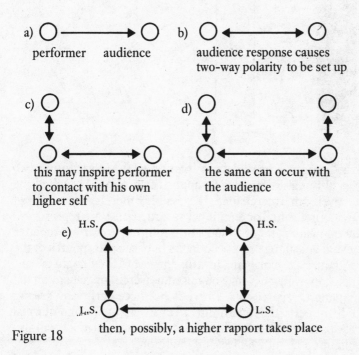

a) performer   audience

b) audience response causes two-way polarity to be set up

c) this may inspire performer to contact with his own higher self

d) the same can occur with the audience

e) H.S.   H.S.   L.S.   L.S.

Figure 18   then, possibly, a higher rapport takes place

Figure 18 shows in simple terms the possibilities of relationship involving higher and lower selves. The process could be envisaged in greater detail in regard to polarities at different levels or planes, and one could use a fourfold or a sevenfold, or any other system. In the esoteric tradition of the West the Tree of Life and the Pillars of the Temple are commonly used as a pattern of the formation of polarities, and their expression in union.

Figure 19:   **The Pillars and Paths of the Tree of Life**

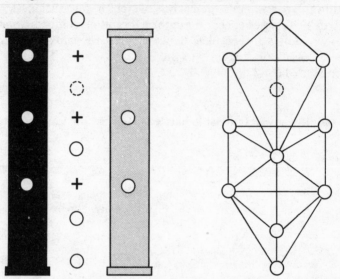

We can imagine the Pillars in Figure 19 as representing two people, although it can also be applied to groups. At each of the main levels an interchange is possible; that is, on levels of spiritual, intellectual or emotional accord. These are represented by the opposite pairs of spheres or Sephiroth. Polar interchange can take place along any of the Paths between the spheres of the side Pillars, and so may be upward, downward, or straight across. That is, consciousness may be raised, lowered, or remain on the same plane of expression. There is not necessarily any greater good in one or the other, for all are legitimate and normal expressions of human activity and interchange, and much will also depend upon circumstances and intention.

As an example, if we take the polar interchange at the level of Personality, we look to the Paths that conjoin spheres seven and eight. This may be directly across, which is that of normal social intercourse, or via one of the central spheres—six, nine or ten—which results in a fruitful and creative union. (For the sake of readers unfamiliar with the Qabalistic Tree of Life we will keep technical terms to a bare minimum but much more can be interpolated by appropriate use of the relevant symbolism by the knowledgeable student).

Sphere Six, (Tiphereth, or the Sephirah of the Sun), represents a creative meeting of souls upon an intellectual level and the generation of ideas that may lead to important projects if duly acted upon.

Sphere Ten (Malkuth, or the Sephirah of the Elements), represents a creative act upon the physical/etheric level. It certainly applies to the physical sexual act, which brings another soul to conception and birth. It is equally appropriate, however, to work undertaken together that has direct physical results, be it the building of a home or a business. In short, any physical activity that results from the pooling of mutual aims, ideas and desires, and the objective results of that activity.

Sphere Nine (Yesod, or the Sephirah of the Moon), is less readily understood by those without an appreciation of the subtleties of the inner planes. This is a physical union that forms an atmosphere in which things can grow and objectify. It is felt in the harmony of a happy home, it may also manifest as *esprit de corps*. It is built on common dedication and mutual trust. Much can result from this powerful treasurehouse and force field which is midway between the abstract ideas and plans of Sphere Six and the physical action of Sphere Ten.

And of course all these expressions of polar interchange and union may occur, to a greater or lesser extent, simultaneously.

The interchange between Spheres Four and Five relates to a Higher Self polarity. Thereafter it descends the planes to be expressed in terms of Personalities who strike an accord with each other, despite apparent differences, and perform some work of destiny together, expressing higher realities in the worlds of form.

A higher creative link is possible at the dotted sphere, known to Qabalists as Daath. This has a formless aspect which, though akin to the Moon sphere of Yesod on a higher arc, is not easily formulated in terms that are understandable to the concrete mind. Thus in the traditional delineation of Paths on the Tree of Life it is not represented and has no Paths to or from it. There are deep Mysteries here concerned with the Fall of Man, that pertain more to the Mysteries of the Holy Grail and the Mysteries of Regeneration. They represent the pooling of human wills in a mutual abnegation that yet has transforming, transmuting function that is perhaps only adequately formulated in terms of

Buddhist metaphysics. These are matters beyond the run of current human experience, but the building of Daath, and of the Paths thereto, is a matter of man's eventual cosmic destiny. Then the Spiritual Will will become fully operational within the Higher Self and all its experience will manifest in the lower planes of form in a Personality of great clarity. Thus will the New Jerusalem come to Earth or, in Grail terms, the enchantment be lifted from the Land of Logres.

In another aspect, the sphere of Daath is likened to an Empty Room. It has no symbols, and is alternatively called the Condemned Cell. It may also therefore be said to represent complete union without 'projection', the naked experience of ourselves and others.

At the highest level there is an interchange of spiritual awareness between Spheres Two and Three. This concerns mutual spiritual destinies over whole evolutionary periods, and at the lower levels will be expressed via Sphere Six, whereby we have the manifestation of two individuals united in the quest of a particular destiny or high ideal in life after life and also between incarnations.

It will be gathered from the diagram of the Tree of Life that there are also vertical polarities within each individual, and it is indeed possible for two individuals to be united at all three levels, expressing union at all levels, from the heights of uncreate reality where the Will of God is known down to complete expression in Earth. The goal of evolution might be said to be the situation where *all* relationships are of this mutually free and expressive numinous nature.

This is but one way of applying the Tree of Life to the intricacies of human polarity, both within the individual organism and without it, in objective inter-relationships. All of this theory and practice, which is the warp and woof of all experienced existence, pertains to the Grade of Guenevere, which is concerned with the science of the aura, delineated by the system of chakras or psychic centres in the East, and by the Tree of Life system in the West.

Thus the building of the Tree of Life in the aura is a fundamental exercise in the Western Mystery Tradition at whatever level one is aiming to function. For these same polarities operate within the individual, and indeed, when interchange between individuals takes place to its fullest extent, it can be envisaged as a dual polar arrangement whereby two Trees of Life are interposed face to face and the interchange of polarity produces another Tree between them. (Figure 20)

Dual Polarity on Two Trees of Life

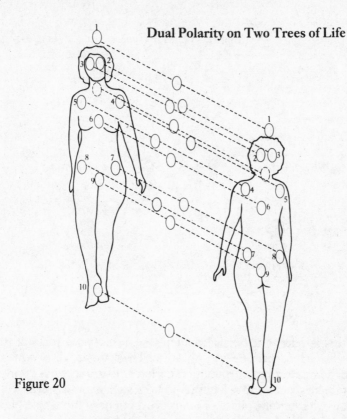

Figure 20

However, we now approach technicalities that are beyond the immediate scope of this book. In practical terms it will prove more useful to leave the more erudite Qabalistic student with these suggestions for further study and pass on to consider facts of polar relationship in more practically human terms.

The knowledge of these magnetic polar relationships, within and without the marital bond, was what was concealed with such emphasis on secrecy by occult groups of the nineteenth and and early twentieth century.

There is a rhythm in these matters of sexual polarity, and it differs between men and women. The psychic rhythm of man is that of the Sun cycle—passing rapidly through all its phases of dawn, noon, dusk and night in twenty-four hours. The rhythm of woman is that of the Moon, which operates over a twenty-eight day cycle—waxing, full, waning, new. (Figure 21.)

Solar and Lunar Cycles

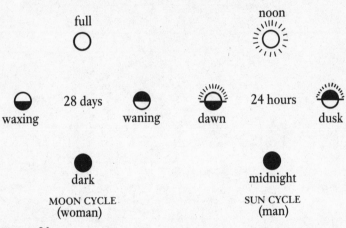

Figure 21

All this is part of a much broader system of cycles relating to successive incarnations and phases of civilizations, all of which have their pattern in astronomical cycles. Life in general is cyclic, or indeed spiral, and whatever point a soul is on a spiral will dictate whether one phase or many is experienced in a single life. Some individuals thus may be observed to lead very placid, stable lives; others may go through a number of different experiences of life conditions in the course of one physical incarnation, almost as if they were cramming many lives into one. It all depends on their point on the spiral. (Figure 22.)

The poet Yeats was much interested in this line of research into what he called gyres. The swing of the spiral curves also gives parallels between different phases of life expression, distanced in time when it is regarded as linear.

These general principles are capable of infinite expansion in that they are the underlying pattern upon which the structure of personal life is built. Likewise there is, in practice, considerable complexity in the way that polar relationships take place but the simplified outline we give can be applied to an understanding of

the most complex of changing and multifaceted relationships.
There are thus two types of achievement for the knights and

Spiral of Manifestation

Figure 22

ladies of the Arthurian legends. There are those who marry and
become the lords and ladies of castles and lands in suzerainty to
the king, forming a local dynasty and ruling the provinces and
parishes of the realm. On the other hand are those who devote
themselves entirely to quests of knight errantry or, in the case of
ladies, to being the paramours of such knights.

At a more spiritual level this finds expression in the virgin Grail
knights and the Grail maidens. However, in this context the terms
virgin or maid are not used in the sense of sexual inexperience but
in terms of an inner quality of dedication and purity of motive.

Another aspect of polarity that must be borne in mind when
considering the role of Arthur and Guenevere is their polar
relationship to the court and realm, being carriers of the archetype of headship, the male head and the female head of the whole
land, as King and Queen. There is a real sacramental charisma
involved in royalty that goes far deeper than conventional ritual
etiquette and ceremonial pomp. Both King and Queen need to be
fulfilled human beings to function properly in carrying the
archetypes.

We have seen that Arthur lacked in this because of the treacherous aspirations of Morgan le Fay, and he was thus a better warrior than he was a ruler. Similarly Guenevere lacked full humanity because of Arthur's inability to relate fully to her, but this role was performed, as well as it could be by one not of the royal line, by Lancelot, the leading champion of all knights of the day. The magnetic interchange that takes place at physical sexual union has lasting effects upon the inner vehicles far beyond the apparent lack of lasting effect upon the physical plane, for there are matings possible at different levels, and any relationship that goes beyond the superficial will have an element of one or more planes.

A sevenfold system of defining these relationships is explored by Dion Fortune in her book *The Esoteric Philosophy of Love and Marriage* which is closely connected with her book on abstract esoteric principles entitled *The Cosmic Doctrine*, and the two could wll be read together as an attempt to relate theory to practice, in much the same way that her later theoretical volume *The Mystical Qabalah* was matched, in her intentions, by the practicalities of the later occult novels *The Winged Bull*, *The Sea Priestess* and *Moon Magic*. How successful she was in this endeavour is a matter for discussion in the light of further experience but that is the way that the subject should be approached. It will be sufficient for our purpose to make a résumé of the system in a comprehensive diagram (Figure 23). It is in relation to this that the relationships of the Arthurian characters can be understood, for they operate against the same background and demonstrate the same teaching.

Life forces run down through the seven levels of expression, and force will go to whatever level that attention (that is, an act of will, whether voluntary or involuntary) is directed to.

In the arousal of the innate life powers, arising from the first and second planes, of the young Arthur and Lancelot, the Lady of the Lake comes to them operating principally on the third and fourth planes, stimulating their affections toward concrete images of the ideal woman that are moulded in the thoughtforms of the lower mental plane, although they represent qualities of the planes above form, the fifth to seventh planes, having their primal spiritual force from the seventh plane, their archetypal principle from the sixth, and mode of expression toward form on the fifth plane.

The mature woman then takes over, whose task is to operate from the level of the Higher Self, directing these aroused forces

The Seven Levels of Relationship

Planetary Plane Symbol			Type of Union	
☉	7th	SPIRITUAL	All is unity, unified in mutual love, but two categories of spirit. Those who have experienced form and those that have not. 'Sages' and 'Fools'.	
♃	6th	SPIRITUAL	First differentiation into 'ray types'. Union by common destiny or basic spiritual type.	HIGHER SELF
☿	5th	MENTAL	Union by intuitional sympathy.	
♄	4th	MENTAL	Union by common content of consciousness, intellectual accord.	
♀	3rd	EMOTIONAL	Union by higher affections.	
♂	2nd	EMOTIONAL	Union by instinctual desires.	LOWER SELF
⊗☽	1st	ETHERIC -PHYSICAL	Physical union.	

Figure 23

back toward the objective planes of form. The difference of her function from that of the Lady of the Lake is principally the fact that she is a human, not an elemental, being, and has a physical body and all the qualities of a human woman that are not present in such complexity and concrete expression in an elemental or fay. Nonetheless, although she has the lower polar vehicles of expression at her command it is important that she does not direct the forces, energies and desires of the young men upon herself. She represents a focus of intellectual sympathy, commonality of interest and warmth and affection but has to do this in what can only be described as an impersonal manner. This is not an aloofness or manipulation but a placing of motivation and values at the level of the Higher Self; that is, in accord with spiritual and moral principles and along the lines of destiny and karmic realization. This indeed is what is known as the 'impersonality of the adept' which is by no means the impersonality of inhumanity of the small minded functionary. The true impersonality needs an exceptional long-sightedness and a rare degree of maturity.

In Morgan le Fay we have the example of an adept using powers in a personal instead of a truly impersonal way. The curent of force which should have found its destination in a young maid awaiting initiation by the young man is short circuited, directed upon herself. That is, in a deliberate rechanneling of the forces, diverting to her own ends powers that, rightfully connected, should have been used for the good and destiny of the race.

We have no record of the initiation of Lancelot but in his case it evidently proceeded safely and correctly. As a consequence he was able to step in and act as an incarnate expression of the forces of all the planes. That is, appearing an ideal hero in the young Guenevere's eyes, bringing down her romantic idealism to focus upon him as a cultured, brave, affectionate physical human being.

19. Arthur, Lancelot and Guenevere

When we examine the relationships that exist between principal characters of the opposite sex in the Arthuriad we find that they fall into three main groups: around Arthur, Lancelot and Guenevere. There is also a parallel pattern at the Court of King Mark of Cornwall which we shall deal with separately. These relationships, which overlap and intersect, may be expressed diagramatically, (Figure 24), and could be added to by inclusion of minor relationships, as for instance those of Galahad, Mordred, Meliagraunce, Gawain, Mador de la Porte, Bors, and others with the Queen. We seek however simply to lay down the main principles, leaving the interested student to apply them to the complex minor ramifications.

In the three principal relationships of Arthur we have first of all the overseeing of his awakening to the powers of manhood by the Lady of the Lake whom we will call Nimuë, who also plays the same role with Lancelot.

This is an inner plane contact; there is no physical pole to attract the youths' virile forces as a focus, which are thus directed upwards towards the ideals of chivalry and service to feminine beauty.

The next phase in Arthur's development is his relationship with Morgan le Fay, where there is an abuse of function on her part. The young prince is seduced into a premature and incestuous physical liaison the result of which is the birth of the evil bastard Mordred. Whether one follows the tradition of Mordred being the son of Morgan, or of the lusty elemental Morgawse, with Morgan as pander, the principles still pertain.

Another consequence is that Arthur is now unable to mate

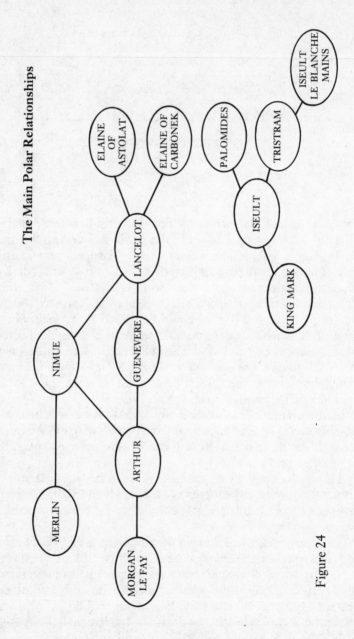

The Main Polar Relationships

Figure 24

satisfactorily with a woman of his own generation. His forces are directed upwards towards a goddess figure in the glamours manifested to him by the seductress Morgan. After this, the simple innocence of a young maid such as Guenevere will seem insipid.

Guenevere is thus wed to a husband who is not interested in her. In one tradition Arthur does not even go to claim Guenevere from her father but sends Lancelot instead. The first contact of the virgin bride-to-be with her groom is an important one. It releases a built up tension of expectation that cements the foundation for a life-long love match. This occurs for example in the case of the first sight of each other by Gareth and the Lady Liones. In Guenevere's case it is Lancelot who appears in the place of her groom.

We pass then to the relationships that Guenevere forms in the face of the indifference of Arthur. As is well known she finds magnetic polarity and sexual physical fulfilment with Lancelot. Thus she is awakened to womanhood and is able to exercise her function as first lady of the court. This includes being initiatrix in chief of all the pages, squires and maids in waiting.

However, Lancelot's liaison with Guenevere is out of accord with the Christian moral code, which is based upon the procreation of children. This has caused considerable difficulty for later monastic scribes, who asumed the only alternative to marriage to be celibacy but, whether inside or outside of the marriage contract, there is a perfectly legitimate form of relationship which enables the inner forces to flow in the interests of mutal fulfilment.

Thus we have the accounts, which are later interpolations, of Lancelot and Guenevere pining their lives away in religious houses filled with remorse. Such, however, would hardly have been so. Indeed, greater remorse would have been called for had Lancelot and Guenevere failed to form a fructifying relationship that, although it did not produce children, and was formed outside wedlock, enabled Guenevere to become the bearer of the Regina archetype. To have left her unfulfilled, unawakened, and uninitiate would have blighted Camelot in the bud.

However, having been awakened to her function, as Queen of the Realm and Mistress of the Court, Guenevere should then have acted in an impersonal fashion expressing love without attachment. But the forces broke bounds in their relationship so that both became victims of a lifelong infatuation. This is the flaw in the relationship that allowed evil to multiply—not the fact that it was outside wedlock.

Lancelot could well have remained in the court, and found his own lady, who would probably have been Elaine of Astolat. The physical side of sexual relationships is not fundamentally at issue here, but rather the 'magical' or emotional and etheric polarities which may or may not be paralleled by making physical love. Physical love making is an 'earthing' of the life forces that can find equally creative exchange at other levels.

The fact that there is widespread scepticism that a platonic relationship can exist between man and woman is a common recognition that there is a strong tendency for the polar life forces to find expression by coming down the planes, but this is by no means a universal law. There are matings at many levels and the initiate or the mature human being should be able to express love and the life forces at will on any level. In a strictly technical sense this is the meaning of the word purity, which is not a condition of inexperienced innocence but simply clear function on any plane without admixture of ulterior motive.

The Morgan/Arthur relationship should have been platonic, that is, confined to levels above the physical, but it was not. The relationship of Guenevere and Lancelot after the first initiatory awakening of her, physically and etherically, to womanhood could have thereafter been expressed entirely in platonic terms, in exactly the same way that Guenevere related to the rest of the knights of the Round Table. This was exemplified particularly in her relationship with Gawain, who was regarded as the Queen's knight without any shadow of suspicion of a physical love relationship. The physical side of the relationship was expressed in the service to ladies in general and the standards of ideal knighthood that the relationship led or inspired Gawain to try to maintain. In turn, this relationship with the Round Table knights reinforced Guenevere in her role as Queen and Head of the Court.

It was the fact that Lancelot and Guenevere became enmeshed in an ongoing obsessive passion that gave Morgan, Mordred and Agravaine the opportunity to stir up scandal at the court. This eventually led to the death of Gawain's brothers at Lancelot's hand and the civil war that was to rend the Round Table Fellowship and allow Mordred to usurp the kingdom.

It also complicated Merlin's alternative genetic strategy following the fall of Arthur at Morgan's hands. He arranged a liaison between Lancelot and Elaine of Carbonek in order to produce a fitting vehicle for the high soul that was to be known as Galahad. The failure of relationship between Arthur and Guenevere had effectively scotched the original plan that this soul should be crown prince of a great new dynasty of priest-kings. The magnetic forces of the Pendragonship had been twisted and perverted into the evil Mordred, a devilish caricature of the intended Galahad. This channel of expression could be used no more. It would likewise not be appropriate for the Queen to give birth to a son that was not of the king's line. Therefore, in order at least to bring to birth the one who could achieve the Grail, Lancelot, the best knight in the world, was chosen to be the father, and Elaine of Carbonek, of the line of the Grail Castle Guardians—another elect order of knighthood with unique spiritual credentials—to be the mother.

As with the details of the conception of Arthur these little understood factors have been interpreted by medieval storytellers in terms of magical trickery. This is not the real tone of these spiritual and dynastic matings however, which were highly sacramental acts of profound import in the old Atlantean manner.

In Malory the higher significance is implied when a hermit arrives at Arthur's court and asks a question that no-one there can answer. This is, why is there one seat at the Round Table, (the Siege Perilous), left vacant? They know that it is perilous and that only one person destined for it may sit there without destruction, but they do not know who it is who will have this destiny or for what reason. The hermit reveals that it is reserved for one not yet born or conceived but who will win the Holy Grail.

When the hermit departs the story immediately takes us with Lancelot over a bridge, which is the usual token of higher adventures to come. He proceeds to a fair tower in a city wherein the fairest lady in the world is kept in the torture of a scalding bath. This, it is recorded, is through the envy and enchantment of Morgan le Fay.

The lady has been in this parlous condition for five years but on Lancelot's approach the iron doors of the chamber wherein she is confined fly open. Lancelot enters the chamber which is 'as hot as any stew', and there 'took the fairest lady by the hand that ever he saw, and she was as naked as a needle'. This ends the enchantment by fulfilling its original condition that it could only be lifted by the hands of the best knight in the world. There is, however, another aspect to the test, which is to slay a vicious serpent or dragon that is concealed in a tomb. Upon the tomb is a prophecy in letters of gold 'Here shall come a lybarde of kings blood and he shall slay this serpent. And this lybarde shall engender a lion in this foreign country which lion shall pass all other knights.'

As with fountains, so with serpents and dragons in the esoteric symbolism of the Arthurian legends; we are at the fount of creative powers, those forces that are also behind such magical weapons as Excalibur. This is the serpent power kundalini. Lancelot conquers this serpent power and thereupon it is revealed that he is within the realm of King Pelles, of the line of Joseph of Arimathea. The Holy Grail makes its appearance in twofold form: as a dove appearing at a window holding a censer of gold from which emanate beautiful savours, and as a young, fair damsel holding a gold vessel before which all kneel devoutly and pray. All this is accompanied by the table being covered with every conceivable food and drink.

It is then revealed that King Pelles knows full well that the knight who will one day achieve the Holy Grail will be called Sir Galahad and the son of Lancelot and his daughter Elaine. The responsibility for bringing this union about is placed in the hands of an initiate priestess named Brisen 'one of the greatest enchanters that was that time in the world.'

As with the shape shifting that occurred in the circumstances surrounding the conception of Arthur, Brisen glamourizes Lancelot into thinking that Elaine is Guenevere. By the light of day, however, Lancelot discovers that he has been deceived but forgives Elaine her part in the enchantment and goes upon his way.

Sir Bors later arrives at the Grail Castle—which is also called the Castle Adventurous. There he sees the newborn Galahad in Elaine's arms, whereupon the Holy Grail appears once again. Bors, whose function later is to bring news to the outer world of the achievement of the Quest of the Holy Grail itself, here, in a similar capacity, brings news of Galahad's birth back to court. Guenevere is at first greatly distressed by it until Lancelot convinces her that he had been deceived by an enchantment.

Shortly afterwards, however, at a great tournament, which is attended by Elaine of Carbonek, Guenevere is overcome with jealousy and condemns Lancelot for his duplicity. Lancelot thereupon loses his reason, for he is torn between two 'realities' of equal contending force. His destiny as father of Galahad is in conflict with his destiny as initiator of the Queen. It should be said, however, that these two destinies need not have conflicted but for the possessive involvement of Guenevere and the degradation of the forces of both of them into a personal infatuation.

For the space of two years he runs wild in the woods, and undergoes great privations and severe afflictions. These include being severely wounded in the thigh by a boar, which is symbolic reflection of his personal debasement of higher impersonal cosmic and racial forces into the channels of personal sexual satisfaction. This is immediately followed by the utmost degradation when he is unceremoniously carried off in a cart, helpless and wounded, in which is also the body of the dead pig that has wounded him. This is also not without symbolic irony when one recalls an episode of his high knighthood when even to contemplate stepping into a cart to save his lady was almost beneath the dignity of a chivalrous knight. Also, being wounded by a pig is, besides being a disgrace for a knight, indicative of the flesh to which his high destiny has fallen prey.

At a deeper level of symbolism, the pig is sacred to the goddess, and to be overcome by one is appropriate indication of the failure to cope adequately with the feminine forces.

Eventually he wanders back to the country of King Pelles where he is healed of his wounds and his madness. In remorse and repentance he vows not to return to the court of King Arthur, and he calls himself, not Lancelot, but Le Chevalier Malfet, that is, the trespassing or sinful knight. He then lives in the company of Elaine of Carbonek in the castle of Joyous Isle until their son Galahad reaches the age of fifteen.

During this time Guenevere is desolate at his absence. She expends a fortune in sending knights in search of him. It is this deterioration in Guenevere's character that explains the later, lower moral condition of the court wherein one knight of the Round Table can attempt to poison another and the suspicion fall upon the Queen, who then has the greatest difficulty in finding anyone who will champion her. These events are in the latter days after the Quest of the Holy Grail, and when Lancelot has returned to the court. Lancelot is, however, absent on this occasion because he has been banished from the court by Guenevere in a fit of jealous pique. In the end he does return, in disguise, and saves her by becoming her champion, and the Lady of the Lake intervenes to reveal the true culprit.

Immediately after this incident Lancelot again incurs Guenevere's jealous wrath when, fighting in disguise at a tournament, he wears the colours of Elaine of Astolat, the daughter of the knight with whom he is lodging. Lancelot is wounded and taken to a hermitage. Elaine of Astolat comes to nurse him during which time she falls in love with him. Upon his departure she begs to be his wife, or failing that, his paramour. The most that Lancelot can or will offer is, however, to be her champion and guardian, but she finds no consolation in this and after his departure dies for love of him. Before her death she arranges for her corpse to be floated on a barge down the river to Camelot so that all shall know that she died for love of Lancelot.

Esoterically considered, we see here an example of life force being projected onto another who cannot or will not react as the opposite pole at the lower levels. When Elaine cannot transfer the projection upon another the frustrated and deflected life force turns back upon itself and destroys her own lower vehicles.

Ironically this is the form of relationship that Lancelot should have maintained with the Queen. Neither Guenevere or Elaine are able to keep the forces contained at a higher level. In the case of Guenevere it results in the relationship being expressed fully down the planes, but to ultimate destruction of the Round Table Fellowship. In the case of Elaine the blockage of a free run down the planes results in self destruction.

Shortly afterwards Guenevere insists that Lancelot wear her favour at tournaments, ostensibly so that he may not be struck down accidentally by his friends again. There is, however, a degree of possessiveness and jealousy in this act.

However, Lancelot is shortly after wounded in a different fashion. This time he is somewhat unheroically struck in the buttock by an arrow from a huntress. This thinly disguised goddess, Diana the virgin huntress, thus exacts a toll for his mishandling of the polar forces. This is another wound of the symbolic type given him by the wild boar when he was mad, and also by Mador de la Porte, who struck him 'through the thighs' when he defended the Queen's honour in the incident of the poisoned apple.

At this point Malory introduces the incident of Guenevere's abduction. This tale was originally a folk tale deriving from ancient myth of the Persephone type, wherein the Spring Maiden is abducted by the dark lord of the Underworld. This was used by Chrétien de Troies in *Le Chevalier de la Charette* and interpreted as a comedy of manners in exposition of the code of Courtly Love. Malory uses it as a means of illustrating the decaying standards of the court for, having rescued the Queen, Lancelot is trapped in clandestine liaison with her by her abductor Meliagraunce. Lancelot saves the day by fighting Meliagraunce with one side exposed and one arm strapped behind his back. This is not merely a show of bravado to ridicule the unpopular Meliagraunce, esoterically it is another indication of the mishandled involvement with Guenevere which causes Lancelot to be more vulnerable and less able than he might otherwise be.

In the Quest of the Holy Grail, Lancelot had failed to achieve the Grail for this very same reason. However, the measure of his potential greatness and the power of grace is shown in the episode of the healing of Sir Urre, a Hungarian knight who had wandered with seven wounds for seven years which could only be healed by the best knight in the world. Lancelot, reluctant to regard himself as such, when pressed to lay hands on Sir Urre, prays for the intercession of Divine Grace. As a consequence there is a run through of force from the spiritual levels, the channel having been cleansed and cleared by his faith, dedication and humility; and Sir Urre is miraculously cured.

In a sense this is a vision of the kingdom as it could have been. Lancelot, in humility and under command of the king, bringing through the powers of the achieved Grail to heal the sick and raise the enchantment.

The whole Arthurian story is based upon principles of polarity working which have rarely been understood. The way ahead is for a proper analytical understanding of the causes of failure, and then a realization of what the proper pattern should have been, for that will reveal the redeemed or the perfect archetypes embodied by the characters.

For instance, in his full glory Arthur the king represents the archetype of the Sun and Guenevere the Moon of the racial forces, with Merlin representing the Starry Wisdom behind them. The two Pillars of the racial temple, which correspond to the Goddesses Isis and Nephthys behind the throne of Osiris in Ancient Egyptian symbolism, are the Lady of the Lake and Morgan le Fay.

It is as representative of the Moon forces that Guenevere appears in threefold form in the Arthurian tales, and this is the base of truth behind the confusion over 'false' Gueneveres and so on. She aligns with the moon's phases like the triune Diana.

This is the glorious goal and truth behind the cautionary tales of the legends wherein Arthur failed to pass on the initiation of the

Lady of the Lake to the human maiden Guenevere because of the wiles of Morgan le Fay. Lancelot was able to help Guenevere but could not control the forces of glamour surrounding his personal experiences within this racial function. Through him Guenevere was able to receive the auric contacts that enabled her to function as Queen and bring through the powers of the Goddess. Lancelot also provided, in the revised plan, the home and fatherhood of Galahad who should, under the original plan, have been the child of Guenevere and Arthur. The relationship between Guenevere and Galahad, stemming as it does from the spirit and close spiritual destinies, is a unique and touching one.

The relationship between Merlin and the Lady of the Lake is also not without its demonstration of the perils of misdirected and personally orientated polarity working. There are, as in all legends, overlays of other material, as we have already described in the function of burial of an ancient priest-king. However, at another level, the disappearance of Merlin from the scene of action early on in the story is hardly helpful to the young Arthur and the guidance of the realm. It is the result of his becoming imprisoned in a hawthorn tower by Nimuë, and shows how the powers of a highly contacted white magician can be set at nought if the universal or racial powers that are using his consciousness as a channel are diverted into a personal vortex.

Nimuë's powers are blighted by this same involvement, although this is not explicitly stated in the legends. This would be the natural result of her enmeshing Merlin in toils of his own making through her ambition for power and knowledge that was not properly hers to work. Her natural function was an inner plane guide and teacher through dream and vision. As it turns out, however, she is decapitated at the beginning of the Grail Quest, an event which causes some chronological anomalies as she appears in the tales later, but which is an accurate symbolic rendering of the spiritual condition she has brought upon herself. However, in the end all is in process of redemption for she appears in the barge that fetches Arthur, accompanying the mourning Queens, with whom she coalesces as an expression of the great overall female archetype.

20. Tristram and Iseult and the Hibernian/Cornish Polarity Workings

The lessons of polarity working are also to be found in the circle of the Cornish court of King Mark, particularly in the tale of Tristram and Iseult. In this tale is portrayed, in a more detailed and personal manner, the deep pain that can be caused by the expression of horizontal and vertical polarities without proper control.

The original relationship of Tristram and Iseult, at the court of her father in Ireland, is one of chivalric honour that has no direct modern counterpart. Its closest approximation is that of a god-father, for the knight stands guardian to the maiden, almost *in loco parentis*. He is her champion, and there is much affection between them, but it is not a love match for the maiden will marry another, as long as he meets the approval of her guardian knight. This is clearly delineated in Malory:

> 'Ah gentle knight' said La Belle Iseult, 'full woe have I of thy departing, for I saw never man that ever I owed so good will to' and therewithal she wept heartily.
>
> 'Madam' said Sir Tristram, 'you should understand that my name is Sir Tristram de Lyones, begotten by a king and born of a queen. And I promise you faithfully I shall be all the days of my life your knight'.
>
> 'Gramercy' said La Belle Iseult, 'and I promise you against that that I shall not be married this seven years without your assent, and whom that ye will I shall be married to and he will have me, if he will consent thereto.'
>
> And then Sir Tristram gave her a ring and she gave him another, and therewith he departed.

Nor is there any agony of heart when King Mark of Cornwall sends Tristram as his emissary to bring back Iseult from her father's court to be his queen. There is, though, an interesting parallel with the situation at Camelot where Arthur sent Lancelot as his emissary to claim Guenevere.

The hopeless lover at this stage of the story is Palomides, the Saracen knight, not Tristram. He is a reminder that the cult of passionate love that saw its literary flowering in the lays of the Trouvères and Troubadours in twelfth and thirteenth century Provence had its origin in Islamic mysticism brought back by the Crusaders, or absorbed from Moorish Spain and North Africa.

Palomides is one consumed by unconsummated love. Of all knights he venerates Tristram the highest, which causes him considerable internal conflict because of his envy and jealousy of Tristram's relationship with Iseult. This is exacerbated when Tristram defeats him in a joust and orders him to avoid Iseult's presence for a year. Iseult, for her part, is heartlessly cruel to Palomides, and uses him as a messenger to Guenevere to proclaim the love between herself and Tristram.

However, the passion and conflict undergone by Palomides is shown to have an ennobling power. This would have seemed incredible to the ancient or the oriental world, where it would have been deemed a weakness; besotted lovers being figures of fun. Yet in stories of the Cornish court we see also the abuse or degradation of the noblizing power of romantic love when it is diverted by Palomides or King Mark or even Lamorak into a self-pitying introspection.

Palomides is later found pursuing the Questing Beast. This may best be defined as pursuing the quest for its own sake, not for any true or proper goal. However, in the end he fulfils his self-imposed vow of a sequence of testing battles before, having found honour and self-restraint in the hard school of experience and sustained aspiration, he comes to Arthur's court just prior to the Quest of the Holy Grail and is baptized and admitted to the Fellowship of the Knights of the Round Table.

The passion between Trsitram and Iseult stems from an older tradition than that of much of the Arthurian legend, in that it is a product of the Hibernian Mysteries. The characters of Tristram and Iseult are more of the Green Ray type, that is, they are closer to nature. They might fit more readily into the cycle of Robin Hood and his Merry Men than into that of King Arthur and his Knights. Tristram is a musician, skilled with the harp, and a hunter. It does not seem out of character for him, as it might a more conventional knight, to souse a rival in a well, or to come running naked through the woods to meet his lover. Iseult, too, is very much the Irish princess, beautiful, impetuous, haughty, conscious of her magnetic power of attraction, and also a healer. When the couple escape together it is to the greenwoods that they go for shelter, not to any castle.

The cause of their emotional entanglement is, in the tales received, almost accidental. It is the drinking of a love potion that had been prepared to cement the marriage of Iseult and King Mark. Versions vary in detail, (and Wolfram von Eschenbach's story is probably better told than that of Malory), but generally speaking the potion was prepared by Iseult's mother and was in the safe keeping of her maid Brangwain.

Brangwain, in an esoteric sense, is a very similar character to Brisen and Linet, who are the introducers to the liaison of Lancelot with Elaine of Carbonek, and of Gareth with the Lady Liones. That is, they are priestess initiators of the old Atlantean school. However, in the case of Tristram and Iseult, the magical force breaks bounds, for animal magnetism, or kundalini, call it what one will, like electrical power under high tension will break bounds at any point too weak to contain it. The psychic circuits are heavily overloaded in the case of Tristram and Iseult and the result is an emotional fusing together instead of the pursuit of their proper dedicated roles, she as Queen of Cornwall, and he as her guardian and champion, and equerry and champion of the king—a role very similar to that held by Lancelot at the court of King Arthur.

An interesting story that makes little sense in ordinary terms is that of the wound of Tristram that will not be healed. Iseult cannot be with him to exercise her healing powers but instructs him to go to England and find another Iseult, (Iseult la Blanchmains) who can cure him. He does so, and even marries this other Iseult, although he does not consummate the marriage.

This strange story makes sense only if conceived as a pattern for the cure of the breaking of bounds of the psychic forces that entangle Tristram and Iseult. The esoteric connections are also demonstrated by the fact that Iseult la Blanchmains has a brother, Sir Keyhydyns, and later, when Tristram takes them both back to the court of Cornwall, Sir Keyhydyns falls into a great love for la Belle Iseult. We have a situation therefore of deliberately set up cross polarities. (Figure 25.)

Pattern of Cross-Polarities

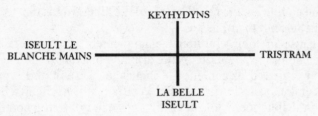

Figure 25

This device could have taken the force that bound together Tristram and La Belle Iseult in a vortex, and directed that of Tristram upon Iseult la Blanchemains and that of La Belle Iseult upon Sir Keyhydyns.

This figure is capable of further extension in that the force could also have been further projected by these means upon inner plane figures, or upon ideals embodied by the contrasexual image. The fact that Iseult la Blanchemains and Keyhydyns are brother and sister indicates that they represent a unified force on a higher plane, of a bi-polar or androgynous nature. Upon this both Tristram and Iseult could focus, thus disentangling themselves from their interlocked lower psychic forces. These dynamics are summarized in Figure 26. The androgynous function is best served by an ideal figure that can be looked up to. (Figure 26.)

However, this remedy is not to be, for La Belle Iseult cannot break free and transfer her projection onto Keyhydyns, although Tristram, thinking that she has, goes, like Lancelot, out of his mind.

The story of Tristram and Iseult then, is one that runs parallel to that of Lancelot and Guenevere, as Iseult well realizes when she sends a message to this effect by Palomides to Guenevere. There is a similar plot to betray each couple, organized by Andret in the court of Cornwall, by Mordred at Camelot. And Morgan le Fay's enchantments are also in the background. She arranges for a horn to be brought to court by Lamorak from which no adulterous woman can drink without spilling the contents. This was intended to trap Guenevere but was diverted to the Court of Cornwall to the subsequent embarrassment of Iseult.

The Androgynous Function

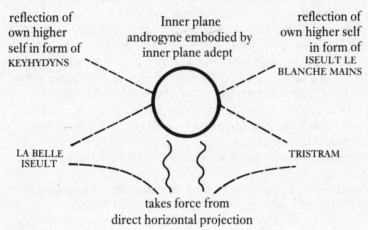

reflection of own higher self in form of KEYHYDYNS

Inner plane androgyne embodied by inner plane adept

reflection of own higher self in form of ISEULT LE BLANCHE MAINS

LA BELLE ISEULT

TRISTRAM

takes force from direct horizontal projection

Figure 26

Morgan le Fay also takes advantage of Tristram's madness by giving him a shield on which is emblazoned a caricature of Arthur, Guenevere and Lancelot. There are interesting technical points of magical symbolism and function here. The horn and shield are both instruments of receptivity (the latter having also the function of a mirror), that are used as a means of revealing truths. The stone that cries under rightful kings is another example. There is here the inner rationale behind systems of divination—all of which are functional forms of receptable for reflection of inner forces to reveal a current condition that may be about to materialize.

The Tristram books in Malory are long and discursive and portray different aspects of love between various knights and ladies. The couples include Alexander le Orphelin and Alice la Belle Pilgrim; Epinogris and his lady; Lamorak and Queen Morgawse; La Cote Mal Taillé and Damsel Beau-Pensante; Palomides and la Belle Iseult; Meliagraunce and Queen Guenevere; and also an important lesson provided by the un-mated Dinadan.

In social and historical terms these stories portray various attitudes to the sexual relationship between men and women during medieval times. These range all the way from viewing woman as a piece of property on a level with horse and armour, to worshipping her from afar as goddess and inspirer to chivalrous action.

The episodes involving Tristram, King Mark and the wife of Sir Segwarides are instructive in this respect. It is over the favours of this lady that King Mark and Tristram quarrel in the first place, for Tristram enjoys them and King Mark does not. She is one day abducted by Sir Bleoberis but Tristram makes no move to rescue her. This, he states, is the duty of her lord and husband Segwarides. Only after Segwarides is overthrown does Tristram go to the rescue. However, he and Bleoberis, the abductor, take a liking to each other and, having fought to an honourable draw, decide to allow the lady to choose which of them she will belong to. They are somewhat disconcerted when she demands to be returned to her husband.

Similarly, the role of woman as mere chattel is shown in the barbaric and bizarre beauty contest held when Tristram and Iseult meet Sir Breunor and his lady. Each lady is turned about three times by her knight, who holds a naked sword, and the one deemed less fair is to have her head struck off.

Of the others of the Cornish court, Meliagraunce is an abductor of Queen Guenevere. In pursuit of his desires he is ready to overthrow all codes of civilization and custom. Behind this story is also the nature cycle of the Persephone/Pluto mythology.

Alexander and Alice portray an idyllic pattern of love in the face of severe odds; and La Cote Male Taillé's story parallels that of Sir Gareth of Orkney. His lady, Maldisant, does nothing but scold and deride him, although in this case it is in order to try to protect him from danger. In the end she is re-named, because of this, Beau-pensante, and they marry.

Epinogris is one who has loved and lost in that he is overthrown in arms and parted from the lady he loves. He enters into some debate with Palomides as to which of them is the more unfortunate: Epinogris who has loved and lost, or Palomides whose passion for Queen Iseult has never been requited. In the end Palomides restores the lady to Epinogres by force of arms.

The relationship between Lamorak and Queen Morgawse is a straightforward lust of the desires of the flesh but as it breaks the bounds of the marriage-tie of the Orkney royal family as well as ignoring an inter-clan feud, it costs him his life at the hands of Gawain and his brothers.

Gawain also plays his part in defining these patterns, although his stories are not part of the Tristram cycle. Most of his story we have covered in considering the Round Table knights, but of particular relevance here is the story of Gawain, Uwain and Marhaus.

This develops from another incident involving Morgan le Fay, who has sent a jewelled cloak to Arthur, apparently as a peace offering. However, the Lady of the Lake reveals it to be a fiery trap for any who are so unfortunate as to put it on. In great anger Arthur banishes Morgan's son Uwain from his court. Gawain, feeling that Uwain has been unjustly treated, accompanies him.

On their travels they come upon twelve damsels spitting on a white shield which they say belongs to a knight who hates all women. This turns out to be Marhaus, whom they fight, but after an inconclusive battle, it is revealed that the twelve damsels are in fact sorceresses falsely maligning Marhaus. The three proceed together to a strange country where they find a fountain with three ladies sitting by it. The ladies are of different ages; one is fifteen, one is thirty and one is sixty. They are bidden each to choose a lady and follow the adventure that results for the space of a year and a day.

The three damsels portray three forms of the feminine principle. The young Uwain goes with the eldest lady and is led to perform chivalrous deeds in rescuing a lady from transgressors and restoring her to her lands. Marhaus, with the mature woman of thirty, is also led to great deeds, proving himself in a tournament, and destroying a giant who has many knights and ladies captive. Gawain, with the young damsel, meets the unfortunate Pellas, (son of the Grail King, Pellam) who is dying for love of a haughty lady who will have nothing to do with him. Gawain behaves seemingly shamefully. He offers to intercede on Pellas' behalf, but when he sees the lady, he feels attracted to her himself, and ingratiates himself to her by saying that he has killed Pellas. He then seduces her. Pellas discovers this treachery but, although tempted to kill them both as they sleep, leaves his drawn sword between them as token that he has discovered them and controlled his passion.

Behind this seemingly callous and cynical behaviour of Gawain there is an initiatory level of higher motives. Gawain demonstrates that fantasies of hatred held by the lady can be diverted into love, on the rebound from believing that they have been fulfilled. That is, that love and hate are like two sides of the same coin. Each is a movement or potential of the emotions, which are not really opposite; the real opposite to either is indifference. However, beyond this demonstration is the provision of an initiatory test for the love-sick Pellas of transmuting his own passion into reconciliation through realization of a higher principle, rather than giving physical expression to disappointment and hatred.

The end of this story is provided by the Lady of the Lake, who causes the proud lady to fall in love with Pellas as uncontrollably as he previously had been with her. As a result she dies from unrequited love.

The Lady of the Lake takes Pellas unto herself into a permanent loving relationship, and Pellas becomes, rather as Arthur had inadvertantly become, one whose feminine ideal and fulfilment is on a higher plane than the physical.

Finally, the figure of Dinadan, the humorous, joking knight, who has no lady love, demonstrates that laughter is an antidote to the toils of uncontrolled emotional entanglement. It is the soul's method of disengagement.

However, adventures of the soul and of the emotions need to be gone into and experienced in order to gain the fruits of life and experience. Thus although Dinadan, through flippancy or cynicism, may find an easy way through the entanglements suffered by the lovers around him, he is a poor and barely competent knight, despite his likeability and charm. It is the spur of the ideal, portrayed by the feminine image, that is needed to make the knight into a man.

PART FOUR: THE GREATER MYSTERIES AND THE HOLY GRAIL

21. The Dolorous Stroke and the Mystery of the Two Swords

The Holy Grail and its Quest represent the Greater Mysteries of the Secret Tradition within the Arthurian Cycle, just as the tales of the adventures of the Knights of the Round Table, of the magical enchantments of Merlin and the faery women, and the polar relationships of the Knights and Ladies of the Court represent the three grades of the Lesser Mysteries.

The Lesser Mysteries lead up to an integration of Higher Self and Lower Self, or, in other words, represent the equilibration and controlling of the forces of the Elemental Kingdoms. The Greater Mysteries aim to bring through the uncreate powers of the spirit and to undertake the work of destiny upon the basis of the successfully achieved Lesser Mysteries.

The Mysteries of the Grail run deep into the roots of the Arthurian legends. They are present in the early tales of Bran, and Keridwen, and their mighty cauldron of regeneration and inspiration. From these primeval beginnings they run in unbroken line to the greatest spiritual heights that the inner eye of man can discern. These have lessons for men of today and of the future, for they set patterns that are the standards and goals of a whole planetary evolution of consciousness.

It is because of this unique run through from the depths to the heights, from beginnings to endings, from elemental to spiritual, that the Arthurian legends are of unique importance. No other system has this complete range in such detail and ramification.

The seeds of the Grail Quest are sown very early in Malory's books, in the story of Balin and Balan and the striking of the Dolorous Stroke; and there is much in this tale that is often overlooked.

This part of the story comes from what is known by scholars as post-Vulgate romance, namely works that, according to present evidence, appeared after the Vulgate cycle. The Vulgate cycle is the great mass of popular material, probably written between 1215 and 1230, that Malory used as his principal sources. In the Vulgate cycle Galahad is the principal Grail winner, and Malory's version is a very close translation of it.

Earlier Grail stories had Percivale as Grail winner. These include the first known written version, that of the courtly Chrétien de Troies, (c.1180) and also the more mystical sequence commenced by Robert de Boron (c.1200). Chrétien did not live to complete his tale and it received no less than four 'continuators' between 1200 and 1230. The first of these placed the emphasis upon Gawain; the others reverted to Percivale as the central character.

Robert de Boron pitched his tale in New Testament times with a romance called *Joseph of Arimathea*, which was followed by *Merlin*. The trilogy was completed by an unknown hand—not that much is known of Robert de Boron himself. The completion is known as the *Didot Perceval*, so-called from the library in which it was found, and it is dated by scholars somewhere between 1200 and 1230.

At around 1210 two other Percivale romances were written. One was *Perlesvaux*, which appears to stem from the monks of Glastonbury Abbey and has been translated by Sebastian Evans as *The High History of the Holy Grail*. The other is the German *Parzival* by Wolfram von Eschenbach, which has, understandably, a considerable following upon the Continent, together with its sequel *Lohengrin*, and was the version used by the composer Richard Wagner for his opera cycle.

We shall follow Malory, and the Vulgate *Queste del Saint Graal* as the main core of the story, paying due attention to the other versions as off shoots from this. We are, of course, dealing with a cord of many strands, intertwined into one great story. The story has different versions reflecting the myriad aspects and emphases that can be placed on very deep and ancient material. To make the most of this material one must consider each version to try to glean the lessons that are to be learned from its particular emphasis. There is no 'one and only true' story that relates all the truths to be found in this complex of Mystery teaching. One also has to be able to cope with anachronisms and even direct contradictions in the material received and recorded. And, as with the rest of the Arthuriad, due allowance has to be made for changes in material at the hands of the scribes who recorded it. Their own attitudes and assumptions may obscure or heighten the lights in the oral material, for at root all of the Matter of Britain is far more ancient than the texts as we have them.

The writers themselves, almost without exception, refer to ancient secret books as their sources. As none of these have been found modern scholars tend to deny their existence, but those of some esoteric experience will not be so ready to dismiss them. Many ancient works have failed to survive the ages. Even those known to have had many manuscript versions have sometimes survived only in single copies or a small handful. How likely is it, therefore, that a secret text of a corpus of Mystery teaching would survive? Particularly if they are records of communications received by occult means from psychic sources. There is no call to assume that such communications started with nineteenth-century spiritualism. As a part of the natural order of life they have always been with us, albeit received and passed on guardedly when 'commerce with spirits' would have attracted severe penalties. To the trained esoteric sense much of the Arthurian and Grail material comes from such sources.

There is a clear distinction between the strands of the Grail Quest legend that surrounds Galahad and that which surrounds Percivale. Galahad represents the natural sequence of the ancient Atlantean dynastic pattern conceived by Merlin, his masters and the faery women. Percivale is a more universal figure who represents the human race as a whole; he is a twelfth-century version of the Fool of the Tarot. Their stories, in the Vulgate cycle particularly, have been merged into one.

In another sense they represent two attitudes to spiritual realities—the one achieving by works (Percivale) and the other achieving by faith (Galahad), although this is a comparatively modern gloss. Equally important to the understanding of the story is the other Grail winner Bors, and also the stories of those who failed, particularly Lancelot, Gawain, and Ector de Maris.

Bors is particularly important as he not only achieved the Quest of the Grail but returned to tell the tale and to continue life at the Round Table and after. In this respect, in spite of the traditional emphasis given to Galahad and to Percivale, his achievement might well be held to have been the greater. However, he would have outshone the others in this way only if he had been able to bring the Grail back with him.

The story of the Grail Quest, as of the Round Table, is one of eventual failure, for just as the Round Table disintegrated into civil war and dissension, so was the Grail never brought to Logres. The enchantment still rests upon the land and the reformulation, in Earth, of the Round Table Fellowship around the manifest Holy Grail, awaits the champions of another generation. Thus the legend has significance for the present and future as well as the past.

The beginnings of the Grail story, as far as the court of Arthur is concerned, commence with the story of Balin and Balan. These two brothers in the end, despite the highest of motives, slay each other; and it is Balin who delivers the Dolorous Stroke that lays the land under enchantment.

There are anachronistic problems here, for the event is the equivalent in Arthurian legendary terms of the fall of Adam and Eve from Paradise. As we approach these Greater Mysteries however, time ceases to have the linear significance that we tend habitually to put upon it. These cosmic events extend through and outside time and the story of Balin and the Dolorous Stroke expresses universals in terms that are related to Arthurian symbolism.

It should be no surprise to learn that Balin is also called the Knight of the Two Swords. That is, he is one of split or divided spiritual will. In this sense the story of Balin is a terrible and pitiful one, and he is, like Percivale, a cosmic representation of the human condition. The difference between the two is that Percivale is the pagan innocent, the natural man who, without the Fall, would have wandered around the cycle of incarnation, blundering at first, but achieving spiritual maturity through natural experience in the created universe. Balin is the pattern of man as agent of a cosmic disaster. His story therefore, in a sense, vitiates that of Percivale, who represents how things would and could have been without the Fall.

After Balin's cosmic disaster the need arises for a spotless Grail winner, a mediating Saviour, which is exemplified in Galahad.

The efforts of all men, that is the heroes such as Bors, Lancelot, Gawain and Ector, is to try to measure up to this standard, which might well be considered an impossible task without the assistance of Divine Grace. This is another aspect of the Holy Grail, for it is an aid as well as a standard that is to be achieved. It brings sustenance and healing to the sinful as well as to the worthy—and has always been available in some form or other, adapted at each stage to the limitations of consciousness of man. Thus to the tribal Celts it was a magical regenerating, bountiful, inspirational cauldron long before it became one of the implements of Christ's passion to mediaeval man. Its role throughout the ages of man's dawning self-consciousness remains the same. It is the presence of the divine Uncreate Reality revealed to a struggling humanity finding its way back to its spiritual home.

With these wider factors in mind, let us return to the beginnings of the Arthurian story. The scene is set in the early days of Arthur's reign when the dissenting barons have been quelled and he is established on the throne. In all beginnings there is a testing point when evil tries to gain sway. This is a universal law, perhaps a reflection of the original Fall. In the case of Arthur's rule it manifests in the evil, marauding King Rience who has invaded a far part of the realm and killed a number of Arthur's subjects.

A general council is called to discuss how best to quell this danger and it is, significantly, at this point that a damsel, richly dressed, arrives at the court, declaring that she has been sent by the Lady Lyle of Avilon. This name, which derives from the Isle of Avalon betokens an emissary from the astral plane—the great world of the inner Isis which shares the good and evil of the physical kingdom.

She reveals a huge sword beneath her cloak, firmly fixed in its scabbard, which, she says, she is forced to wear until she finds a knight able to remove the sword from its scabbard. This can only be done by one who is quite free from felony or treason.

Arthur and all the assembled knights attempt to draw this sword but all fail until finally a poor and impoverished knight in rags and tatters, who has been recently imprisoned in the dungeons on suspicion of murder, steps forward and asks to make the attempt. In spite of his unlikely appearance, to the amazement of all he successfully draws the sword. This hitherto obscure and maligned knight is Balin.

In his general appearance and attitude he has similarities with the uncouth young Percivale.

The test of withdrawing the sword is by no means the normal test of worth such as that which proved Arthur to be true king when he drew the forerunner of Excalibur from the stone. This particular sword has a curse upon it. This is that its winner shall slay the best friend that he has, and that the sword will also be the agent of his own destruction.

This sinister background is further revealed by the arrival of the Lady of the Lake as Balin is about to leave the court. Immediately the esoteric significance of the sword is re-emphasized for she announces that she is come to claim the boon that is her due for giving Arthur Excalibur.

To the astonishment of all, the prize she claims is a severed head; either that of Balin or that of the damsel who brought the sword to court. Arthur tries to persuade her to ask for something more acceptable but suddenly Balin steps forward, accuses her of murdering his mother, and strikes off *her* head.

There are plainly deep mysteries at work behind this bizarre story. The severed head is a symbol connected with the Holy Grail as far back as the severed head of Bran the Blessed, the winner of the ancient cauldron of regeneration and inspiration. His severed head entertained his companions on an island, (traditionally Grassholm), in their seven year mission to take it to bury it under the White Mount, upon which the Tower of London now stands. This symbolism has a later parallel in connection with the Grail when it is held by some to be the dish that held the blood and the severed head of John the Baptist, the forerunner of the Christ.

There is considerable esoteric import to be read into Salome's dance as a means to obtain the head of John the Baptist, and in our considerations of the significance of the Grail we shall have much occasion to deal with this strange mix of ancient pagan beginnings and peripheral and apocryphal appendages to the Gospel record. They have the aura of alchemical symbols or surrealist paintings, pregnant with some kind of undisclosed meaning that disturbs and defies the logical structure of the concrete mind.

Merlin then tells the symbolic story behind the incident of the damsel with the cursed sword. It revolves around the fact that the weapon is the focus for motives of revenge. The damsel, who is described by Merlin as 'the falsest that liveth' had a brother, 'a passing good knight of prowess and a full true man' who slew a knight who was, at the time, her lover. Consequently the damsel took her lover's sword to the Lady of the Isle of Avalon in order to use it as a means of revenge.

There is sorcery of a very deep and terrible kind involved here. The Lady of the Isle of Avalon is, like that of the Lady of the Lake, a generic title for the powers and beings of the astral plane, and plainly this is an approach to these inner powers with a view to diverting the discarnate will and inner forces, (symbolized by the sword), of her slain lover into a means of retribution and attack upon her brother.

The Lady of the Isle of Avalon, or Lady of the Lake, responds in the obscure and ambivalent way that inner plane powers traditionally express themselves when sought for purposes of personal malice or gain. An answer is given, or the request granted, but in such a way that the recipient is none the better off. In this way do the inner powers neutralize attempts to abuse them or to disturb their natural balance.

In the story the Lady of the Lake seals the sword in its scabbard and decrees that no-one shall be able to draw it unless he be 'one of the best knights of the realm' and 'hardy and full of prowess' but that if it is in fact drawn it will slay that knight's brother.

This is a natural piece of inner plane cauterization or sealing of the door where evil dwells. Only one of very considerable worth will be able to release these forces. The evil will of the sword cannot be destroyed by the powers of the astral forces, but at least they can only be released by one who will stand a reasonable chance of being able to cope with them.

The kind of forces of misrule embodied by this sword are to be discerned by the complexities and misunderstandings that arise when Balin draws it. The Lady of the Lake is immediately conjured to presence by these activities, which are a parody of her own custodianship of the good sword Excalibur. She identifies the damsel with the sword as the slayer of her (the Lady of the Lake's) father. In this we may discern not so much an actual physical murder but its inner equivalent. The Lady of the Lake is an astral being and the murder of her father represents, in the context of sorceress, almost certainly the illicit use and binding of Elemental forces.

The Lady of the Lake, with her inner sight that traverses time and hidden spiritual conditions, also identifies Balin as the murderer of her brother. In this we should understand Balin's role as striker of the Dolorous Stroke, which not only has dire human consequences but brings death, destruction and suffering to other orders of creation too.

The vile subtle power now in Balin's hands clouds his judgment. As with Percivale, the other representative of all humanity, Balin has difficulties in the relationship with his mother. In the case of Percivale, the innocent pilgrim soul, it is a matter of neglect. He comes forth into manifestation completely forgetting his origins in the womb of the Cosmic Mother. In his case, the unfallen innocent, it is depicted as a matter simple neglect. To Balin, who is enmeshed not only in matter but in the toils of sin, this fault is denied and is projected forth as anyone else's fault but his own. Thus he blames the Lady of the Lake, the inner plane being, for the 'loss' of his mother.

Cutting off her head is a bizarre way of righting the imagined wrong but, as so often in these matters, it is a distorted reflection of an inner truth. An aspect of the Holy Grail is a severed head; a concept perhaps most easily understood by Qabalists as the directing Crown of Creation, and the 'head centres' of the Supernal Sephiroth, divorced from the rest of creation below Daath. In other words, we are currently inhabitants of a 'headless' universe. That is, the spiritual will of God is ignored by the deviant wills of the creatures of the body of creation.

King Arthur banishes Balin from the court. His murderous attack on the Lady of the Lake is a dire infringement of the principles of the king's hospitality and protection, which are basic to ordered society. Balin leaves, resolving to reinstate himself in the king's favour by seeking out King Rience, and thus drive evil from the land.

After he has left the court, a further twist to the significance of these events is put in train by the desire of Sir Lanceor to follow after Balin and exact the king's retribution upon him. Arthur gives permission for this and Lanceor hotly pursues Balin.

Balin is hereafter known as the Knight of the Two Swords, which is an inner condition as pathological as being Siamese twins, for no man can have more than one spiritual will, more than one system of inner vital forces. At the same time this mirrors, in a general cosmic sense, the condition of mankind. There is for each human being the original will of God, which is sometimes referred to as destiny, or *dharma*, the pattern held for him by each human being's Holy Guardian Angel. The other is each fallen human's own deviant personal will, which is the agent of his misfortunes and problems, or *karma*. However well intentioned the individual human being may be in his formulation and attempted implementation of the plans of his own will, they will be in conflict with the individual plans of others. Unbeknown to himself, mankind's dual spiritual nature has become the agent of conflicting spiritual forces that will work their way out in accordance with laws far beyond his own comprehension or visionary scope.

This works out in many strange ways in the case of Balin,

accompanied by awesome prophecies given by Merlin or by other means. The first of these is the confrontation with the pursuing Lanceor. Balin slays him in combat but Colombe, Lanceor's lady, has followed her lord, and is so distressed by her lover's death that she takes up Lanceor's sword and kills herself in front of Balin.

Lanceor is a knight of Ireland, in fact he is the King of Ireland's son, and is therefore a representative of the Hibernian Mysteries. These, as we have seen in the cycle surrounding Tristram and Iseult is very much concerned with horizontal polarity and the projection of the contrasexual image. It is not inappropriate therefore to find King Mark of Cornwall now appearing, apparently coincidentally. He erects a rich tomb upon which is inscribed 'Here lieth Lanceor, the king's son of Ireland, that at his own request was slain by the hands of Balin', and 'this lady Colombe and paramour to him slew herself with his sword for dole and sorrow.'

Then Merlin appears and announces that this tomb will be the site of 'the greatest battle between two knights that ever was or shall be, and the truest lovers; and yet neither of them shall slay the other.' He then inscribes the names of these two knights upon the tomb in letters of gold; they are Lancelot and Tristram.

Merlin upbraids Balin for standing idly by and allowing Colombe to kill herself. It is to no avail that Balin protests that it all happened too quickly and unexpectedly. Merlin prophecies that it is because of this suicide, that Balin allowed to happen, that he will be the one who strikes the Dolorous Stroke.

> Because of the death of that lady thou shalt strike a stroke the most dolorous that ever man stroke, except the stroke of our Lord Jesu Christ. For thou shalt hurt the truest knight and the man of most worship that now liveth; and through that stroke three kingdoms shall be brought into great poverty, misery and wretchedness twelve years. And the knight shall not be whole of that wound many years.

Merlin then vanishes. Balin's brother Balan also arrives after the death of the Lady Colombe, from a place known as the Castle of the Four Stones. This place appears nowhere else in the Arthuriad but would seem to be a symbolic state of balanced poise, after the fashion of a magic circle or mandala. This is commensurate with the fact that Balan can esoterically be interpreted as representing the Higher Self of Balin.

It is Balan who announces Balin's new cognomen as the Knight with the Two Swords to the enquiring King Mark. Balin and Balan then pursue their journey in search of the evil King Rience (or Royns) in which they are assisted by Merlin. With his help they overcome Rience and send him in submission to Arthur's court, where Merlin tells their story and gives them full credit for the deed.

There remains however a more sinister figure behind King Rience of North Waalis, and that is King Nero, who has, with a great host, arrived before the Castle Terrable. Arthur enters battle with him and is assisted by valorous and wondrous deeds by Balin and Balan. King Nero is vanquished, partly through the help of Merlin's craft and strategy, and also because he did not have, on this occasion, the aid of his ally King Lot of Orkney and Lothian. King Lot and his host come forth to do battle as soon as they receive news of King Nero's defeat but they too are defeated. This is the occasion when Lot is killed by King Pellinore, a fact which later brings revenge from Gawain and his brothers, who are the sons of King Lot and Morgawse.

There is a symbolic element to this great double battle. Nero, apart from being a memory of Roman imperial might, is at root a figure of cosmic evil, who works through primeval barbarous agencies such as King Rience and King Lot. Lot's enmity to Arthur was largely caused by the early machinations of Morgan which led to Lot's belief that Arthur had lain with his wife Morgawse.

It is recorded that twelve kings were slain by Arthur's forces. Merlin by 'his subtle craft' fashioned a complex of tombs each with an effigy of a slain king holding a perpetual light. Above these he fashioned an image of Arthur with drawn sword in token of being vanquisher of them. This is symbolic confirmation of Arthur in the role of solar hero, in the tradition of Hercules, having overcome the powers of the twelve constellations of the zodiac. The rest of the slain are buried in a great rock at Camelot. The tomb of the twelve kings is also said to be at Camelot, in the church of St Stephen.

This is also the occasion when Merlin pronounces mighty prophecies about the future of the kingdom, and in particular cautions Arthur about the safekeeping of the scabbard of Excalibur. These revelations apparently cause a sickness to fall upon Arthur, who may have realized that he has already failed in this respect. As he lies stricken in a pavilion a grieving knight goes by. Arthur despatches Balin to discover the cause of this distress.

This is the commencement of the action that leads directly towards the striking of the Dolorous Stroke.

As Balin returns to Arthur with the grieving knight the latter is suddenly struck down by Garlon, an evil knight who has the power of invisibility. The dying knight charges Balin to take up his quest with the damsel whom he has been accompanying, and also to avenge his death should opportunity arise.

Balin and the lady meet another knight shortly afterwards but he too is struck down treacherously by the invisible Garlon. They are, although they know it not, in the lands around the Grail Castle, for, as later occurs with the sister of Percivale, they come to a castle where maidens are required to give of their blood in an attempt to cure a lady who is sick. The damsel with Balin is, however, not pure enough for her blood to effect a cure, and so, after resting, they are allowed to pass on. Later Percivale's sister dies at this place, for her blood is of sufficent worth to effect a cure, although only at the cost of her death. There are, in this event, deep matters of the feminine side of the Grail Mysteries, for by her royal and holy blood Percivale's sister is, in effect, a feminine saviour.

Shortly afterwards, at a castle, Balin finds another who has been grievously used by Garlon. A knight had bested Garlon twice at a jousting and, in revenge, Garlon, using his cloak of invisibility, seriously injures the knight's son. It is said that only some of Garlon's blood can cure him. Again, in these realms around the Grail Castle, we have emphasis on the significance and healing power of blood. Blood, in esoteric terms, is indeed regarded as the bearer of the spirit.

Balin learns that Garlon is the brother of King Pellam of the Grail Castle. Accompanied by the knight with the wounded son and the lady whose champion was slain by Garlon, Balin makes for the Grail Castle to seek revenge. A tourney is being held at the castle and Garlon is pointed out to Balin. He is black faced, which, in the symbolic conventions of the times, indicates that he is of the devil. The fact that he is brother of the good King Pellam shows a strand of Persian Manichean dualism in this story.

Garlon takes offence at Balin gazing at him and strikes him across the face. This may well be regarded as a deliberate act of provocation, for the powers of evil well know the weaknesses of all men and use them as a means to evil and misrule. Balin, with the same impetuosity that disgraced him at Arthur's court, slays Garlon at the banqueting table. At very least this is a serious breach of the principles of hospitality and the king's peace. It is also a grave cosmic blasphemy for the banqueting table, or feast, is a deeply religious symbol for the harmony of heaven. It is not for nothing that the central sacrament of the Christian church takes the form of an enactment of the Last Supper. The Grail, too, brings food and drink to all it serves. Thus this action of Balin's, whatever its motives or provocation, is counter to, and in disregard of, all the principles of heavenly or earthly civilization. In short, the ends do not justify the means, and good cannot be engendered by acts of barbarism.

Consequently all hands are turned against Balin. Pellam, the Grail King, takes upon himself Balin's retribution, whose treasonable deed against civilized values and murder of the king's brother is punishable by death. It is significant, in view of his being called the Knight with Two Swords that Balin's sword breaks in his hand at the first blow from the righteous wrath of Pellam.

Balin flees through the castle, seeking a substitute weapon, and finally comes upon a holy chapel where, above the altar, there is a great spear. Notwithstanding its obvious sacramental nature Balin seizes it and strikes Pellam. Immediately the whole castle crashes to the ground, killing most of those present, and Pellam and Balin are struck down prostrate for the space of three days.

Finally Merlin arrives and sends Balin upon his way. As for the King of the Grail Castle, the text of Malory has it that:

> King Pellam lay so many years sore wounded, and might never be whole til Galahad the High Prince healed him in the Quest of the Sangraal. For in that place was part of the blood of Our Lord Jesu Christ, which Joseph of Arimathea brought into this land. And there himself lay in that rich bed. And that was the spear which Longinus smote Our Lord with to the heart. And King Pellam was nigh of Joseph's kin, and was the most worshipful man alive in those days, and great was the pity of his hurt, for through that stroke came great dole, pain and sorrow.

Balin's wanderings take him through wasted lands with people slain on every side and those surviving crying out against him 'Ah Balin, thou hast done and caused great vengeance in these lands. Because of the dolorous stroke and thou gave unto King Pellam these three countries are destroyed. And doubt not that vengeance will fall upon thee at the last.'

The wasting of three countries means inner plane devastation as well as dire results upon the physical world. This is expressed in Qabalistic terms by the dragon with seven heads which rises up unto Daath, that is, to just below the head centres; and the surviving head is another form of Grail symbol.

Balin's capacity for sowing discord and tragedy continues. He meets a knight who has lost his lady. Balin finds her for him but she lies in the arms of another most foul and evil looking knight. Balin seeks to help the knight to overcome his feelings of unrequited love by confronting him with the falsity of his lady. However, when Balin takes him to where the couple are, the knight slays them in a paroxysm of rage and grief and then takes his own life.

Balin goes on from this disaster conscious of a sort of malign fate overshadowing him, for he deliberately passes a sign on a cross that states that no knight should ride past it alone to the castle beyond. This is yet one more aspect of the situation of the Two Swords. It emphasizes that no man achieves by his own merit alone. In a world founded on love, the isolated self-sufficent one is one who is lost. Self-will, however well intentioned, is no substitute for God's will and compassion, which transcends personal glory and self-interest.

An old man repeats the warning and vanishes away, after which Balin hears a horn blow and realizes it to be the call of his own fate. 'That blast', says Balin, 'is blown for me, for I am the prize, and yet I am not dead.'

He comes to a castle where he is welcomed and they tell him that the custom is that he joust with a knight who keeps a nearby island. He is also offered a shield that is larger than his own, which he accepts. A damsel close by laments this fact, for by changing his shield he loses his identity. From this, which is akin to losing one's own true sword, she sees that there can only come great sorrow. Indeed, this comes because the knight of the island is Balin's brother Balan. The brothers fight without recognizing each other and in the battle each is wounded fatally.

At the burial of Balin and Balan, Merlin appears and performs four symbolic actions. He makes a strange bed in which no man can lie without going out of his mind. He puts another pommel onto the ill-fated sword of Balin. Upon it are prophecies that it can be handled only by Lancelot or Galahad; and that Lancelot will kill his best friend with it. The sword is then placed in a stone until the time that Galahad shall draw it. He makes a strong but perilously narrow bridge to the island; one which only a worthy man, 'without treachery or vaillainy' may safely cross. And he places the scabbard of Balin's sword where Galahad will find it.

Interpreting these actions, we have seen how the sword that the evil maiden brought to Arthur's court represents the deviant spiritual will, conceived as it was in a spirit of revenge by methods of dark sorcery. It can only be redeemed by being taken up by the utmost pure and exemplary knight, the Grail winner Galahad. In lesser hands, even one so noble as Lancelot, it will bring brotherly discord and tragedy. In fact when in Lancelot's hands it kills Gawain, and it is the conflict between these two that leads to the destruction of the Round Table Fellowship. The sword is the Arthurian counterpart of 'original sin'. It can only be put to rights by one entirely without taint of it—by the absolutely pure willed, whose will is at one with God.

The result of Balin's dual spiritual motivation leads to the ill-fated progress in which all he touches turns to tragedy. Of all his acts, the Dolorous Stroke at the Grail Castle is the most dire in that hallowed objects are used by Balin for his personal defence; that is, the spiritual principle is subserviant to the immediately expedient. Inevitably this leads to the confrontation between Balin and Balan, that is, between the Higher and Lower Self. There is, in the current condition of human consciousness a divorce between Personality awareness and that of the Higher Self. In Arthurian terms this will be resolved by the Achievement of the Quest of the Grail. In the meantime the narrow bridge that Merlin constructs to the island of the higher consciousness is a temporary expedient whereby meditation and contemplation by those of sufficient vocation can make the connection.

The test of the strange bed is concerned with the laying to rest of old primeval sins and errors, a harrowing of hell, a confronting of the Dweller on the Threshold, the dark shadow of the repressed elements of what is nowadays called the subconscious mind but which also contains unresolved and unbalanced racial and personal memories and traumatic experiences. But for the event of Christ 'descending into Hell' after the Crucifixion, none would be able to withstand the undertow of these mighty currents from the underworld. This is one aspect of the redemptive sacrifice of the Incarnation that is little understood.

22. Joseph of Arimathea and the Order of Grail Knights

Before we follow the adventures of the Arthurian knights upon the Grail Quest it will be helpful to trace back the antecedents of King Pellam and the Grail Castle.

These go back to New Testament times and to the figure of Joseph of Arimathea, who is mentioned in all four gospels as one who obtained permission to take custody of the body of Jesus, (the *corpus Christi*), and to bury it. For this purpose he used his own tomb, a cave with a large rock over the entrance.

Joseph of Arimathea is largely overlooked, or taken for granted, in most Christian considerations of the events of the Passion. However, his actions are crucial to the full story of the Resurrection, of the removal of the stone, the folding of the grave clothes, the overcoming by sleep of the guards, the appearance of the angel to the women in the garden, the disappearance of the body. None of this, it might be argued, is crucial; Jesus could still have risen from the dead had his body been left hanging on the cross or cast into a communal grave according to the Roman custom. But the events as recorded give a setting and dignity to the central fact of Christian belief. Joseph of Arimathea therefore might almost be regarded as the architect of the Resurrection. He provided the physical setting for it—even if the power and the glory came from God. He is therefore a very important figure in the Christian story.

In the Gospel of John a certain Nicodemus is also mentioned as the companion of Joseph of Arimathea at the deposition of Jesus from the Cross. 'He was joined by Nicodemus (the man who had visited Jesus by night), who brought with him a mixture of myrrh and aloes, more than half a hundredweight.'

By the fourth century Nicodemus has become an important Apocryphal figure, and there is indeed a Gospel of Nicodemus, alternatively called the Acts of Pilate. In this early Christian document Nicodemus is portrayed defending Jesus at the trial before Pilate. One of the charges the Jews bring in their general indictment is that Jesus is born of fornication. This, however, is denied by a body of twelve Jews, who swear that they were present at the espousals of Joseph and Mary.

Those who were healed by Jesus also testify, one that was crippled, one that was blind, one that was crook-backed, and one that was a leper. They are followed by the woman who was healed of an issue of blood by touching the hem of his garment. This encourages a multitude of others to bear witness to Jesus' good and miraculous works, including the raising of Lazarus from the dead.

After the crucifixion, in revenge, the Jewish authorities seek out those who had defended Jesus before Pilate. All go into hiding except Nicodemus, who is described as a ruler of the Jews. He goes forth to meet his persecutors, accompanied by Joseph of Arimathea.

Joseph is seized and locked up over the sacred Passover period to await execution. There is no window in his prison tower and the door is sealed and guarded. However, when his captors come for him they find that he has gone. As they wonder at this disappearance news comes of the similar disappearance of the body of Jesus from the tomb. At this they are afraid, but bribe the soldiers to say that disciples stole the body of Jesus in the night.

However, later reports tell of Jesus having been seen, with his disciples, on a mount in Galilee, from whence he finally ascends into heaven. On the assumption that Jesus may have been lifted up by a spirit and cast down upon another mountain they go in search of him. Although they find no trace of Jesus they do discover Joseph of Arimathea safely at his home.

None dare lay hands on him and they ask him how he escaped from the tower. A delegation of seven men is sent from Jerusalem to request Joseph to come and testify to these occurrences. Joseph therefore returns to Jerusalem, where he stays at the house of Nicodemus.

The next day, under sacred oath, he tells how, as he had prayed within his prison, at midnight, the place seemed to be taken up by the four corners, and a great flashing light appeared before him. He was bathed in a shower of water, and annointed, and then tenderly greeted by Jesus, whom at first he did not recognize. Jesus then proved his identity by showing Joseph the place of Resurrection, which was of course Joseph's own tomb. Joseph then found himself transported to his home, and laid upon his bed, despite the doors being shut for the night. Jesus, as he departs, tells Joseph not to leave his house for forty days, during which period Jesus goes to his disciples in Galilee.

This news spreads consternation among the Jewish priestly authorities as they realize that they may well have been in the wrong. Accordingly, they send for the three witnesses who have reported seeing Jesus teaching upon the mount prior to his Ascension. These three are rabbis and they confirm that they had seen Jesus on Mount Mamilch teaching his eleven disciples, and that they themselves had also seen Jesus carried up to heaven.

With the realization on the part of the Jews that Jesus must be a holy one such as Enoch or Moses, the first part of the Gospel of Nicodemus ends. In the second part the three rabbis tell how, on the way from Galilee, they had met two dead men, risen from their graves, who told them about Jesus' descent into Hades. At Jesus' approach this dark abode of the dead had been lit as by a great light and its doors were flung open so that all those captive were released. At the same time Satan, its prince, had been cast into its toils himself.

Hell is seen in this account as being fearsome but righteous in the sense that it only punishes those who transgress through sin. It has no power over those without sin. However, because of the fall of mankind Satan had been able greatly to extend his kingdom.

When Jesus became man, although he was without sin, he had been falsely accused and crucified through the wiles of Satan. Satan thus had overstepped his mark. The unfallen, sinless nature of Jesus the God-man, releases all sinners from Satan's clutches and Satan himself alone remains in the confines of Hell. This has for long been his mighty empire but now is his cell of solitary confinement. All his legions are routed; and it would appear to follow from this that all demons are but 'creations of the created', born of human sin and not of God. Therefore upon the redemption from sin of mankind all the legions of hell, whose sustenance and mode of being comes only from sin, must, by that fact, be destroyed.

In various appendices to the Acts of Pilate or Gospel of Nicodemus are accounts of St Veronica curing the Emperor Vespasian with the cloth which bears the imprint of Jesus' face.

As a consequence Vespasian makes a pilgrimage to Jerusalem, where, according to this version, Joseph of Arimathea is still imprisoned. He releases Joseph and razes Jerusalem to the ground. The destruction of Jerusalem is an historical event of AD 70 around which the legend has developed.

There was, therefore, a considerable body of tradition surrounding Joseph of Arimathea. Some was in Latin, some in Greek, and some later in Anglo-Saxon, that was available for the development of the Grail tradition. The development of this is revealed in full flower by the work of Robert de Boron. He is a little known Burgundian whose style gives the impression of his having been both knight and priest. His poem is called *Joseph of Arimathea* and, as so often in the Arthurian canon, he claims that the source for it is another great book which contains the secret of the Grail.

De Boron's story reproduces the story of the Gospel of Nicodemus and associated material and takes up the story from when Vespasian is converted by Joseph of Arimathea in AD 70, some forty years after the crucifixion. It then introduces two important new characters—the sister of Joseph of Arimathea, called Enygeus, and her husband Bron (or Hebron).

As they wander in the wilderness Joseph himself is instructed from heaven to make a replica of the Table of the Last Supper. Bron is then told to catch a fish and to place it upon this table whereon the cup used at the Last Supper also stands. This, it is said, Joseph had obtained from Pilate and used to collect the blood of Jesus.

Before going further we should take particular note of this Cup, (here the form taken by the Grail), which is here a surrogate for the body of Christ, the *corpus Christi*. It is highly unlikely that Pilate would have had custody of the actual Cup of the Last Supper, but he did have custody of the body of Jesus. As Joseph now uses the Cup as a container for the blood of Jesus we have a clear identification of the Grail with the physical presence of God. Esoterically the blood is carrier of the spirit, which in this unique context is also the Holy Spirit. In Old Testament terms the Cup of Joseph would therefore be the equivalent of the Tabernacle containing the Ark of the Covenant, the place of the Shekinah, or Presence of God. This was later to be replaced by the Temple of Solomon—so the Temple Mysteries also relate to the Grail.

Robert de Boron's poem, which was a long trilogy comprising not only *Joseph of Arimathea* but also *Merlin* and *Perceval*, survives only in fragments. Malory, compiling his translation and unification of the material 250 years later, relied on an intermediate text called *Le Grand San Graal* which was based on de Boron's work. Malory however, presupposes rather than retells most of the material that occurs before the coming of Arthur. We shall therefore recapitulate this earlier subject matter.

Le Grand San Graal is itself important in that it not only takes in de Boron's work but also expands it to tell how the Holy Grail came to Britain. In doing this it gives expression to another very old strain of tradition which is that the Christianity of Britain was, in its origins, independent of Rome. This is a matter of accepted historical fact. Britain was largely Christian in later Roman times and reverted to paganism only with the barbarian invasions. It was then reconverted in the sixth century by Augustine of Canterbury. However, in the far West the original Celtic church still flourished and there was, to begin with, considerable conflict between the two Christian institutions. Finally the Roman prevailed at the Synod of Whitby in AD 664.

However, the traditions of the Celtic church, despite official rulings, pronouncements and accommodations, continued for a considerable time after this, and is to be found exerting its influence on the Arthurian legend. Wherever one finds hermits or anchorites dwelling at shrines in forests or other lonely places we have the influence of the old Celtic church. Its emphasis was on the individual rather than the monastic institution, on the nature mysticism of the country rather than the urbanized mysticism of Rome.

In a sense it was an expression of an independent spirit that later manifests as a unique form of Protestantism. The original Church of England, under Henry VIII, was regarded as the Catholic church in England, rather than part of the Reformation represented on the Continent by Luther, Zwingli, Calvin and others. Henry always considered himself a defender of the faith and the legend FID DEF appearing on coins of the British monarchy represents a title originally conferred upon by him the Pope for his theological refutation of the Protestantism of his day.

Long before this, however, this national independence had also manifested in a movement which was sufficiently strong to be condemned as the Pelagian Heresy. Pelagius was a British monk who promulgated the belief that it was possible for man to be responsible for his own salvation. He taught that man was not entirely dependent upon Divine Grace as administered in the sacraments by the church.

In this he was reacting against a trend resulting from the teachings of Augustine of Hippo who, in turn, was reacting from the excesses of his own youth. The assumption was that man was so corrupt that there was hardly any point in trying to live a better life; one simply relied on the grace of God and the efficacy of the sacraments. Obviously such a system of belief was open to certain abuse and indeed this controversy was all part of the perennial dichotomy between whether it is faith or works that is paramount in the Christian life.

It is also possible that Pelagius, (whose name is a Greek form of Morgan), was much influenced by Druid teaching and was attempting a synthesis between Augustinian Christianity and the pagan spiritual heritage. This attempt in other areas of Christendom brought about the promulgation of the Hermetic tradition.

Jean Markale, Professor of Celtic History at the Sorbonne, points out in *Celtic Civilization* that although Pelagianism was certainly not Druidism;

> its basis in total human freedom is very clearly Celtic in its leanings. It is also distinctly anti-Mediterranean since it emphasizes the solitude of man, while the ancient religions of Greece and Rome assume that human acts are all prompted or abetted by some divinity. The very concept of grace is Greco-Latin in origin, being an extension of the superstitious belief that man was incapable of acting alone and required the help of some impartial *numen* or divine will. By denying the power of grace Pelagius was fighting against the superstition, re-establishing the notion that man is entirely responsible for his own acts and restoring to human dignity a respect which the early Christian leaders with their erroneous ideas of evangelical humility sought to remove.

There is little doubt that Pelagius overstated his case and there grew up a strong movement of semi-Pelagianism which took up a middle position saying that man was not morally dead as Augustine assumed but neither, on the other hand, was he as morally healthy as Pelagius argued. Mankind was best regarded as morally sick and in need of Divine Grace. This could be obtained by anyone who sought for it but at the same time did not negate human free will.

It is not our purpose to pursue these doctrinal arguments at length but simply to record that a considerable body of belief reflected Celtic as opposed to Graeco-Roman ideas. Pelagianism has even been described in a standard work on Celtic Christianity as 'the national heresy of the Britons' (Gougaud = *Les Chrétientés celtiques*. Paris 1911). The Pelagian teaching was preached against by special missions of 429 and 447 and was the subject of an admonition by the Pope to the church in Ireland in 639: 'We have learnt that the poison of the Pelagian error has reappeared among you. We urge you to reject this odious doctrine. Is it not blasphemous to claim that man can be without sin?'

The independence of the Celtic Church, brought about by its isolation after the departure of the Roman armies, is important. St Patrick is a key figure here. A native of North-west Britain, he was captured and enslaved by Irish pirates in his youth and, on obtaining his freedom, later decided to return to convert his former captors. He landed at the Boyne, the ancient site of primeval religious activity, and within ten years had founded the See of Armagh.

Patrick was very much a Roman type of administrator and was created a bishop in 432 by St Germanius, who had organized the anti-Pelagian missions. Although historical details are dim, he brought about a wide ranging organized hierarchy, with Rome as the ultimate seat of authority. However, things did not remain in quite the way he intended.

One of his early converts, the Fenian chieftain Cailte, became author of a collection of tales about the old days called *The Colloquy of the Ancient Men*. This, whatever its intentions, preserved and indeed even revived the old legends of kings, gods and faery denizens of the countryside.

The old Irish traits of supreme individualism, tribal loyalties and internecine strife soon eroded the Roman ecclesiastical system after Patrick's death. This was the beginning of what is now known as Celtic Christianity, and Ireland was pre-eminent in its formation. In a strange parallel with the earlier days of the builders of stone circles, Ireland became a centre of civilization and culture in the far West. So it remained after the rest of the Celtic domains in mainland Britain and Gaul had fallen into the dark ages of barbarian invasion from the North and East.

An example of this influence is Columban, or Columbkill. He was of the royal blood of the O'Neills, and founder of the Celtic monastery of Kerry. The Northern O'Neills at that time were in conflict with the Southern O'Neills, as a result of which he was exiled, in 563. A relative, King Dalriada, gave him the Scottish island of Iona, and here he founded another monastery which he used as a base for missions to the wild tribes of Scotland. It was as a result of these activities that the Gaelic tongue was introduced to Northern Britain and the Irish word 'Scot' came to be applied to its inhabitants.

His disciple Aiden founded Lindisfarne as a base from which to convert the Saxon areas of the North, and following a similar pattern a whole network of influence spread southwards until the Celtic Church became a separate entity from the Roman Church of continental Europe.

The close links between Celtic Christianity and the old Druid religion are evident in Columban's ruling that every chief should have an official bard. This practice was still law in Wales 500 years later. The bards, or *filids*, were a class made up for the most part of Christianized Druids. Through them there remained a strong influence of the old legends, customs and religious rites and beliefs. Perhaps as a consequence many Celtic saints may be identified with old gods and heroes: St Brendan with Bran, St Corneille with Cernunnos, St Anne with Ana, and particularly importantly St Bridget or Bride of Kildare with the similarly named daughter of the Dagda, chief of the Tuatha de Danaan.

Bridget is important to our considerations of the Holy Grail. There is a tradition that she founded a convent for both men and women—an institution unthinkable in the rest of the church. There was certainly a general custom in the Celtic church of giving shelter to women, whether refugees from tribal warfare or more domestic violence, and allowing them to live with the monks. These women were called *conhospitae* and were apparently allowed to serve at the celebration of the mass. A letter from the Bishops of Tours condemns the practice in Brittany in 515–520: 'You continue to carry from hut to hut among your countrymen certain tables on which you celebrate the divine sacrifice of the mass with the assistance of women whom you call *conhospitae*. While you distribute the Eucharist, they take the chalice and administer the blood of Christ to the people. This is an innovation, an unprecedented superstition.' (Dom Louis Gougaud: *Les Chrétientés celtiques*, Paris 1911).

This is particularly significant when we consider that the most sacred elements of the Holy Grail legends are administered by maidens. This circumstance would be unthinkable in the Roman church even to this day.

Professor Markale stresses in *Celtic Civilization* the very different attitude to women in Celtic society compared to the peoples of the Mediterranean. We have indeed only to recall the traditions of the Irish Queen Maeve, and the revolt of the Iceni against the Romans under Boudicca. Old Celtic heroes are also referred to as being the sons of a particular mother, rather than father, which suggests a matrilinear method of succession in earlier times. There are also Greek and Roman records of communities of priestesses at Mont St Michel and on an island at the mouth of the Loire. These communities sent women once a year to make love to young men on the mainland, and to initiate any who dared return with them. There is a suggestion here of the queens in the dark boat who came to take away the wounded Arthur.

In the end, as a result of political changes, the Celtic church was absorbed into Roman organization and practice. It might perhaps have survived in the far West but for the depredations of Viking pirates who overran the great Celtic monasteries of Ireland and North Wales.

In mainland Britain it was destroyed by the subordination of the Britons to the newly converted Saxons, who looked to the Roman ecclesiastical hierarchy. In Ireland, when the Vikings had been driven back, the church was reinstated under Rome. It is an irony of fate that the mainland Saxon culture should later break away from Rome whilst traditionally independent Ireland should remain Roman Catholic.

It is of the old Celtic Christian hermits and local saints that we find a distant echo when we read of the adventures of the knights of the Round Table, who frequently meet them. They have however, undergone a sea change through the additional stratum of medieval conceptions, and particularly in the Grail Quest, those of Cistercian monks under the influence of the towering figure of St Bernard of Clairvaux. His insight and zeal reformed the monastic system, and introduced to the church the Cult of the Blessed Virgin Mary which might be considered a christianiz- ation of the movements that had surfaced to express themselves as the worship of the feminine in the Troubador minstrelsy and the rites of Courtly Love.

First, however, we must complete the formulation of the Grail story before the Cistercian influence.

In *Le Grand San Graal*, which stems directly from Robert de Boron's lost poem, the tradition of an order of Grail Knights is formulated. This goes back in time to the early Christian era with, as its leaders, the direct descendants of Joseph of Arimathea.

The Secret Tradition in Arthurian Legend

According to this tradition Joseph of Arimathea, upon his release by Vespasian, set off with his followers on a journey carrying the Grail. They made their way to the city of Sarras. This is a type of talismanic mission, for the intention is that the supreme Mysteries shall be unfolded at the place where Mahomed taught a false religion.

It will be obvious that we are here in the field of twelfth century symbolism and its concern with Saracen conquest of the holy places of Jerusalem. There is no physical city of Sarras and, at the time of Joseph of Arimathea, Mahomed was some 500 years unborn. However, the inner dynamics of the tale are beyond space and time, and Sarras as here presented is a symbolic city of infidelity and misbelief, which can also represent the whole world.

The King of Sarras, Evelach, worships the Sun, and is currently at war with Tholomes, the King of Egypt. Joseph traces a red cross upon his shield and promises him the victory contingent upon his faith. Subsequently, after being captured, Evelach gazes in faith upon the cross and Jesus appears before him. Evelach cries to him for help, whereupon an invincible knight on a white charger appears, bearing a white red cross shield and wins the day for Evelach.

In this tale there are various historical and quasi-historical elements. Tholomes' name derives from the Greek Ptolemaic dynasty that ruled in Egypt from the death of Alexander until the time of Antony and Cleopatra (323 to 30 BC). The theme of the story runs very close to that of the Roman emperor Constantine, whose early connections were British, and who was converted under similar circumstances after winning a crucial battle through contemplation of the cross, thus giving a very material interpretation to the pious phrase *In hoc signo vinces*. As a result of Constantine's conversion Christianity became the official religion of the Roman Empire.

Evelach, after his conversion, takes the name Mordrains, and his brother Seraphe takes the name Nasciens. Changes of name in such circumstances are important in that they represent and identify a change of purpose or aspiration for the incarnate spirit.

At Evelach's conversion there appears the first Grail vision. Josephes, the son of Joseph of Arimathea, witnesses the whole sequence of the Passion of Christ, and the Risen Christ comes to him in a red burning robe, accompanied by five fiery angels also clad in red, with flaming wings and swords. This is accompanied by the text, in Hebrew, 'In this likeness shall I come to judge all things in the Day of Terror.'

Joseph of Arimathea beholds lesser mysteries. It is a characteristic of the Grail that each percipient receives that which is appropriate to his particular needs and current spiritual status.

The sequence closes with a procession from the Ark of the Covenant, when Jesus Christ, vested as a priest, and accompanied by angels bearing incense and candles, celebrates the mass and annoints Josephes bishop of a land yet unknown: la Bloie Bretagne.

It is also recorded that with the remainder of this annointing oil miraculously preserved, all the kings of England were annointed until the birth of Uther Pendragon.

Joseph and his company then proceed, through long wanderings and various adventures, to Britain where, in an Eastertide lit by a full moon, the Grail is finally brought to Logres. The inner circle of the company around Joseph, who have faithfully kept to Holy Law, arrive miraculously, walking upon the waters, carrying the Ark of the Grail. Those less strong in the faith are transported later by the Ship of the Church.

It will be noticed that we have, in this story, very fundamental claims about the importance of the church in Britain, before Augustine or any Roman influence, and deriving its authority directly from Joseph of Arimathea, and also, through Josephes, from the authority of Christ himself in a special re-enactment of the events of the Passion. This implicitly gives Josephes a status close to that of the original apostles, together with a specific mission toward the Isles of Britain.

The Siege Perilous is in the table constructed by Joseph as a pattern of the table of the Last Supper. It may thus be construed as the place of Jesus himself, whose role of God-man is one that no man born under the shadow of original sin can undertake. Ambitious or vainglorious mortals who attempt to sit there are swallowed up in a fiery end; and one is reminded of the Old Testament incidents wherein even the touch of the Ark of the Covenant could kill; and of the early Christian church when the Holy Spirit struck dead Ananias and Sapphira for duplicity in the faith. The pure spirit, untrammelled by the channels of normal manifestation, has a corrosive, explosive or violently transforming effect upon anything that is not pure or good. Thus also the tradition that no-one can see the face of God and live, from which may stem the seemingly hard saying of Jesus that 'No man cometh to the Father but by me.' That is, mediation by God-in-manifestation is the way to God-the-Uncreate.

In the course of time Joseph of Arimathea dies and is buried at Glastonbury. Josephes, his son, who is the first Bishop of Britain, by the direct consecration of Christ, also dies in due time. The red cross shield which converted Mordrains (Evelach) is preserved as a relic, resting in the tomb of his brother Nasciens (Seraphe) until the coming of Galahad. The origin of Galahad's sword is also described, which differs from the Balin story although it is not symbolically contradictory. Here it is described as a saracen's sword which broke in the act of wounding Joseph. When it is welded together again it can become mighty for the power of good in the hand of Galahad.

King Galafres, a convert, builds a castle for the Grail keepers in the midst of a forest. In this forest a white hart ranges, accompanied by four lions. In allegorical terms this represents Christ and the four Evangelists, which is an interesting melding of apocryphal Christian tradition into a Celtic legendary setting.

The orthodox Church has never been too happy about the Holy Grail, perhaps because the Grail does not seem easily contained by any human institution. It is, rather, the presence of God in nature, in the whole creation, without organizational limits. It is similar to the Holy Spirit which 'bloweth where it listeth' and is no respecter of organizations or persons.

Other versions of early Grail history differ in detail from the story as here outlined. A link between Christian apocryphal and Celtic legendary material is also to be found in the character of Bron. In a sense he is the old Celtic Bran the Blessed, married to Joseph of Arimathea's sister, and thereafter becoming Joseph's successor as Grail custodian. In some versions he is made the equivalent of Josephes, the son of Joseph of Arimathea. This would perhaps be more acceptable to the mediaeval monkish mind because he is thereby celibate and in holy orders, distinctions which neither Bron nor Joseph of Arimathea can claim.

There is also a Joseph of Arimathea tradition, separate from the Grail stories, which associates him with Glastonbury. Some versions consider him to have come with the tin traders to Cornwall in earlier times, and to have brought the young Jesus with him. Hence the words of William Blake's *Jerusalem* 'And did those feet in ancient time, walk upon England's mountains green? And was the holy Lamb of God, on England's pleasant pastures seen?'

These legends became grafted on to the very ancient traditions of Glastonbury which, until 1184, had a very old mud and wattle church which was believed to have been built by twelve disciples of Saint Philip and Saint James at the command of the Archangel Michael.

Other legends considered this ancient church to have been built by no man's hand. Joseph of Arimathea was, by others, considered to have been in the party with Philip and James from Gaul. In the course of time he became one of the patron saints of the abbey. In the fourteenth century a chapel was dedicated to him and an image of Our Lady ascribed to his workmanship.

The Holy Grail was never emphasized in this process and he is associated with the more orthodox scene from the Passion of the Deposition from the Cross, distinguished by the accoutrements of the two cruets, containing the blood and sweat of Christ. By the sixteenth century the legend of the holy thorn had become current. This was said to have sprung from his staff and to bloom at Christmas.

It is a mistake, however, to dismiss legends on chronological grounds. Late legends can be as valid as earlier material for all legends are facets of a timeless reality. They bear witness to inner conditions that may crystallize about a certain geographical locality.

The powerful and sacred site of Glastonbury thus attracts many Arthurian and quasi-Arthurian legends to itself. These range from that of a great circular zodiacal earthwork depicted in the surrounding countryside to the discovery of two bodies assumed to be those of King Arthur and Queen Guenevere. In many people's minds Glastonbury is also very much associated with the popular image of Camelot. This is an idealized medieval picture that could hardly have physically existed but which nonetheless has its own reality as a force centre on the inner planes. It is spontaneously built by the popular imagination as a need of the racial soul, and from it inspiration and strength may be gained.

23. The Knights on the Grail Quest

The beginning of the Quest of the Holy Grail is heralded by a fair lady galloping into Camelot at Pentecost. She summons Lancelot to go with her, in the name of King Pelles, although she will not disclose the nature of the errand.

She leads Lancelot through a forest where, in a great valley, they come to a nunnery. There he is made welcome and meets his kinsmen Bors and Lionel, who are on their way to Camelot. Twelve nuns then enter the chamber accompanied by a fair youth who is in fact Lancelot's son Galahad. They ask Lancelot to make him a knight on the morrow, which he agrees to do, and the next day the four knights pass on to Camelot.

Meanwhile considerable excitement has been caused at the court by mysterious writings that have appeared around the Round Table. Each place is now designated with the name of the knight who should sit there. In esoteric terms this is an externalization of the inner powers; a crystallization of the forces of destiny, wherein cosmic principles are united to the actual names of those human beings who are destined to express them. About the always vacant Siege Perilous is found the statement that its place will be filled on this day, which is held to be 'four hundred winters and four and fifty after the Passion of our Lord Jesus Christ.'

At the same time the court is told of a great stone of red marble that is floating in the river with a fair sword therein. Upon this is inscribed 'Never shall man take me hence but only he by whose side I ought to hang and he shall be the best knight in the world.'

King Arthur naturally assumes this to refer to Lancelot, but Lancelot realizes that it is not in fact for him, and that, by implication, he is no longer the best knight in the world.

There is also an ominous warning that any who attempt to draw the sword who are not worthy of it will receive a wound from it that will bring about their death. Such indeed is the peril of vaulting ambition and vainglory in the context of high spiritual powers. Arthur, however, prevails upon Gawain to try to draw it. Inevitably he fails and in due course, after the Quest, when the sword comes into the possession of Lancelot, it does bring about his death.

Arthur, somewhat regretting what he may have inflicted upon Gawain, asks Percivale also to attempt to draw it. Percivale complies, not in expectation of being able to do so but in order to establish comradeship with Gawain in his peril. He thus enacts two of the fundamental virtues of knighthood, allegiance to the king and to one's fellow companions, no matter what the peril.

However, the young Galahad is soon to arrive who will draw the sword. This occurs when the company are seated for the feast of Pentecost. The doors and window shutters of the palace suddenly close, as if the Holy Grail were about to appear, and Galahad is brought before them, led by an ancient man dressed in white. Galahad himself is armed in red and has at his side a scabbard without a sword.

The old man addresses King Arthur with the words: 'Sir, I bring you here a young knight the which is of king's lineage and of the kindred of Joseph of Arimathea, whereby the marvels of this court and of strong realms shall be fully accomplished.'

The old man then disarms Galahad and takes him, in his red coat with ermine mantle, to the Siege Perilous beside Lancelot where, lifting up the cloth with which the miraculous letters have been reverently concealed, it is seen that the writing has changed to read: 'This is the siege of Sir Galahad the High Prince.'

Galahad bids the old man to return 'to my grandfather King Pelles, and to my lord the Fisher King.' The old man departs, accompanied by twenty squires, to the great excitement of the court at these events—and not least in amazement at the extreme youth of Galahad and also his physical likeness to Lancelot. Galahad is taken to the sword in the stone which he easily draws and places into his empty scabbard.

Galahad takes all these marvels as a matter of course, for spiritual certainty is his. 'It is no marvel' he says, upon drawing the sword that defied the efforts of Gawain and Percivale, 'for this adventure is not theirs but mine.' He also knows the whole story of the origins of the sword, with Balin and Balan, and that it is his own destiny to heal King Pelles of the wound received by the Dolorous Stroke.

A lady is then seen riding at a great pace down by the river's edge. She announces to Lancelot what he already knows, that he is no longer the best knight in the world. She also announces to Arthur, on the authority of Nasciens the Hermit (one of the early Grail custodians) that to Arthur shall befall the greatest worship that ever befell a King of Britain, for this day the Sangraal will appear in his house and feed him and all the Fellowship of the Round Table.

Indeed, at that evening's banquet the Holy Grail does appear, to the sounds of 'cracking and crying of thunder, so that they thought the palace should burst asunder.' Then in the midst of the blast enters a sunbeam, seven times brighter than daylight, and they are all illuminated with the grace of the Holy Spirit. Then all see each other fairer than they had ever seemed before, and all are struck speechless.

The Holy Grail enters the hall, covered with white samite, though no-one can be seen bearing it. The hall is filled with fine odours and each one present is offered such meat and drink as he loves best in the world.

When the Holy Grail departs they all regain their speech.

It is Gawain who announces the Quest of the Holy Grail. As the precious thing was covered and could not be seen he declares that he will spend twelve months in the quest of seeking to view the Holy Grail unveiled. Did he but know, the Quest is an impossible one in the terms that he conceives it, for naked spiritual realities are not so easily run to earth, nor so easily apprehended 'face to face' even when they are personally encountered.

However, each according to his realization vows also to embark upon the Quest, and the whole Round Table Fellowship, after a celebratory tourney, departs in different ways upon the Quest, all 150 of them according to Malory. Arthur and Guinevere are left to grieve at the court; he for the dispersed fellowship, she for the parting from her lover Lancelot. As Arthur intuitively realizes, this great Quest betokens the beginning of the break up of the Round Table Fellowship.

Indeed, after the conclusion of the Quest, the human bickerings and misunderstandings break out, and lead with tragic inevitability to the self destruction of the whole company and its leading protagonists. Gawain and his brothers die at Lancelot's hand, and Arthur is mortally wounded in the act of killing his bastard incestuous son, the usurper Mordred.

However, all this lies in the future, and the first event in the Grail Quest is the winning by Galahad of his shield. This, like his sword, is perilous to the unworthy, as King Bagdemagus finds to his cost.

It is held in a white abbey, behind the altar, and is white with a red cross upon it. The monks warn that it may only be worn by the worthiest knight in the world and that whoever else tries to take it will be either dead or maimed within three days.

King Bagdemagus, who is at the abbey along with Galahad and Uwain claims the right to try to take it. Accordingly, he is allowed to, but has not gone two miles before he is struck down and wounded close to death by a white knight on a white horse from a nearby hermitage, who sends a squire with the message that the shield is destined only for Galahad. The White Knight then instructs Galahad on the origins of the shield, which we have already discussed.

Like the sword and scabbard, which signify important elements in the make-up of man, namely the indwelling spiritual force and its bodily expression of containment, so the shield is of paramount symbolic importance. It signifies self-knowledge and the aware-ness of the bedrock of our own personal identity. In esoteric symbolism the inside of a shield is polished like a mirror to reveal the bearer's identity to himself, whilst its outer side bears the heraldic symbol device that reveals his identity or aspirations to others, rather like a 'magical name'. In the Arthuriad we see the dire consequences of a false belief in the identity of oneself as shown in the fate of King Bagdemagus who is maimed as a result of his spiritual presumption, and also the fatal confrontation between Balin and Balan brought about by the confusion of shields. It is indeed a not uncommon motif throughout the Arthurian tales.

With Galahad now fully equipped, his Grail Quest can com-mence. In the tales of the Quest we also follow other knights, principally Percivale, Lancelot and Bors but also with some attention to those less successful, such as Gawain and Ector, Lancelot's brother.

It soon becomes apparent that the tests of the Grail Quest are not only those of knightly prowess but also of moral and spiritual worth. Allegiance to an earthly code of loyalty to monarch, and love and service to ladies and comrades is now not enough. In addition to this an unreserved dedication is required to a code that derives from a higher level of reality. Even Merlin's magic is not sufficient in these areas; Galahad's armour is more of a piece with that graphically described in the New Testament in Paul's Letter to the Ephesians:

> be strong in the Lord, and in the power of his might. Put on the whole armour of God, that ye may be able to stand against the wiles of the devil. For we wrestle not against flesh and blood, but against principalities, against powers, against the rulers of the darkness of this world, against spiritual wickedness in high places. Wherefore take unto you the whole armour of God, that ye may be able to withstand the evil day, and having done all, to stand. Stand therefore, having your loins girt about with truth, and having on the breastplate of righteousness; and your feet shod with the preparation of the gospel of peace; above all, taking the shield of faith, wherewith ye shall be able to quench all the fiery darts of the wicked. And take the helmet of salvation, and the sword of the Spirit, which is the word of God.

The story of the Grail Quest shows first the testing of Percivale's character. He is found worthy and thus is able to join Galahad later on the strange ship that sails the mystic seas.

Then the moral condition of Lancelot, Gawain and Bors are tested and only one of them, Bors, is found worthy to join Percivale and Galahad. These three then pass on to the higher adventures of the Quest.

Percivale is a Grail winner who brings with him much that is outside the mainstream of native Arthurian tradition. His tale is developed particularly by the German Wolfram von Eschenbach, whose *Parzival* is regarded by many as one of the two great peaks of mediaeval visionary poetry, the other being Dante's *Divine Comedy*.

However, the origins of Percivale would seem to be the Northwest of Wales and as Peredur he is to be found in the *Mabinogion*, which although a late manuscript source plainly contains very ancient elements. In the opinion of the translators of a recent edition of *Parzival* (Helen M. Mustard and Charles E. Passage) the *Mabinogion* stands closer than any other surviving manuscript to the Welsh prototype that must have existed in the mid-twelfth century before the tale of Percivale was taken up by Chrétien de Troies. From his rendering of the old Welsh stories into courtly French came the inspiration for Wolfram von

Eschenbach and the writers of the Nibelungen sagas to produce their own cycle, which culminated in the opera cycle of Richard Wagner.

It is worth saying that both Chrétien de Troies and Wolfram von Eschenbach make reference to unknown manuscript sources. Chrétien says that his *Conte du Graal* is based on a book lent him by Count Philip of Flanders. Chrétien did not live to finish his Grail poem and it was taken up by no less than four continuators. One of these also refers to a vast source attributed to Bleheris, a figure who is mentioned by other twelfth century writers. One is reminded of the shadowy figure of Blaise, to whom even Merlin seemed accountable and whose function seemed to be to record all the ancient annals of Britain.

Wolfram, on the other hand, refers no less than six times to a certain *chanteur* or *enchanteur*—that is, singer or enchanter—known as Kyot, a Provençal, who in turn obtained it from a heathen tongue, (presumably Arabic), in Toledo. Toledo was a great cosmopolitan intellectual melting pot of a city, renowned for magic, which was synonymous with all scientific knowledge in those days, where scholars were fluent in both Latin and Arabic through the penetration of the Moors to the Iberian peninsula. Wolfram also states that Kyot's version is the true original that was incorrectly adapted and rendered into French by Chrétien.

We may take an accommodating view that Chrétien's tale is based mainly upon old Celtic sources, via the Breton, adapted to Norman French court tastes; and that Wolfram's, whilst ultimately coming from the same root, has been infused and transformed by later esoteric teaching from the Near East. That is, in much the same way that the doctrines of Courtly Love found their way to Provence, and also became part of Arthurian narrative—the later Mystery teaching cleaving, as like to like, to the old.

In Peredur, the Percivale of the *Mabinogion*, we have the earliest form of Grail hero. North west Wales, (or Gwynedd, from the Roman name for the local tribe, the Venedotia or Guenedocia) was, by its very location, a meeting place for both Welsh and Irish (Brythonic and Goidelic) traditions. Thus one finds that elements of Percivale's childhood closely parallel the *enfances* of the Irish heroes Cuchulain and Finn.

In its earliest form we might equate the Grail with the Principle of Sovereignty where, in the halls of the ancient Irish gods, horn and platter provided endless feasting, and Eriu, the Sovereignty of Ireland, presented their great talismanic treasures to them.

Eriu could appear either in loathly hideous form or beautiful and radiant. These aspects she has in common with other ancient goddesses such as Isis, and also with the dual figure of the loathly damsel who acts as Grail messenger and the beautiful damsel who is Grail bearer.

As guardians of great treasures, including the proto-Grail, the early band of hero gods is a prototype of the Order of Grail Knights that is described particularly by Wolfram von Eschenbach. He derives it however from the line of the Fisher King, who was the brother in law of Joseph of Arimathea and fed the pilgrim missionaries on their journeys through the waste lands. He did this by catching and serving to them a miraculous fish.

The fish embodies several levels of symbolism. In the early church the emblem of Christ was a fish. It also has an astrological signification in the precession of the Equinoxes when, for approximately two thousand years, the Spring Sun rises in Pisces, the Fishes. The importance of the fish is brought out in the miracles of the feeding of the multitudes, when in addition to the bread of life, the acceptance of the Incarnate God-head is also the food of the spirit. In later alchemical symbolism the fish represents the soul and spirit swimming in the waters of manifest life, and this may also be applied to the Cosmic Christ swimming into the depths of creation. The disciples of Jesus are originally called from amongst the fishermen of Lake Galilee and are called to be fishers of men. Also, after the Resurrection, the Risen Christ joins the disciples in a meal and partakes of fish. It is a long way from the miraculous salmon of all wisdom of ancient Irish mythology but the symbolic connections are there.

In the Parzival story the Fisher King is called Amfortas and is the head of an Order of Knights called Templeisen, who guard the sanctuary of the Grail. They are vowed to celibacy, like the monk-knight orders of the Knights Templar and Knights of St John who were contemperaneous with the literary rendering of these stories. The Templeisen are not so much derivative of these orders, though, as an ideal to which members of such an order might aspire. The Grail Knights were held to be chosen by God himself, and besides guarding the Grail sanctuary rode out, like the Knights of the Round Table, on hazardous missions.

The difference between the Templeisen and the Knights of the Round Table is that the former are possessors and guardians of a great holy treasure; the latter are seekers of such, even when they realize its existence or significance. The former tend to be more purposive, sent out like missionaries to do a specific deed; the latter are more speculative, often seeking adventure or engaging on quests in a more haphazard manner.

With the Templeisen are an order of ladies of noble birth who serve the Grail with precise ritual ceremony; and the Grail Bearer is a queen of unsurpassed beauty, stainless purity, and arrayed in all the silks of Arabia. The source of her finery, like much of the symbolic wisdom within these stories, is significant of the influence of Islamic mysticism.

The Grail, as here portrayed, is not carried to a secret chamber to sustain the life of a maimed king but is placed in open court before the king, Amfortas, himself, and it serves the whole company with whatever food and drink they desire.

Its form is that of a stone rather than a cup or dish, and it is variously described as a 'fair blossom of Paradise garden' or 'the crown of all earthly wishes.' One of its functions is also to choose the kings of distant lands. This is a direct link with the principle of Sovereignty, represented in the Irish tales by Eriu, and also with the Crown of the Tree of Life in the Qabalah. In this function it aims to preserve upon earth the principle of just kingship, rule and law, as a mirror of the sovereignty of God over the whole creation.

The role of the Grail winner is to continue to guard and serve the Grail in its castle, which confers rulership of the land surrounding the castle and removal of the enchantment therefrom.

The Grail castle is traditionally located upon a mountain top and is surrounded by water. In physical terms it has been associated with various geographical places, principally Montsegur in Southern France and Monserrat in Spain. However, the image is such as to have universal symbolic significance and this is the pattern for many holy places, not least the Earthly Paradise or Garden of Eden which tops Mount Purgatory in Dante's visionary poem.

The Grail castle is more universal than the parallel associations of any particular place and time, for it is a principle of location for a universal and uncreate reality. In the Arthurian legends the Grail may appear at any place and any time completely unexpectedly, like the Holy Spirit 'blowing where it listeth'. So too, in the Parzival tradition, it is recorded that originally the Grail 'had no fixed place, but floated, invisible, in the air.' Albrecht von Sharffenberg describes in a poem on the young Titurel how this grandfather of Parzival founded the castle for the Grail to indwell.

It is a description of a 'model universe' so familiar to students of magic from Marsilio Ficino to the present day. It stood on top of a high promontory, polished like a mirror to reflect heavenly realities, and was constructed in jewels and precious metals to represent the domed vault of the starry heavens, with a gold sun and a silver moon in movement, and cymbals striking the passage of time.

This description by Albrecht, once considered literary fiction, has since been discovered to resemble closely the seventh-century palace of the Persian king Chosroes II on the holy mountain of Shiz. This was the reputed birthplace of Zoroaster and site of a sanctuary of the Holy Fire, for there had been a circular temple on this site long before Chosroes. Chosroes captured Jerusalem in 614 and carried off the True Cross, which he incorporated into his palace, or Throne of Arches, now called the Throne of Solomon. He was, in turn, defeated by the Byzantine emperor Heraclius in 629, who destroyed the holy place, rescued the Holy Cross, and took it to Byzantium.

These events made a great impression upon the mediaeval world and from this line of tradition there sprang certain elements of a heretical tendency in the Grail Legend. This Persian influence, with its tendency to dualism, the created universe seen as a battleground between two equal forces of light and darkness or good and evil, lends an Eastern touch to the legends. Also, in its extreme form it led to the Earth denying heresies of the Cathars, who considered the physical world evil and to be escaped from by heroic spiritual virtue.

The Grail itself, in this cycle, has a more cosmic and pre-Christian ambience. Wolfram, in an obscure passage, describes it as some kind of stone, and also as an emerald fallen from the crown of Lucifer when he fell from grace. In this sense it could represent the 'goodness' of the fallen Archangels, their original spiritual destiny in the scheme of things, presumably as light bringers and light bearers. Since their defection, which led to the Fall of Man, the Earth has struggled in turmoil and darkness as 'the Dark and Sorrowful Planet'.

Esoterically this emerald stone has been equated with the 'third eye' of Lucifer, the brow centre of the fallen Archangel. This will also bear a similar interpretation to the above. The nearest human equivalent is man's sense of destiny in the lower worlds, which is by virtue of his intuitive knowledge of the higher realities.

Percivale is the human 'Fool'. His story commences with him as an uncouth rustic, unaware of his own high lineage or of the very fact of knighthood, yet who nonetheless through his own inherent, unrealized virtue, finds his way to knighthood and eventual achievement of the Holy Grail.

In Chrétien de Troies *Conte du Graal* he is shown having to find his own way to the happy middle way or mean, by swerving against and being battered by the opposite poles of, on the one hand, too much reliance on the precepts of others and, on the other, too great a spirit of self-will and independence.

On his first coming to the Grail Castle he fails to ask the Grail Question because he has been taught the virtues of silence. Following this humiliation, which lays the land waste, he spends five years in personal aimless errantry, out of touch with court, church, Grail quest or his lady, Blancheflor. Finally he follows the advice of a hermit and mends his ways, taking up his individual responsibilities to God and man.

There is a strand in some versions of the Perceval story wherein he is of an especial lineage, like Galahad—as in the *Didot Perceval*. Here he presumptuously sits in the Siege Perilous at Arthur's Round Table which cracks and casts the land under a spell which can only be raised by the best knight in the world finding the Fisher King's castle and asking the Grail Question. It is, after many vicissitudes, Percivale himself who achieves this, and Bron ascends, released from his pain, to heaven; the split in the Siege Perilous at the Round Table closes with a great noise and the enchantment of the land is brought to an end. This story of Percivale causing the wasting of the land by overweening pride of sitting in the forbidden siege, and then by his own efforts setting things to rights is a version of the Fall of Man and his subsequent redemption. The fact that this is by his own efforts would be enough to cause a certain coldness of the Church toward the Grail stories, for in canonical belief it is only by the mediation of the Church and the Grace of God that man can be saved.

The Percivale of Malory is based closely on *Le Grand San Graal* which was written very much under Cistercian influence, the order of monks brought into being by the immensely powerful and charismatic medieval figure, Bernard of Clairvaux. He was a great mystic and organizer and in 1120 helped to draw up the Rule of the Knights Templar whom he considered to represent a new breed of men. He debated whether to call them monks or soldiers and wrote: 'To tell the truth both names are appropriate for they lack nothing, neither the gentleness of the monk nor the cool courage of a soldier. What can I say but that it is the Lord's doing and marvellous in our eyes!'

This might almost be a formula for Galahad, or Lancelot, or any of the more spiritually vocational knights of the Round Table.

The Cistercian story tends to contrast, perhaps too starkly, the qualities of spiritual and earthly knighthood. It tends, for instance, to put almost an obsessive emphasis on chastity as an essential virtue. If, for this chastity, one were to read purity there would be no quarrel between the esoteric and the Cistercian viewpoints. Chastity in this sense is not mere absintence from sexual experience but a purity of motive, a condition of the heart rather than of the body.

There is perhaps also rather too much exegesis given by holy men, who are often wearing the white Cistercian habit, to the knights on their wanderings. Gawain is capable of giving short shrift to such advice on occasion.

Certainly there are rather deeper lessons to be drawn from the Grail symbolism than the rather shallow comparisons between the old law of Moses and the new law of Jesus, yet Synagogia and Ecclesia are two allegorical names frequently thrown into opposition or even conflict in a way that is perhaps less than helpful.

Malory plays down this element where he can. His Cistercian influenced original tends to emphasize a contrast between earthly and divine chivalry with the former shown as much the inferior. By the rule of St Bernard a soldier could become a monk, but a monk could not be allowed to revert to a soldier, not even to a soldier-monk of the Templar or St John Orders. Malory, on the other hand, strives to show the Grail Quest as the opportunity for the earthly knight to obtain greater glory, in and for *this* world. He saw no dichotomy between heavenly knighthood and secular knighthood but a synthesizing grace in virtuous living. This is surely the more fruitful attitude, and because of this it appeals more to the imagination. Malory rescues the tale from becoming a doctrinal exposition on grace and makes it a living legend once more.

This accounts for his somewhat crude substitutions of pious phrases for equivalent Arthurian ones. Thus the injunction 'pray to Our Lord to have mercy on my soul' is rendered 'when you come to court recommend me to my Lord Arthur and those that be left alive'; and appeals 'for God's sake' become appeals 'for Arthur's sake'.

Percivale in this Grail cycle has lost many of the attributes that are part of the continental Eastern derived Parzival tradition, and also his Celtic roots in Peredur or Prediwi. He no longer has a lover Blancheflor or Kandwiramur. He is no longer part of a dynastic Grail line which leads from Titurel, builder of the Grail castle, to Lohengrin the swan knight. Rather is he a monkish figure whose tests are for the most part concerned with resisting the seductions of carnal knowledge. However, his sister, un-named but who might, as Charles Williams suggests, be called Dindrane, is an important figure. She brings an important femi-nine element which can never be divorced from tales of the Grail without completely losing their vitality.

The Grail Quest of Lancelot is one that brings Malory into greatest difficulty with his Cistercian source material. This makes his liaison with Guenevere the reason for his being unable to achieve the Grail. Lancelot is indeed treated much as a recalci-trant medieval monk would have been—stripped and buffetted and left out in the cold, barred from the divine service within. However, as we have earlier discussed, the liaison between Lancelot and Guenevere is not, in itself, an illicit liaison, but one designed for the continued function of the Round Table and Courtly formula.

Where Lancelot does fall short is in his inability to focus upon the aweful purity of the Holy Grail because part of him is still projecting the vision of the ideal upon Guenevere. Where your treasure is, there will your heart be also; and with Lancelot his treasure is not wholly with the uncreate Mysteries but in con-siderable part caught up on the glamour of Guenevere.

This human devotion is not necessarily a fault in itself. It is simply inappropriate in the context of one who desires to make the unreserved dedication to the service of higher forces and is impelled thereby to fall away.

Gawain's Grail Quest, such as it is, demonstrates the same mechanism but at a lower level. In this version, Gawain does not represent a candidate for higher initiation as does Lancelot. Therefore he goes through no agonies concomitant with falling away from a glimpsed higher ideal that he cannot quite achieve. He has no real desire for, or appreciation of, this ideal in the first instance. Therefore, like Ector and most of the other knights, his Grail Quest is uneventful. Nothing very much happens. That which does, he finds unfortunate or difficult to understand. Thus, like the mass of mankind in the face of Mysteries beyond their immediate comprehension, he is impatient of any advice on the matter and soon finds good reason to give up the apparently useless and fruitless Quest.

Ector's experience is similar, except for the interesting fact that the closest he comes to the Vision of the Grail is through the expression of brotherly love, when he is seeking Lancelot. This is in direct contrast to Lionel, whose hatred of his brother Bors has to be met with divine intercession.

In the Cistercian story Bors is criticized for having once fallen from chastity, which accounts for his having a son. However, properly understood, and divorced from medieval monastic values, Bors is as important and exemplary a figure as Galahad. He represents the initiate, achieved in and rooted in the world, who can maintain the responsibilities of a man in the world, and yet still achieve the Vision Splendid. It is not insignificant that it is upon him that earthly knowledge of the achievement of the Grail Quest relies. He alone of Galahad, Percivale and Dindrane returns to tell the tale. He survives also the final break-up of the Round Table after the Last Battle and the eventual deaths of Lancelot and Guenevere.

Galahad himself is the figure around whom the higher, 'uncreate' realities of the Grail Quest revolve. It is the Galahad story that sets the seal on the religious national ideal that Christianity in Britain sprang directly from Christ himself. The nature of the Grail Quest is to restore it to the land from whence it has been lost. This restoration will at the same time be a purification of the national life. This crowns and fulfils the very objects of Merlin when he raised Arthur to the throne and created the Round Table Fellowship.

The Grail, with its roots in ancient Celtic myth and legend, is transformed into a pure ideal of Christian mysticism, into an exalted vision and delicacy of realization that is not found anywhere else in literature outside of Dante. It indeed parallels the *Divine Comedy* of Dante as a search for the revelation of Divine Beauty, which is the eternal quest of the soul, in and out of space and time.

The Grail, as the presence of God within the Creation, is not limited by the acts or realizations of men. It resides in a castle set apart for it, Carbonek. Or it may be conceived as the focus of civilization in an 'inner' city, Sarras. It is, however, also to be seen, as it listeth, wandering free and appearing unexpectedly in the Land of Logres.

There is a lesson here for all religious institutions that the Spirit of God is not so readily confined to official channels as they might prefer to think. In a more universal sense, the castle or city of the Grail is a mode of appearance of the Earthly Paradise which has its legendary location in many places, from Shamballa or Shangri-la of Eastern Tradition, to the Isles of the Blessed or the Kingdom of Prester John in the Western world.

Nonetheless the Quest of the Holy Grail, like the establishment of the Pendragon dynasty of divine kings, and the Order of the Chivalry surrounding the Round Table, is one that ends in failure so far as its physical expression is concerned. It remains however as an inspiration and ideal within the hearts of men, and the truth of its vision has enabled it to retain vitality and immediacy over centuries and it still remains meaningful in the radically changing world of today.

Something of the gap that remains between vision and reality is to be found in the portrayal of Galahad's character. Like Jesus, he tends to be rendered into an unhuman idealized figure. This reflects and reveals a gap that exists in human perception and consciousness.

Galahad is, however, a knight of formidable prowess, no fairy figure or effete allegory. His relationships to his father Lancelot and Queen Guenevere are important, and that between him and Dindrane, the sister of Percivale and daughter of King Pellinore, should not be overlooked. It is her damsel that summons Galahad to her castle from whence she leads him to the boat of mystical consciousness, in which, along with Percivale and Bors, he is led to the Ship of Faith—the symbolic vessel of Nasciens, Mordrains and the early company of Grail bearers who came to Britain.

This ship is a treasure house of symbolism that stems from the Mysteries of the Temple of King Solomon; and the spindles of red, green and white wood come from the original Tree of Life. It also bears the Sword of David, the father of Solomon and the first King of Israel, which is, symbolically, the Will of God made manifest in Earth. The sword is also called the Sword with Strange Hangings, for its scabbard is supported by the hair of Dindrane herself. One may take a hint from the little understood symbolism of the *Zohar*, which goes, at great length, into the symbolic significance of the beard and all the hairs of the head of the Great Countenance, of God the Father of All. We may thus regard the golden hair of Dindrane which is used to support the scabbard (which is made from the Tree of Life) and the sword of the Divine Will itself, as the spiritual emanations of the highest centres of the being of Dindrane, the perfect female initiate. The hair is the expression, in physical terms, of the emanations of the head centres, in terms of the human aura. In literal fact it is a 'crowning glory'.

Dindrane's transposition to the 'inner' city of Sarras takes place by means of her voluntary sacrificial death, when she gives her life's blood, the carrier of the spirit, to heal the sick.

At the celebratory Feast of the Holy Grail at Carbonek which marks the achievement of Galahad and the other Grail winners, the vision of Christ consecrating the first Bishop of Logres is repeated, and the achievement is witnessed by the presence of other knights, from all the four corners of the world.

Jesus, proceeding from the Holy Grail itself, speaks to them, saying: 'My knights and my servants and my true children, which be come out of deadly life into spiritual life, I will no longer hide myself from you, but ye shall see now a part of my secrets and of my hidden things. Now hold and receive the high meat which ye have so much desired.'

They are all then fed by Christ himself with the 'good of immortality'. This open vision of uncreate reality that is granted to them bears them away from the Land of Logres, which is never again blessed with the veiled presence of the Holy Grail. This is explained by Christ himself as he says to Galahad as he partakes of the Mass of the Holy Grail:

> . . . you must go hence and bear with you this holy vessel, for this night it will depart from the realm of Logres, and shall never more be seen here. And do you know why? For it is neither served nor worshipped to its right by them of this land, for they be turned to evil living, and therefore I shall disinherit them of the honour which I have done them.

Galahad, Percivale and Bors accompany the Holy Grail back to Sarras, from whence it came. The maimed king is healed and the three knights are borne away in the ship with the silver alter above which hovers the glory of the Holy Grail.

In Sarras, persecution comes to them, presumably in accordance with the hard saying that whom the Lord loveth he chasteneth, or as in the circles of Mount Purgatory in Dante that lead to the Earthly Paradise. This gives place however to great honour, and in due time Galahad's wish is granted, and he leaves this life and ascends to the realities of the uncreate God-head. Percivale remains in Sarras, and only Bors, commanded to do so by Christ, returns to tell the tale. In this sense Bors is in the line of succession of great revelatory mystics and prophets, and the keepers and sustainers of the inner Mystery traditions.

It is these traditions that survive as an eternal hope and inspiration to a Logres that is deserted, fallen from the potential of its high destiny. The object of the Table Round had been to bring Logres under a new law, a plan that embraced the vision and works of Merlin on the one hand, the missionary journeyings of Joseph of Arimathea and the Grail on the other.

In the end however, the Pendragon line peters out, almost before it began, the Round Table Fellowship disintegrates into internecine dissension, and the Holy Grail is withdrawn to the inner planes. As we have earlier said, the Arthurian cycle embodies both the vision of achievement and the consequences of failure.

The story does not end in ultimate defeat however, for the story is not yet ended, and it remains as an inspiration, instruction and challenge for later generations to build the realm of Logres and all that can go with it. In other words, it is a living Mystery Tradition, for Mystery Traditions embody the ultimate Vision of Perfection, reinterpreted throughout the ages for different times and seasons.

24. Esoteric Origins and Implications of the Grail

If one were to trace back the Greater Mysteries of the Holy Grail tradition, and this can be done only by recourse to the akashic records, as little physical evidence remains, one would find its focus in Syria, in one of the greatest esoteric brotherhoods that the world has ever known. It has come down to us as little more than a name, in the tradition of the Essenes. Certain Jewish teachers claimed connection with them and it is even said that Jesus trained amongst them, although his mission was to all mankind and thus couched in universal terms rather than in the technicalities of a secret doctrine designed to teach chosen initiates the means of handling inner forces.

They were a great power on the inner planes, with considerable astral working knowledge. From them the Tree of Life of the Qabalah, with its immense store of knowledge and power, derives.

Mount Carmel was an important Essene centre, and in the Old Testament the prophets Elisha and Hosea give hints of having belonged to them. But whilst the orthodox Jewish tradition was outwardly so patriarchal in development, the Essene inner tradition was well aware of the feminine side of Almighty God. In fact they used this power, of the Sephirah Binah on the Tree of Life, a great deal, and it was this that formed, many centuries later, the basis of the Templar teaching.

The symbolism of Binah has much to do with the Temple and the very name Knights Templar, although outwardly connected with their guardianship of the Temple of Jerusalem, inwardly signified the 'inner temple' and the great esoteric grade of Binah, known as the Magister Templi. This inner teaching came from a small body of Essenes whom they contacted, and whose influence had already percolated into the Mysteries of the Saracen knights.

The mechanism of this onward transmission of ancient Mystery traditions is due to a particular property of the astral plane. If a group meditates upon a constructive image sufficiently intensely it will become imbued with power and knowledge which will remain available for another group at a later time, who will be able to draw from this form as if it had an independent existence of its own.

In this way the Essenes guarded within their secret doctrines the inner knowledge of a great being known as Melchizedek, who is mentioned briefly in Genesis xiv 18–20, and to whom Jesus is likened in the New Testament Epistle to the Hebrews, attributed to Paul but by an unknown Christian initiate. There is a vast amount of knowledge still to be realized surrounding this great figure, who brought bread and wine to Abraham after the slaughter of the Kings of Edom, and to whom even the patriarch gladly gave a tenth of the spoils. The Table of Melchizedek was a great and secret formula, with which the Round Table of Arthur has much in common, as also the Table of the Last Supper. All this is bound up in the Round Table Fellowship and the Quest of the Holy Grail and later traditions associated with the Rosicrucians.

A certain group of medieval personages are important as being in the direct line of transmission of these Mysteries, who were incarnate in Norman Palestine at the time of the Second and Third Crusades (c.1170–90).

One of these was Humphrey IV of Toron, who was the first husband of the much married Isabella who later became Queen of Jerusalem. Humphrey was captured by the Saracens and remained a prisoner for a considerable time during which he learned Arabic and became conversant with the philosophy of Islam. He was later a friend of Richard the Lionheart who employed him as a translator in the Third Crusade.

In this way Humphrey was a human bridge between the cultures of Islam and Christendom. Associated with him was Balian of Ibelin, who was commander of the army that defended Jerusalem against the Saracens before they recaptured it. He took Humphrey under his protection when his life was at risk in the troubled policits of the times.

The contact between East and West that occurred at that time had within it three streams of wisdom, each of which was important in bringing through unbroken an inner doctrine. These came from Arabia which was at that time a storehouse of ancient wisdom garnered by the impressionable hordes who had spread worldwide at the behest of Mahomed in the seventh century, conquering with the sword as they went, but at the same time absorbing the essentials of the diverse cultures that they met.

The three streams of wisdom were alchemy, Sufi mysticism, and the traditions of the Holy Grail. Each of these carries within it a knowledge of the feminine side of God in contradistinction to the masculine perspective of the Judaic tradition.

The Arabian alchemists knew very well that what they were doing in transmutation was not merely an external process, and they knew what they meant when they said that Maria is the *Prima Materia*. Maria is from Mara, the Great Sea, with the creative sperm, Yod, or hand of God, within Her. She is the great Chaos, the First Mother out of which the process begins that ends in the creation of the Lapis. In Qabalistic terms she is signified by Binah (the Throne) within the sphere of creation, and as Ain Soph (the Limitless) beyond it.

From the many alchemical diagrams it is apparent that the conjunction of Sol and Luna is one of the essential stages of the process. This also has a significance in historical and cultural terms for its signifies the coming together of the heraldic sign of Christendom, the Sun, and the cresent Moon of Islam. Thus is the Royal Marriage accomplished.

The Troubadours in their lays, which superficially had a personal and romantic connotation, were in fact conveying to those who could understand them, the hieroglyphics of the inner wisdom in another fashion. The images within their verse were very close to the patterns of symbolism to be found in the Tarot, which likewise served as a bridge with the ancient Mysteries embodied in the ancient Egyptian Bembine Tablet of Isis.

The Knights Templar were profoundly influenced and changed by their contact with Islam, and therefore became what the Christian church of the day regarded as heretical. A close association developed between certain loyal members of the Orders of Knighthood that were in the Holy Land and the Troubadours. Thus the continuation of knowledge was preserved, the knights being in direct touch with the preserved tradition which was disseminated by the Troubadours in their free passage through various countries.

The Sufi element linked this contemporary process with the lengthy tradition that sprang from the Essenes—for the Sufi mystics were also aware of the centres of essence which the Hebrew mystics referred to as the Sephiroth of the Tree of Life; and indeed they were to appear before the Qabalah became known to Gentile Europe in the works of the Spaniard Ramon Lull (1234–1316).

Whatever may have been said of the Templars at the time of their denunciation in later years, as being worshippers of Satan, their stronghold at Acre never inclined toward this error. Indeed it was from this centre that the transmission from one culture to another was preserved in its greatest maturity. It was the one stronghold to which carriers of the ancient wisdom could come and go, to and from any point of the compass, without fear that that which they carried would be taken from them or that they would be persecuted for holding it.

Christianity at first could not accept the figure of the goddess and the divine feminine principle. It is for this reason that the intermingling of East and West at the time of the Crusades is important. Much of the ancient wisdom of Greece, that could not be accepted directly by the early church, was received by the East and later re-transmitted to the European culture. In particular this concerned the concept of the Mother Goddess.

Two other important figures in this re-seeding of the West, were Avicenna, an Arabian physician and alchemist of profound wisdom, and Geber, who preserved in direct translation from the Greek that part of Gnostic and inner tradition which is kernelized in the Emerald Tablet of Hermes Trismagistus. The particular element of this great body of wisdom we seek to stress is that of the role of the Goddess as the Holy Grail.

Symbolically, it could be said that the body of the Goddess is offered willingly upon the cubic silver altar of the Grail and at the partaking of the sacrament there exists a moment of conception, which is the birth of the Elixir, of the Lapis. That is to say, that out of the human soul (which is a form of manifestation of the Goddess), laid on the four elements as a willing offering, there can come the final fruition of the ultimate wisdom. In terms of another system of symbolism this is the blossoming of the Rose upon the Cross.

The Christian church, inheriting the Judaic tradition, finds something profoundly shocking in the sexual imagery of a sacrificed virgin upon the altar. It has indeed in our day been twisted into a travesty of the original profoundly sacred mystical significance. It is part of the *mise en scène* of the popular 'black magic' film or novel. But beyond such misinterpretation and later per-version the inner meaning remains, that the feminine, both as Goddess and as human soul, must offer itself upon the altar of earth, air, fire and water before there can come into it the seed of the fifth element, which brings about a new birth.

To bring this into alignment with the geographical pattern we have already outlined we should mention Damascus, Frederick II's Kingdom of Sicily, the great Western cosmopolitan centre of Toledo, and the routes between them, upon which an important staging post was the island of Malta.

Damascus was a centre on one of the great trading routes between East and West where there still remained echoes of the religion of Ishtar, who was a form of the Goddess who had the capacity to become the Grail. In the Old Testament canon, hers is the influence in the erotic mystical imagery of the Song of Solomon. That is to say, Ishtar could contain the ancient feminine religious dynamic in a new form.

Sicily, in the time of Frederick II, was profoundly interested in the sciences, philosophy and the occult arts. A dual Christian and Islamic civilization, its form of government and administration, embodying enlightened tolerance, made it a kind of island uni-versity where astrologers, occultists, philosophers, alchemists and mathematicians and other seekers after learning could gather together.

Toledo in Spain also had the Saracen and Hebrew influence from whence the inner wisdom of both Islam and Israel could intermingle with the Christian ideas of the times.

Malta was of course one of the strongholds of the Knights Hospitaller and a very ancient religious site, and to and from it the marine routes of esoteric knowledge and wisdom came and went.

This whole mosaic came into being roughly between the ninth and twelfth centuries, although there had been infiltrations at an earlier point in time.

In modern times we have become aware, through the psychol-ogy of Jung, of the psychological significance of alchemical images, seen as part of an internal process occurring within the psyche, but this is only half the story. The ultimate goal is the transformation of the environment which the alchemist perceives.

It could be said that the 'whitening' in the alchemical process is the stage that corresponds to the subjective purification of the vehicles of the operator. This is the equivalent of producing silver and refers to the subjective sphere of Yesod on the Tree of Life, wherein the soul becomes as a perfect magic mirror of the higher realities.

When the inner vehicles have been purified however, they can then enkindle the 'reddening', the state wherein the operator's realizations may bring about change in the environment. This will be refining in its effect. That is to say, it will bring about, in figurative terms, the transformation of base metal into gold.

The word for the alchemical furnace was, with the Arabs, the *athanor*. By this is to be understood the concentration of intensity and heat of the magical will. This occurs with the circulation of the light, as Chinese alchemy calls it, or the raising of the serpent in the Middle Pillar as it is referred to in modern Qabalism or kundalini yoga. In this enclosed intensity of passionate will to achieve, the human personality becomes the receptacle for the transformation process. This is an outer as well as inner rebirth— for the terms inner and outer are but terms for two aspects of an illusion of duality that is in fact a unity.

The process may be understood as being in three stages. At the simplest level the operators think the work they are doing is on material or spirits or essences outside of themselves. This state of comparative ignorance, or initial innocence, does not preclude results from occurring because the higher wisdom behind the conscious ego is projecting into matter the elements of the spiritual work.

At the second stage there comes the sharp division between exoteric and esoteric alchemy. At this stage the more enlightened alchemists cease to think of what they are doing in terms of the process of transmutation of outer material, and come to recognize that their work is in states of being and the transmutation is of the personality itself.

At the third stage however there can be a return to the original innocence but at a higher level. Such a person has gone through the primal unity, and then the division into opposites, to the awareness that 'as within—so without' and thus is able to realize that what changes within is inevitably accompanied by changes without. A dialogue, or vortex, between 'inner' and 'outer' is established which continues in an ever enriching spiral of trans- cendental energy.

It is now possible to make more clear why so much secrecy and obscurity had to be involved in the alchemical writings of the parallel Grail experiences. The processes which were being restored were the very ones that would call down a condemnation of heresy from the church. The Gnostics in the early church preserved a true intuition of the redemptive work that was being carried out when they spoke of the spirit being lost in matter and having to be redeemed from it. They fell into the error, some of them at any rate, of regarding matter to be intrinsically evil. This error was avoided by the Hebrew inner wisdom and the Islamic traditions of alchemy.

The alchemists knew that matter was fallen, but they also knew that it was not evil, but an aspect of the One (the feminine aspect). This the Hebrew Qabalists also knew. Therefore both these currents of wisdom spoke of the need and duty of man to redeem matter, first in his own person and then in the world. In this way could man act as an intermediary between the One and the Kingdom in such a way as to redress the Fall in which man had himself been implicated.

There is in this paradox a key to the whole problem of evil, suffering, redemption and transformation. This, if used in the right way, will illuminate many apparently diverse subjects. For instance, the position of the Fool in the Tarot has caused much discussion and heart-searching among students of the modern Qabalistic tradition. Some say the Fool belongs to the centre and the circumference of the circle; some wish to associate it with Kether, with the beginning and the end. However, there is a sense in which, because the Fool is Zero (another Arabic mathematical concept) it may be regarded as the redeemer of all the Paths on the Tree of Life.

That is to say, the Fool adds nothing and takes nothing away. He has an attitude of total trust, a will committed to experience to the full and accept whatever he encounters. The fool represents an inner attitude, of divine innocence, which redeems whatever it meets. The quality of the Fool in all relationships, by this act of humility, prevents adverse elements in the situation from causing disequilibrium. Any adverse aspect present is brought to the heart of its positive nature. Thus one can say that the Fool, being present in any situation, redeems it. In terms of symbolic mathematics, the zero of the Fool adds and subtracts nothing to any other number but raises it by a power. That is, for example, by it, 1 becomes 10, 100, 1000 etcetera.

In so far as the Grail Hero is the Arthurian equivalent of the Fool, (particularly in the case of Percivale), one may read into this another aspect of the Grail Quest.

An important stage in the Grail Quest is the asking of the Grail

Question—a part of which is 'What is the Grail?' There are, as in most Mysteries, various levels of reply to the question. As we have already indicated, in one sense it is the soul of man as alchemical *athanor*. At another level it takes us into the deep waters of what unredeemed man would or would not accept, for the Grail might also be described as 'that which was excluded from the Trinity'.

That which was excluded from the Trinity was the divine feminine principle. In terms of the exoteric Jewish tradition, which the Christian church inherited, woman was as Eve, or Lilith, a temptress, an agent of ~vil. Therefore one has to say to the question 'What is the Grail?' that the Grail is the soul, that the Grail is also the woman, that the Grail is that which was branded as evil, that which was the scapegoat, that part of himself and of God that man would not accept.

These are sayings both dark and bright and from them can be drawn conclusions relating to many fields of experience and moral attitudes. They are issues which have to be put, and resolved, for they become more critical with the evolution of human consciousness.

The dilemmas involved are exemplified in the accusations levelled against the Templars; of their alleged worship of a devil-like figure called Baphomet and their attitude to the cross.

The figure of Baphomet is not dissimilar to the figure in the Tarot which is vulgarly called the Devil. This figure stands for a force or power, which, if identified with, may lead to diabolism and perversion. If, however, it is understood and brought into proper relation with the other figures, it is an essential pre-requisite for the deliverance of the ego from a false belief in its own godliness, called by the Greeks hubris or spiritual pride. The Caliban-like figure is an image of the un-godlike aspects of human nature, which often set themselves up as gods. In this respect it is also what is sometimes called the Dweller on the Threshold or the Shadow. One cannot rise to the spiritual heights without confronting it and coming to terms with it. Those who try to do so represent a false kind of spirituality, not uncommon in religious and esoteric circles, where 'niceness' takes the place of the awesome beauty of reality.

Historically, however, a number of other currents have coloured this image, for by its very nature it can be abused and perverted by evil or atavistic elements. Unfortunate connotations derive from the averse initiatory cults emanating from Mendes in ancient Egypt. There is also an atavistic contact with the old horned god of the pagan wilds, not intrinsically evil but, except for a few souls whose destiny it may be to maintain custodianship over these old treasures of the past, now considerably out of place in time so far as the majority of souls in incarnation are concerned. These elements were also picked up and to a greater or lesser degree distorted by the eighteenth-century Hell-fire clubs from which the modern popular image of devil worship derives.

In this popular image of the Black Mass we do have, however, quite accurately portrayed, the intimate association of the Virgin and Baphomet. The naked virgin lies upon the altar of sacrifice behind which towers the horned Pan-like monster. In terms of folklore and fairytale it is Beauty and the Beast. It signifies that the shadow side of the human being must be present and visibly consenting to the offering of the soul as a receptacle for the higher realities. It is this hidden brute driving force of the *deus absconditus* that enables the human being to transcend, offer up and transmute the self and therefore resurrect the intrinsic spiritual nature of the soul.

The figure of Baphomet represents also the force of desire which brings souls into incarnation without knowing what it does. Yet by this very fact of being precipitated into physcial incarnation the soul gains the possibility of self-transcendence and redemption. As the Tibetan Buddhists point out, incarnation as a human being is a rare privilege and great opportunity. We should see that we do not waste it.

To revert to the fact that the earlier strands of the Grail tradition emanate from the Essenes, and to relate this to the present day and the immediate future, we should consider the great interest that the Essenes had in the stars, as indeed one would expect from a tradition that descends esoterically from Melchizedek and the plains of Chaldea, whose clear skies show the stars better than anywhere else in the Northern hemisphere, and where there was an immense knowledge of ancient star lore. Some of this lore we have referred to at the beginning of this book; much, however, has been lost but it can be recovered by meditative means.

Astrological elements are interwoven into alchemical wisdom and we ought to take note of the symbolism that is revealed in the stars in our own space and time. It is not that the destiny of man is influenced by the heavenly bodies; rather is it a case that the great 'without' partakes of the same nature as the great 'within'. Therefore those with sufficient subtlety of wisdom (and they are few), may learn to extrapolate, to a certain degree, from the development of the planetary cycles, the corresponding patterns of development taking place within the human souls inhabiting the Earth, and indeed with the development of the whole collective atmosphere of Earth.

For instance, in 1962 there occurred a much publicized conjunction, or more accurately a close configuration, of the Sun, Moon, Mars, Venus, Mercury and Jupiter, and many astrologers prophesied some apocalyptic event for the immediate future, or alternatively the birth of a new Messiah.

What we would say of that configuration is that it exemplified in the heavens what is to be taken as the spiritual task of the current age, which is what St Paul called 'the Christification of the many'. Thus 1962 was not a point in time at which a redeemer was born, it was a point in the evolution of human consciousness where the carrying of inward 'Aquarian' responsibility began to be sounded as a note which future generations would have to embody as the keynote of their epoch.

A similar configuration of planetary bodies occurred in 1186, which takes us back to the dawn of the dissemination in written form of the Arthurian and Grail stories—and the return of the excluded Feminine into Western Christainity.

It can now be seen that in the present age a further stage in these matters has to be undertaken. Man's attitude to the world since the end of the twelfth century has gone through the extreme divorce of the two principles—seen in terms of a materialist 'masculine' science opposed to an inner 'feminine' faith—and it is time that they met in a complementary and reciprocal relation.

This might be called the age of the Aquarian Grail—the highest spiritual teaching of which this Age is capable. It is the Age of the coming of the Cosmic Christ, not to any special group or church, but to the individual spirits of men and women who prove worthy of it. None should make the mistake of setting on one side the teachings of Jesus. Search these well and one will find the pre-knowledge and preparation for this Age, not a setting forth of an outworn ideal belonging to an Age that is passed.

The great religious teachings of the past Age have too often been mis-translated and mis-applied in order to bear out something which it was wished to keep in the Church's creed. These things should be considered from another standpoint, for Christianity should become a movement in the individual rather than within a particular organization.

Those who work from the inner planes need help from us even as we need help from them, for the whole creation is joined together. No part is meant to work alone.

A valuable contact may be established by building strongly and systematically in the imagination the pictures of Monsalvat and of Avalon, and beyond them the great church or temple of the Grail. This is a very real edifice if the hearts and minds of men will make it so. On the way to it is the sacred chapel of Monsalvat, where the contemplation of the spiritual Mystery is profound and where much teaching may descend to the faithful and believing soul who endeavours to worship therein.

The contemplation of the well-known (and not so well-known) stories of the knights and ladies of the Round Table is also one of the paths to that great inner plane Temple wherein the mightiest loving guides of the human race and the planet Earth await the questing soul.

INDEX

Index

General Index

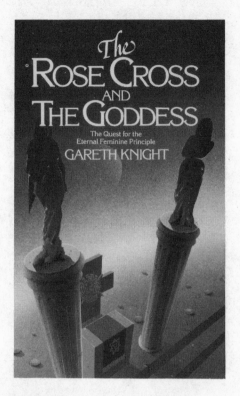

ROSE CROSS AND THE GODDESS

The Quest For The Eternal Feminine Principle

Gareth Knight, one of Britain's most respected occultists, states that the true threat to the world is not pollution, nuclear weapons or over-population, but is actually the psychic unbalance of mankind. He shows how, by balancing the four elements within each of us, the dilemma can be resolved and the Rose of the Spirit bloom again.

A Guide to the Grail Quest
in the Aquarian Age
John Matthews & Marian Green

THE GRAIL SEEKER'S COMPANION

*"The myth was to each according to his need
This and his powers determined what he heard."*
Anne Ridler *Taliesin reborn.*

John Matthews and **Marian Green.** Thumb-nail sketches of the people, items and places surrounding the Grail – that mythical/tangible receptacle of wisdom, which tradition insists will spontaneously appear 'when the soul is ready'. *Everything you need to begin the quest for your true self.*